Advanced Business

Exponentially Increase Stakeholder Value

Donald Mitchell

Author of *Excellent Solutions* and *Business Basics*
Coauthor of *The 2,000 Percent Solution* and *The 2,000 Percent Squared Solution*

400 Year Project Press
Weston, Massachusetts
United States of America

Other 400 Year Project Books by Donald Mitchell

The 2,000 Percent Solution (with Carol Coles and Robert Metz)

The Portable 2,000 Percent Solution (with Carol Coles)

The 2,000 Percent Solution Workbook (with Carol Coles)

The 2,000 Percent Squared Solution (with Carol Coles)

The Irresistible Growth Enterprise (with Carol Coles)

The Ultimate Competitive Advantage (with Carol Coles)

Business Basics

Adventures of an Optimist

Witnessing Made Easy (with Bishop Dale P. Combs, Lisa Combs, Jim Barbarossa, and Carla Barbarossa)

Ways You Can Witness (with Cherie Hill, Roger de Brabant, Drew Dickens, Gael Torcise, Wendy Lobos, Herpha Jane Obod, and Gisele Umugiraneza)

2,000 Percent Living

Help Wanted

The 2,000 Percent Nation

Excellent Solutions (For-Profit and Nonprofit Editions)

Excellent Leadership

Advanced Business
Exponentially Increase Stakeholder Value

ISBN: 978-0692413876
0692413871

For information, contact:

Donald W. Mitchell
400 Year Project Press
P.O. Box 302
Weston, Massachusetts 02493
781-647-4211

Published in the United States of America

This book is dedicated to:

Members of The Billionaire Entrepreneurs' Master Mind

May quickly and easily adding exponential value
for all stakeholders always be ahead of them!

And their spouses, their children and grandchildren,
and their descendants

May this book help them to always focus
on the Lord and doing His will!

Contents

Acknowledgments

Oh, give thanks to the LORD!
Call upon His name;
Make known His deeds among the peoples!

— 1 Chronicles 16:8 (NKJV)

I thank Almighty God, our Heavenly Father, for creating the universe and all the people on the Earth; our Lord and Savior, Jesus Christ, for providing the way for us to gain Salvation; and the Holy Spirit for guiding our daily paths towards repentance and righteousness. I also humbly acknowledge the perfect guidance I received from the Holy Spirit and God's Word to write this book.

I am deeply honored by Professor Banja Junhasavasdikul, Ph.D., writing the book's excellent foreword. Banja has been one of the world's most effective entrepreneurs for many years, focused on adding value for all stakeholders. Based in Thailand, his companies have expanded throughout Asia by providing innovative materials to many customers that are world leaders. I am honored to have been Banja's Ph.D. advisor during his studies. He has done a superb job of capturing this book's essence in a few brief words. Such is the genius of this man.

I am grateful to Peter Drucker for encouraging me to write about 2,000 percent solutions (ways of accomplishing twenty times more with the same or less time, effort, and resources) and to seek ever-simpler ways to help people learn to employ them. His faith in this method for solving problems caused me to take much more seriously the opportunity to share what I had been doing.

I appreciate all those who have permitted me to share with them 2,000 percent solution methods and the work of The 400 Year Project. I thank those who have applied what they learned for all the insights I have gained from observing their wonderful work.

I can never thank my family enough for allowing me the time and peace to work on such a huge and awe-inspiring project for God. They made many sacrifices without complaining and have been a continual inspiration.

I appreciate my many clients who held off on their demands for my help so that this project could receive the attention it required. Their financial support also made it possible for me to give this time to the Lord and to invest in the expenses for creating this book.

Finally, I am most appreciative of the many fine improvements that my editor, Bernice Pettinato, made in the text. This is the sixteenth book where she has helped me to make the messages clearer and more pleasant to read. As always, she was a delight to work with. Her kindness made the writing much easier. I value all she has taught me about writing. I look forward to learning new lessons from her during future books.

I accept sole responsibility for any remaining errors and apologize to my readers for any difficulties and inconvenience that they encounter as a consequence.

Foreword

The global economy is turbulent today. Money flowing from one country to another country can be a powerful force facilitating economies or spreading a global economic crisis. You can't succeed by looking at the world from just one location, one perspective, or one set of interests.

Trade is borderless. The market continually shifts the links in the total supply chain between countries that produce raw materials and the countries that manufacture and supply global customers and end users. To stay ahead of the current complexities of today's business environment requires that business leaders have a deep understanding of how their organizations connect now and should connect in the future to the total value chain for the industry they serve. In doing so, today's businesses touch more lives and affect more interests than ever before, increasing the challenges of adding value for all stakeholders.

What happens when the world changes faster than our organizations do? Donald Mitchell's book, *Advanced Business: Exponentially Increase Stakeholder Value*, answers that question and provides solutions for becoming the driving force for making improvements.

Part One describes the better choices for adding value to eleven classes of stakeholders, from end users to the communities a firm serves. Part Two spells out how investors determine value. Part Three identifies ten strategies that can add value for all stakeholders. Part Four relates three operating methods for increasing value. Part Five has four human-resources practices for enhancing value. Part Six addresses seven financial techniques for boosting value. Part Seven contains seven communications practices for value expansion.

Part Eight pulls together in six lessons how to develop and implement an optimal value-improvement program.

Advanced Business is the most excellent business management book that I have ever read. This book covers the basics of how to be successful in the modern business world by creating increased benefits and value for all stakeholders, rather than just for the company's owners. This book will benefit both business students and leaders of organizations by guiding them in how to put Dr. Mitchell's expert business concepts into practice.

Dr. Donald Mitchell was an excellent advisor to me when I worked on my Ph.D. program at Rushmore University, suggesting that I develop the optimal order for expanding the value of an organization and its stakeholders. Reading and applying the lessons in *Advanced Business* will enable you to gain from his expert advice, as well.

I was pleased to see that some of the concepts in *Advanced Business* have been successfully practiced in our organization and many large companies. For example, 30 years ago I set up as a small trading company distributing DuPont's products in Thailand. I learned how DuPont grew its business from a gunpowder maker to become a leader in the chemical industry by increasing stakeholders' value. We and end users of DuPont's products fully benefited from its expanded offerings.

Currently, our business, Innovation Group, has grown from being a distributor of DuPont products to being one of the leaders in polymer technology. We have become a global company supplying rubber compounds, parts, and technology services to major brands of car makers in many countries. Innovation Group is one of the main suppliers of rubber products for Japanese cars and has learned from the concepts of Japanese car manufacturers in increasing technology value along the supply chain. They are becoming technologically competitive and cost efficient by building cooperative, long-term profitable relationships with business partners along the total supply chain.

All these successful business concepts are fully described in Dr. Mitchell's book.

Advanced Business is an excellent book that I fully recommend you read and apply.

Dr. Banja Junhasavasdikul, Ph.D.
Chairman of the Board of Directors
Innovation Group, Thailand

Bangkok, Thailand
February 2015

Introduction

Yes, the L*ORD will give* what is *good;*
And our land will yield its increase.

— Psalm 85:12 (NKJV)

The information in *Advanced Business: Exponentially Increase Stakeholder Value* has been selected from among The 400 Year Project's most powerful, easily appreciated, and readily applicable lessons accrued during the project's 19 years of research and practice. Many of these lessons were initially developed during 2010 and 2011 for The Billionaire Entrepreneurs' Master Mind, a consortium of entrepreneurs for learning and applying the latest generation of The 400 Year Project's best practices to achieve more than breakthrough success. Versions of seven lessons in *Advanced Business* also appear in the for-profit edition of *Excellent Solutions* (400 Year Project Press, 2014). All the lessons also have deep roots in earlier research and testing done by Share Price Growth 100, a partnership of global leaders that Carol Coles and I directed in developing many of the current best practices for expanding shareholder value. All fifty lessons have been updated, expanded, and improved to increase their usefulness.

Advanced Business: Exponentially Increase Stakeholder Value is different from many other value-improvement books in that it pays attention to ways of benefiting all stakeholders, rather than just the company's owners. If you aren't familiar with the term "stakeholder," let me explain what I mean. Anyone who is substantially affected by an organization or a company has a *stake* in how its activities are conducted. The concept of an individual or organization having a *stake* has been used to describe such an individual or an organization by the word *stakeholder.* Such individuals and organizations include all those who contribute to, benefit from, or are significantly affected by a company's existence and its actions, potentially including some of the following: end users of offerings and benefits, customers, customers' customers, distributors, dealers, agents, suppliers, suppliers' suppliers, employees, employees' families, partners, shareholders, lenders, lessors, neighbors, the communities in which the organization operates, and anyone else who is substantially affected by the organization.

Some might be tempted to dismiss such a broader focus on who should benefit from a company as being some form of impractical idealism. While many of those who advocate such a broadening of who should benefit from a company or an organization base their thinking solely in what increases their emotional comfort, *Advanced Business: Exponentially Increase Stakeholder Value* takes its guidance differently. First, the direction comes from God's Word, the Bible. Second, insights into how to apply the Bible's guidance have been gained from the Holy Spirit concerning the many practical ways that providing more benefits to more stakeholders enhances the value of what the stakeholders contribute to making the company more effective. Such increased stakeholder contributions, in turn, can power virtuous cycles of expanded stakeholder and company capabilities, resources, accomplishments, and benefits for sharing.

To demonstrate these perspectives concerning stakeholder value, each lesson includes pertinent selections from the Bible and explains how they apply to expanding value and improving stakeholders' lives. The lessons also describe ways that the interests and efforts of stakeholders and the company can be aligned so closely that any improvements will automatically translate into much more effectiveness and benefits for all.

Let me also explain what I mean by "value." When academics refer to shareholders, this term has primarily come to mean having a higher current price for all of a company's shares. In ordinary language, of course, value also suggests acquiring something for less: a bargain. In contrast to the first two meanings, we often think of a value as describing what we esteem for guiding our lives, regardless of its current or potential financial worth. While this book often overtly focuses on value in financial terms, either owning something that increases in economic worth or acquiring offerings at less cost, the book also advances Biblical values by basing the advice on the perspective of what God values. While we may not know exactly how to measure value in God's terms, we should certainly not pay any less attention to advancing it.

For instance, consider Jesus' words in Matthew 6:24 (NKJV): "No one can serve two masters; for either he will hate the one and love the other, or else he will be loyal to the one and despise the other. You cannot serve God and mammon." (If you aren't familiar with the word *mammon*, it refers in this context to worshiping *riches*, as though they were personified as a god.) In relating ways to acquire more financial resources and pay less for what is needed, we should always keep in mind that any such benefits should be directed towards advancing God's Kingdom, rather than some selfish purpose of our own. Otherwise, we will simply be worshiping money rather than God, a great sin. We should see using any money developed in this context as simply a means for accomplishing that most important purpose, God's will.

I mention this point now because I have seen variations of some methods described in this book applied solely for selfish purposes. What's the lesson from such applications? I cannot recall seeing any lasting good come from such misdirected uses. So I hope you will apply this information to demonstrate God's greatness to the world and to use the resources He supplies through these methods to glorify Him while serving His purposes.

Other 400 Year Project books contain useful guidance for ways to use increased resources for God's purposes. If you aren't yet familiar with these books, I suggest that you read some or all of them before or while you read and apply this book. A good starting point is *2,000 Percent Living* (Salvation Press, 2010), which describes how to be 20 times more fruitful for the Lord. If you want do delve deeper into the subject of being fruitful, I also suggest *Help Wanted* (2,000 Percent Living Press, 2011). For those who want to focus on witnessing, I recommend *Witnessing Made Easy* (Jubilee Worship Center Step by Step Press, 2010) and *Ways You Can Witness* (Salvation Press, 2010). For anyone who wants to help make a whole nation more fruitful for the Lord, be sure to read and apply *The 2,000 Percent Nation* (400 Year Project Press, 2012).

As you read about the many ways to increase value for all stakeholders, you may find it helpful to think about how the knowledge could help with increasing and improving a community of believers. Such a reference should increase your focus on making fruitful use of what God provides through these amazing methods, reducing your temptation to use the resources in un-Godly ways.

By implementing the 50 lessons in *Advanced Business: Exponentially Increase Stakeholder Value* in conjunction with the 50 lessons for expanding market growth, slashing costs, and eliminating unnecessary investments in *Business Basics* (400 Year Project Press, 2012), a company can increase total value for its stakeholders by 160,000 or more times. Future volumes in the Advanced Business series (*Advanced Business for Innovation* and *Advanced Business for Social Benefits*) will demonstrate how to build stakeholder value from this level to 3.2 million or more times through encouraging competitors to innovate more as well as copy your innovations, and then by 64 million or more times through also profiting from serving important social needs. Be sure to read and apply these two additional sets of value-expanding lessons when they become available later in 2015!

While some might see these potential gains as either being impossible or not very probable, keep in mind that the for-profit edition of *Excellent Solutions* already provides two improvement processes that can be used to expand stakeholder value by over ten trillion times. In addition, The 400 Year Project has already produced such degrees of expanded benefits through the many people who have applied its God-directed research.

Business Basics and *Advanced Business: Exponentially Increase Stakeholder Value* can also be used as sources of helpful perspectives and ideas for applying the astonishing value-expanding processes presented in *Excellent Solutions*. For instance, lessons in *Business Basics* and the Advanced Business series can help identify possible value elements to be included in an excellent solution that is developed by using one of the two *Excellent Solutions* processes.

Let me explain other ways to use *Business Basics* and *Advanced Business: Exponentially Increase Stakeholder Value* to create the stakeholder benefits of an excellent solution. If any of the six complementary improvements described in *Business Basics* or the three Advanced Business books' lessons is enhanced for a second time with a new complementary 2,000 percent solution, total stakeholder value would expand by 1.28 billion times. By sequentially improving any one of the six complementary dimensions on four different occasions by 20 times each (or improving for a second time any four of the combined six dimensions on one occasion by 20 times), total stakeholder value would then grow by 10 trillion times. By expanding performance in these six complementary dimensions through the lessons supplied in these books, most company leaders would be able to design and implement such large value-improving solutions much more rapidly, with reduced effort, and less expensively than by separately developing ten complementary 2,000 percent solutions to gain the same result.

As I discuss in *Adventures of an Optimist* (Mitchell and Company Press, 2007), two other value dimensions that are partially addressed in *Business Basics*, *Advanced Business: Exponentially Increase Stakeholder Value*, and *Excellent Solutions* can also complement these six value dimensions:

1. Lower the cost of capital by 96 percent.
2. Engage many underutilized people (such as those who are unemployed or underemployed) in highly productive activities.

You can find more information about the first of these two dimensions in some of this book's lessons concerning how to increase equity value. As you think about these ways of expanding value by lowering the cost of capital, I'm sure your imagination will be stimulated to identify still other opportunities. *Excellent Solutions* sufficiently discusses topics similar to the second of these two added dimensions to eliminate the need for additional lessons here.

Are there any other complementary dimensions that a for-profit company can use as performance enhancements for greatly expanding stakeholder value? Yes, I believe that there are many more than just the two dimensions I've just mentioned. I list here two others:

1. Invest in upgrading the skills, knowledge, and resources of many underdeveloped people, especially those with little education and experience, so they can make maximum contributions to all stakeholders and then continue operating in partnership with those who can, as a result, accomplish still more.
2. Redirect the public's agenda, attention, and resources into improving or increasing highly valuable activities and resources at little cost.

Feel free to add any other complementary performance dimensions that you prefer.

Let me also note that this book is about for-profit businesses. However, aspects of the discussions about increasing stakeholder value are equally, if not more, applicable to nonprofit organizations.

If you have questions or would like to discuss any of these dimensions, processes, or methods, askdonmitchell@yahoo.com is my e-mail address.

To make the lessons in this book easier to understand and use, they are divided into eight parts, which concern the following subjects:

1. What stakeholder benefits to provide
2. How investors assess value
3. Business strategies that add value
4. Operating methods that increase value
5. Human-resources practices for growing value
6. Financial techniques for boosting value
7. Communications procedures for value expansion
8. Identifying the optimal value-improvement program

I encourage you to direct your colleagues to those parts that will be most relevant to their responsibilities. Doing so will make it easier to redirect your activities in the most fruitful ways.

Let me briefly explain the potential benefits of studying and applying each part. Some readers will not be able to fully identify who a for-profit company's stakeholders are and what kinds of benefits are usually most available and appropriate to provide and increase for each one. Reading the first part will eliminate any of such knowledge gaps. With a broader perspective concerning who is to gain value and of what sort, studying the subsequent lessons will be enriched by appreciating more kinds of useful applications.

Improving value for shareholders can be a key ingredient for expanding value for other stakeholders, as well. In particular, for-profit companies can use stock-price expansion to create financial resources other stakeholders can use to add value beyond what the company can do directly. Paying attention to this subject has another benefit: Many people have not been exposed to the most accurate information about how investors decide whether to purchase, hold, or sell an equity security. Naturally, those who normally don't think about financial markets have even less knowledge on this subject. The second part's lessons in this regard are simple enough to be helpful to such readers. In addition, the lessons address common misunderstandings found among some of those who are literate, as well as expert, concerning financial markets. Even if you have earned a finance degree in business school, you may find some of this information expanding the ways you can apply your knowledge.

Traditionally, business strategies have emphasized outperforming competitors in profiting from attracting and retaining more customers. In doing so, potential effects on many types of stakeholders have too often been ignored. For example, just think about how discarded water bottles might eventually cover an ocean's surface from continent to continent if different approaches aren't adopted. Consider, too, how a better kind of bottle floating in those waters could conceivably be designed to dissolve and supply helpful nutrients for making the oceans more bountiful. As this example shows, examining business strategy in the context of expanding value for all stakeholders often leads to applying quite different concepts and means for implementing them. In the third part, you will find your perspective on business strategy redirected into such broader and more fruitful directions.

Conventional approaches to examining business operations have emphasized increasing accounting profits, operating cash flows, returns on capital or equity, or similar financial metrics discounted into the future. In seeking such financial goals, many companies have actually reduced total stakeholder benefits, sometimes intentionally and other times accidentally. Some leaders who intended to expand shareholder value have been subsequently disappointed by their stock-price results. In the fourth part, we look at business operating methods that many executives do not realize can produce substantial benefits for all stakeholders, while also increasing financial returns.

Human-resources practices are usually aimed at achieving a narrow set of financial goals. In the fifth part, we look more broadly at how stakeholder value can be expanded by pursuing more appropriate goals, as well as how employees and employees' families can be better served in ways that will also increase company effectiveness.

While many executives see the term *value* as being synonymous with financial measures, most companies still ignore many powerful financial opportunities that could have huge positive impacts on monetary value for stakeholders. As an example of such a narrow focus, many companies for which I have consulted once saw the role of the financial staff as merely to find profit-expanding accounting methods and obtain low-cost loans. In the sixth part, we demonstrate the much greater potential of finance to complement what the rest of the organization and its stakeholders are accomplishing. While some of this material will only seem appropriate for financial executives, I encourage all readers to gain a conceptual understanding of the possibilities from these lessons, so that they can advocate more appropriate roles for financial executives in increasing stakeholder value.

Company leaders have always been concerned about not disclosing sensitive information beyond those with a need to know. In some cases, such concerns relate to keeping competitors in the dark to gain or retain an advantage in the marketplace. In other instances, the difficulties of correctly anticipating the future make leaders reluctant to make public commitments that they might not be able to keep. In still other circumstances, some have not appreciated the potential value of communicating more fully, incorrectly seeing this activity as relatively unimportant. In particular, almost all companies are ignorant of the value-improvement potential of assembling the right group of shareholders. The seventh part explains the critical roles for communications in expanding stakeholder benefits. We also look at what kind of shareholders to seek and encourage.

Having read my brief comments about the lessons in the first seven parts, your head may be filled with unanswered questions about how to implement what you will learn: where to start, which directions to take, and the right order for your actions. It's natural to have such a reaction. You have an almost infinite number of choices. Yet only a tiny fraction of 1 percent of these actions and the permutations for sequencing them will lead to huge increases in value for all stakeholders. In the eighth part of the book, I describe a proven, long-practiced method for developing and applying the necessary information to make the optimal choices. Unlike many other decision processes involving complicated choices, the process described in the eighth part is quite easy to understand, learn, and apply. In fact, after the necessary information is in place, most leaders will be able to develop and evaluate high-value choices quite quickly and accurately without assistance from anyone with special technical skills or experience.

By the time you finish reading *Advanced Business: Exponentially Increase Stakeholder Value*, your perspective for what it means to "do business" will have permanently become more fruitful. You will understand many new ways for stakeholders to make unique and important contributions to your firm's success and enhance value for all. In addition, you'll see how the task of effectively leading a company is made much easier by doing more for stakeholders. Shifting to this approach will feel as if a large number of people have suddenly started lifting their fair share of the heavy weight you have been carrying alone: Your burden in increasing stakeholder value will be much less, and you'll be highly encouraged to have so many helpers assisting with any new loads.

Be sure to read the Appendix, as well, where I describe my Christian experiences and testimony. Feel free to share this information with anyone you feel would benefit from learning about how God has touched and improved my life.

We now begin in Part One by looking at what stakeholder benefits to provide.

Part One

What Stakeholder Benefits to Provide

You have increased the nation, O LORD,
You have increased the nation;
You are glorified;
You have expanded
all the borders of the land.

— Isaiah 26:15 (NKJV)

Let me remind you that in referring to stakeholders I mean to include *all* those who substantially contribute to, benefit from, or are affected by a company and its actions: end users, customers, customers' customers, distributors, dealers, agents, suppliers, suppliers' suppliers, employees, employees' families, partners, shareholders, lenders, lessors, neighbors, the communities in which the firm operates, and anyone else who is significantly impacted by what the company does. Although most of these stakeholders have no ownership in the company, be sure to consider how encouraging and facilitating such ownership could be an effective way to expand stakeholder value for many more people.

Here are a few of the possible stakeholder-value improvements to help you begin to appreciate what benefits could be provided:

- End users can gain knowledge and practical advantages that expand the types, quantities, and usefulness of the benefits they receive from the company's offerings. Readers who successfully apply the lessons in *Advanced Business: Exponentially Increase Stakeholder Value* will have received one kind of substantial value improvement from this book.
- Similar effects can also occur for your customers and their customers, often in terms of their obtaining greater numbers of and more profitable customers for their own organizations, along with knowledge and practical advantages that can be used to increase the value of what your customers provide to their own customers and end users.
- Distributors, dealers, and agents can gain from having more appealing offerings that add much increased value for those they distribute to, deal with, and sell to, as well as for their own organizations.
- Suppliers and their suppliers can benefit from becoming vastly more effective, often gaining market share by selling more to your company, as well as to your competitors.

- Employees can see their lives improve through sharing in some of the company's success while enjoying better, more satisfying working conditions, career opportunities, and personal lives.
- Employees' families can experience better lives through any increased time they can spend with the employee, a better working environment for employees that facilitates improved family relationships, any company-provided family-enhancing benefits, and whatever increased income and wealth the employee obtains that is used for the family's benefit.
- Partners can gain wealth and knowledge to apply in their own businesses through ownership and participation in joint ventures, as well as through investments in and with your company.

- Shareholders can be directly enriched through the expanded value of their equity ownership. The value growth from an initial investment of $10,000 in an advanced-business company can be sufficient to support many future generations of the equity owner's family.

- Lenders will have less risk of not being repaid, as well as an opportunity to share in the expanded ownership value of your company whenever your company borrows money through debt instruments that are convertible into equity.
- Lessors can enjoy similar benefits to those gained by lenders, while also gaining the opportunity to do more business with your organization.
- Neighbors and the communities you serve can benefit from your company eliminating any problems it causes while these stakeholders can also receive new benefits designed to make it more attractive for the company, its employees, and neighbors to spend time in the vicinity of the company's activities.
- Anyone else substantially affected by your company can gain from any negative effects being eliminated, receiving more of any existing benefits, and gaining access to any new benefits.

As I mention in the Introduction, please note that effectively adding such stakeholder benefits can be done in ways that greatly expand profits, cash flow, and ownership value for your company. Such consequences follow because these sorts of stakeholder benefits also increase stakeholders' interest in, types of activities for, and effectiveness in usefully contributing to your company's success. Keep these connections in mind as you look for such ways to add to stakeholder value.

In Lesson One, we look at enhancing the economic value of benefits received by end users of a company's offerings. End users are those who actually employ what your company offers, rather than either selling or providing the offering to someone else. Ways to increase such value include adding more helpful features and qualities to an offering, making it easier or less costly to gain benefits from using the offering, and enhancing the ability of end users to gain full advantage from using the offering. Consequently, your company will benefit from their expanded usage.

In Lesson Two, we consider what can be done to increase value for customers and their customers so that they will greatly expand their purchases. We study transferring knowledge, as well as at supplying offerings so valuable that they almost automatically enhance value for customers.

During Lesson Three, we examine improving relationships with distributors, dealers, and agents. Instead of the company and these stakeholders taking a self-centered, short-term focus, such relationships should take a long-term perspective on becoming more mutually rewarding. Doing so means finding important values that distributors, dealers, and agents can provide to enhance benefits for customers and end users. Upgrading the effectiveness of such organizations can also be done less expensively by allowing them to obtain stock options in your company tied to their excellent performance.

Adding value for suppliers and their suppliers is the topic of Lesson Four. Many times your organization will not be able to add much more value for stakeholders unless suppliers provide you with goods and services that allow you to effectively enhance your capabilities and choices. In this lesson, we reverse the focus from Lesson Two on how to add value to customers to look, instead, into the supply chain to see what can be done there by your organization that will ultimately improve benefits for your customers and end users.

Lesson Five considers how to better compensate employees in ways that will increase the firm's value. In addition, we look at how to overcome the most common causes of employee complaints: lack of respect from supervisors, inadequate preparation and insufficient resources to do a good job, overly demanding work environments, unrealistic expectations for the employee's performance, and unpleasant relations with peers.

In Lesson Six, we discuss improving the impact of the employees' work on their families. This lesson describes ways that a company can make it possible for families to enhance their lives in all dimensions, from the spiritual to dealing with worldly problems.

Using partnerships to add more value is Lesson Seven's topic. Adding complementary skills, knowledge, and resources can lead to huge value improvements. However, such partnerships too often focus on outperforming the competition at the expense of adding more value for other stakeholders. We look at the importance of changing the focus of partnerships in this lesson.

For Lesson Eight, we explore the effects on shareholders of accomplishing the stock-price-value-improvement goal of the fourth complementary 2,000 percent solution. This lesson also discusses the need for owners to understand the importance of adding stakeholder value for one and all.

Benefits for lenders and lessors is the topic of Lesson Nine. Creating a more financially sound organization with much enhanced access to low-cost capital decreases risk for lenders and lessors. By allowing these stakeholders to participate in your expansion of shareholder value, you can enrich their organizations while also expanding how much profitable business you provide to your lenders and lessors.

Lesson Ten considers neighbors and how they can benefit from your company seeking to add value for them. Opportunities exist to reduce negative impacts, increase the value of real estate they own, and provide other noneconomic benefits, such as more desirable choices of residences and neighborhoods. Companies benefit by having fewer restrictions placed on them and being able to enter new neighborhoods more easily and less expensively.

In Lesson Eleven, we complete this part by looking at ideas and examples of what companies and their leaders can do to enhance value for the communities in which the firms conduct business.

Lesson One

Stakeholder Benefits for End Users

"Give, and it will be given to you:
good measure, pressed down, shaken together,
and running over will be put into your bosom.
For with the same measure that you use,
it will be measured back to you."

— Luke 6:38 (NKJV)

End users of offerings can be individuals, families, small groups, non-profit organizations, and governments, as well as for-profit companies. How might end users gain immense increases in the value of their benefits? While there are many potential value-improvement triggers for end users, including customers and other stakeholders teaching end users how to increase all forms of stakeholder value, value increases more typically occur due to your company or the end user's supplier providing offerings that automatically deliver either all or most of the value improvement.

Let me supply an example related to 2,000 percent solutions (ways of accomplishing 20 times more with the same or less time, effort, and resources, as described in *The 2,000 Percent Solution*, AMACOM, 1999). If I write a book that tells end users how to make 160,000 times more profits (as *The 2,000 Percent Squared Solution* does by directing that the lessons in the book be repeated for expanding revenues by 20 times and reducing costs by 20 times), end users who buy, read, successfully apply, and keep effectively reapplying the lessons of that book can eventually enjoy 160,000 times more profits. In the process, the economic values of their businesses would typically increase by about 160,000 times, as well.

Now, let's now consider working on expanding cash flow by 64,000,000 times, such as by repeatedly applying the lessons in *Business Basics*. When done correctly, cash flow will increase by that amount, as will the economic values of the businesses to which the lessons were applied.

The offering doesn't have to be a product to cause large value increases. The offering can be a service. Let's consider The Billionaire Entrepreneurs' Master Mind. After learning how to expand the market and revenues by 20 times and to reduce costs by 96 percent for each offering, end users of this service who apply the lessons can gain 400 times more profits. If end users then also learn and apply how to reduce investment intensity by 96 percent, their cash flow also increases by 8,000 times (a 20 fold increase over just applying the first two complementary 2,000 percent solutions). Putting in place a third such improvement will equate to adding another 20 times increase in economic value for end users over the two complementary solutions. If end users then successfully reapply each of the three lessons twice, their cash flow expands by another 511,999,992,000 times. And the master mind doesn't charge 511,999,992,000 times more ... so the value for members of The Billionaire Entrepreneurs' Master Mind compared to the cost in time, effort, and money just keeps getting better and better as they apply more of what they learn.

These product and service examples relate to knowledge transfer for end uses. Benefit transfers through offerings that add stakeholder value can be more direct than that.

Here's a product example. The Amazon.com Kindle reader and the company's support systems for producing and distributing written materials have revolutionized the potential for someone to learn.

On a Kindle reader, hundreds of books can be stored and easily accessed for comparing one source to another. The type size can be adjusted to make reading easier. Each book costs less because it is in a digital version. Because a whole library is now portable, study can be done in more environments, including while traveling or during breaks at work. If we include the value of the space-saving feature of substituting for physical books to reduce how much office or living space someone needs, the economic benefits are undoubtedly much greater than 20 times the cost of a Kindle for anyone engaged in a learning project, such as writing a thesis or dissertation. And to gain the benefit, a learner just has to buy and use the product and related books in this form.

Let's look at a service example of direct increases in the value of benefits. Imagine that an end user's supplier has valuable rights that the end user is allowed to exercise. Such rights might involve being able to share valuable information with other people in a network, perhaps something like an individual controlling a Facebook-like page on an access-controlled network that provides large numbers of people with extremely easy ways to share highly useful information. Another analogy might be a Web site on an Internet-like network accessible by specialized search engines capable of always taking you to exactly where you need to go. In such cases, the supplier's network is made more valuable by having more end users who share greater amounts of helpful information. The same value-multiplying effect on benefits also applies to the supplier's ownership value.

A practical example of this service concept would be a highly efficient branded cooperative that made small companies more effective. The cooperative might do almost everything for the small companies except actually deal with their customers. As a result, each end-user company would gain the same low-cost benefits as everyone else in the cooperative, while also benefiting from owning part of the cooperative. The value of each end user's company could then expand even more if the cooperative could legally assign territories so that the number of end-user companies was held at the optimum level relative to the number of their customers and prospects. In a country that lacked enough qualified providers of a certain essential type (such as plumbers, for instance), such a cooperative might also be able to advocate more appropriate standards for government licensing and gain a virtual monopoly over training providers. If done properly, the cooperative might help a youth with no skills become the successful owner of a highly profitable and rapidly growing business.

You can see from many of these examples that gaining a 20 times value enhancement for end users will not always be automatic. There may be some learning, thinking, and working involved for the end users. In many cases, it may well be that the supplier's supplier (and so on) will have to play an important role in creating the step-up value for the end user before the large increase in economic value will occur.

Think of the potential. If an end user can gain 20 times more economic value from an offering, the value of the end user's activities related to the offering is often going to go up by more than 20 times the combination of the offering's value, plus the time, money, and effort involved in using it. When that's the case, what are end users going to do? Well, they are probably going to find a way to buy and use more offerings from the supplier. When that happens, the end user's economic value will continue to soar in exponential ways. It's like having the ability to turn lead into gold at little or no cost.

What can end users do with that potential? They can cut costs of what they do by 20 times. They can work 96 percent less. They can increase their incomes by 20 times. They can invest 20 times more. And so on. The choice is the end user's. Such flexibility should make a person feel more peaceful before going to sleep each night.

You may be wondering how all of this potential applies to those who have no enterprise to benefit from using offering enhancements. In such cases, freed-up time can be used to engage in other personally or economically valuable activities. Or for someone who feels he or she has enough personal value in hand, the time can be solely applied to being more fruitful for the Lord. Naturally, the potential value increase will not always be realized unless end users are provided with information and encouragement to make constructive use of whatever value they obtain.

What's the key lesson? *By increasing personal or economic value for end users by 20 times as part of the fourth complementary 2,000 percent solution, an end user can gain by applying the benefits to enhance many other dimensions of value. In addition, end users can apply the economic benefits to gain even more benefits by purchasing more offerings, absorbing and applying more transferred knowledge, or selectively reinvesting in valuable activities.*

Your Lesson One Assignments

1. How can your organization's offerings be improved in ways that will increase the economic or personal value of your end users or their activities by 20 times?

2. How can your organization transfer knowledge to raise end users' economic or personal value by 20 times?

3. How can your organization provide exclusive arrangements to end users that will increase their economic or personal value by 20 times?

4. How can you teach end users to increase their value by 20 times, independent of any increased value of offerings, any operational knowledge transfers, or any exclusive arrangements?

5. How can these end-user benefits be transformed into improved relationships that will make it easier for your company to increase by 20 times its economic value and ability to provide for other stakeholders?

Lesson Two

Stakeholder Benefits for Customers and Customers' Customers

"So he went to him *and bandaged his wounds,*
pouring on oil and wine;
and he set him on his own animal,
brought him to an inn, and took care of him."

— Luke 10:34 (NKJV)

Because businesses are often in closer contact with their customers than with their end users, opportunities to notice and serve customers' needs can often be more easily grasped than for adding value to end users. Improving value for customers and their customers can also be a powerful way to extend value to end users through making customers more effective.

How should we treat customers? In Luke 10:34 (NKJV), our Savior used the parable of the Good Samaritan to explain who our neighbor is (anyone we come into contact with) and what it means to love our neighbors as ourselves (to provide whatever assistance we would want provided for ourselves if we were in someone else's circumstances). Surely, applying the stakeholder concept to customers should be based on Jesus' teachings about how to love our neighbors.

We should also see our customers' customers as stakeholders in the sense of their being just like slightly more distant neighbors. Here's a way to think about this similarity. Since you have direct contact (or easily could have in most cases) with your customers, you can see them as being like the neighbors who live next door to you. While you may never see or speak with your customers' customers, their impact on your customers can be just as great as yours is ... or possibly even greater. It's as if a customer's customer lives on the opposite side of your customer's house from where you live, as your customer's other next-door neighbor.

Let's shift now to considering what kinds of benefits can be supplied to customers and their customers. While there are many potential ways to improve value, including teaching customers how to increase value for their stakeholders, more typically the increased value is derived by the supplier company (your firm) providing offerings that deliver either all or most of the value improvement. In that sense, the opportunities are much like those I describe in Lesson One concerning the advantages delivered by the combination of the Amazon.com Kindle reader and the related digital offerings and services.

Let me provide another product example to show how value can be provided to customers. Let's imagine that your company makes a very desirable electronic product, such as an outstanding smartphone that never needs recharging. If you only sell this phone through one service provider, then anyone who wants this smartphone is also going to buy a service contract from that carrier. If the prices and profits on those plans are high and tens of millions of people buy, the exclusive carrier selling the phone can increase its shareholder value by 20 times while similarly increasing value for many of its stakeholders. To ensure that the equity-value expansion isn't hidden, the phone carrier could offer for sale public shares representing a small percentage of ownership in a subsidiary that only provides service for your outstanding smartphone. Those few shares would skyrocket in value, and everyone would know the worth of the subsidiary's shares that the carrier still owned. In most cases, the value of the carrier's shares would also expand by a high percentage of that subsidiary's premium public value.

You may quibble with this example as it applies to adding value for the customers' customers. What about the person who buys and uses the phone in her or his work? That customers' customer (if not an end user) can also enjoy a 20 times larger value by being able to accomplish more profitable activities, due to the phone making it possible to work a higher percentage of the time while mobile. For instance, just imagine the increased value to a salesperson needing to obtain and quickly communicate much information while traveling. There are also bound to be more applications written for use on this phone than on others, applications that will further enhance the value of its unlimited mobile usefulness.

You might respond with a question about where the 20 times increase in value is for ordinary people who buy (customers' customers) or receive (end users) the smartphone for personal applications. Of course, the value of benefits depends on how they employ the phone. If they want to find bargains so they spend less, such a phone could allow them to do more of that, say, while searching for a low-price foreclosed home to buy in a good neighborhood. If they want to do homework more conveniently so that they can spend more time practicing the piano and thus sooner become a concert performer earning a high income, such a phone could help. Naturally, if the increased benefits relate to advancing God's Kingdom, the value of the benefits can be eternal and priceless.

I believe you can see from many of these examples that customers obtaining a 20 times value enhancement will not be automatic. There may be some learning, thinking, and working involved for the customer. But such a large advance in economic and other forms of value could be captured.

Once again, think of the potential. If a customer gains 20 times more economic value, that must mean at a minimum that the value of the customer's activities connected to using the offering is often going to go up by more than 20 times the cost of the offering, plus the time, effort, and money involved in using it.

When that's the case, what are customers going to do? Well, they are probably going to act like end users and find a way to buy more offerings from the seller. When that happens, their economic value will continue to soar in exponential ways. It's like having the Midas touch so that whatever you come into contact with turns to gold, but with the advantage of the touch's effect being selectively up to you to apply so that no loved ones become golden statures by mistake. How nice!

What can customers do with this potential? As with the end users, customers can cut costs by 20 times. They can work 96 percent less. They can earn 20 times more. They can invest 20 times as much. And so on.

And, naturally, the same is true for customers' customers, providing even more value for the customer by expanding its business volume.

What's the key lesson? *By increasing value by 20 times for customers and customers' customers as part of the fourth complementary 2,000 percent solution, a company's customers and their customers can gain the choice to increase benefits in many other dimensions of performance in just the ways that each stakeholder prefers. In addition, customers and their customers can use any economic benefits gained to acquire even more of such benefits by purchasing more offerings, learning and applying more transferred knowledge, or selectively reinvesting in valuable activities.*

Your Lesson Two Assignments

1. How can your organization's offerings be improved in ways that will increase value for your customers and their customers by 20 times?

2. How can your organization transfer knowledge in ways that will raise value by 20 times for customers and their customers?

3. How can your organization provide exclusive arrangements with customers that will increase their value and that of their customers by 20 times?

4. How can you teach customers to increase their value by 20 times, independent of any increased value of offerings, knowledge transfers, or exclusive arrangements?

5. How can these customers' and customers' customer benefits be transformed into improved relationships that will make it easier for your company to increase its value and that of its other stakeholders by 20 times?

Lesson Three

Stakeholder Benefits for Distributors, Dealers, And Agents

"Again, the kingdom of heaven is like treasure
hidden in a field, which a man found and hid;
and for joy over it he goes and
sells all that he has and buys that field."

— Matthew 13:44 (NKJV)

We've been looking at several different sources of economic value in the first two lessons. In quoting Matthew 13:44 (NKJV), I want to remind you that what God values is worth far more than all the economic worth we could possibly assemble. If you doubt that, think about how helpful money and a positive net worth will be for you after dying.

Although the potential benefits for distributors, dealers, and agents are similar to what we discussed in lessons one and two, I decided to discuss this subject separately from those stakeholders because most companies have conflicted objectives concerning and relationships with their distributors, dealers, and agents. In fact, most organizations see such organizations and individuals as temporary accommodations to be replaced just as soon as their company reaches sufficient scale to efficiently take over the activity for itself.

At the same time, distributors, dealers, and agents know that the companies they serve may not be willing to continue with them in the long run. As a result, distributors, dealers, and agents often take short-term views of how to gain a little profit before being squeezed out. Doing so often means performing so poorly that the squeezing out occurs sooner.

What does such a relationship look like in practice? The distributor, dealer, or agent typically requires a minimum payment from the company in the early going, one that's paid regardless of the sales level achieved. And the distributor, dealer, or agent will probably also expect to have almost all of the sales leads be provided by and difficult parts of the selling done by the company being represented. The company hopes that at some point the people from the distributor, dealer, or agent who go along on sales calls will learn how to sell the company's offerings, and these people will begin to do so in sufficient quantities for company profitability to occur. Such hopes are often unfulfilled.

Such relationships remind me of all those old jokes about four pickpockets who went out together for an evening, but who were not able to enjoy themselves because of being constantly on guard so that the other pickpockets didn't steal from them. From such untrusting relationships, little benefit may result.

The exception to such doomed relationships can come in industries where there will always be a need for distributors, dealers, or agents. Frozen food in supermarkets in the United States is a good example of where distributors will be needed for many years to come. People who work in supermarkets usually don't keep the frozen food displays well stocked because it's unpleasant to do so. (Do you remember our old friend, the unattractiveness stall, from *The 2,000 Percent Solution*?) The frozen-food section is also the part of the supermarket where there's the biggest turnover of employees, meaning that stocking performance seldom gets any better.

Frozen-food distributors have taken on much of the stocking for most supermarkets, the primary task they are paid to do by the food companies they represent. The distributors' people go from store to store replacing and restacking the company's offerings. It's such a big fixed expense to visit a store that no single company can ever hope to afford to be able to do this task efficiently for just its own offerings.

Because the frozen-food distributors feel safe in their roles, they make investments in selling more and providing better service. Because the frozen food companies need the distributors and cannot afford to replace them, the food companies bend over backwards to be helpful and to make this work profitable for the distributors.

This relationship can provide a helpful model for all companies that have distributors, dealers, and agents: Find valuable tasks for distributors, dealers, and agents to do that aren't economical to perform in any other way; encourage distributors, dealers, and agents to do such tasks; and provide them with solid reasons to believe in gaining lasting profitability from a relationship with your company.

In such a relationship, it's important that the company help the distributors, dealers, and agents to develop strategic advantages that permit them to be more effective than their competitors in adding value for stakeholders of your company and to attract more accounts that will increase their effectiveness for all organizations they represent. In many cases, it will be desirable and valuable to help build the company's distributors, dealers, and agents into the most effective and profitable ones in any part of your industry.

How can that be done? The answer will differ from industry to industry, but the first step is to evaluate the opportunities with the distributor, dealer, or agent in ways that make it clear your company wants to be more helpful. In doing so, it will normally be desirable to use supplying such help as a means to becoming the largest account of the distributor, dealer, or agent. Where there is no well-functioning organization, achieving effectiveness may mean helping a successful salesperson for your company to start up her or his own company and to gain other product lines to represent. By turning such employees into successful entrepreneurs and expanding their worth in self-esteem, credibility, and wealth, there's a potential to create a greater bond that may better survive and provide more. With smaller or not well capitalized firms, the company may need to subsidize some early investments so that the distributor, dealer, or agent will be able to provide superior value through service to customers.

Helping distributors, dealers, and agents add value also means giving them exciting new offerings to provide, and making those offerings easy to sell and handle without a lot of specialized investment. To do so may mean directly providing more support for customers, but in ways that do not lead the distributor, dealer, or agent to think that he or she will eventually lose the business by your company going direct to sell and serve these accounts.

Companies will need to take extra time to seek out distributors, dealers, and agents who will do a superior job, make the necessary investments, develop and maintain strategic advantages with appropriate assistance from the company, and be in business for many years. Since distributors, dealers, and agents are often small, family-owned operations, that last point is critical. Either work with young people who appear to be stable or with organizations that have matured to the point where they have succeeded in making several transitions from one set of managers to another.

Whoever is chosen, the lesson is the same: Look for ways to enhance the value of distributors, dealers, and agents as seriously as you do your own value and in so doing don't fight over dividing the benefits gained. Instead, cooperate to create more benefits for the company, your distributors, dealers, and agents, as well as all other stakeholders, especially customers and end users.

Keep in mind that one potential tool for value enhancement is providing distributors, dealers, and agents with stock options in your company that are tied to their performance. In this way, distributors, dealers, and agents have a second means to add value for their companies and their stakeholders. Stock options may be a critical benefit to enable distributors, dealers, and agents to attract and maintain the kind of sales and service forces that you would like them to have. Some of the company stock options may even be directly used as incentives for outstanding performance by individuals in the distributor sales and service forces.

What's the key lesson? *Build cooperative, long-term, profitable relationships with distributors, dealers, and agents that add value by 20 times for them and all other stakeholders. In doing so, seek to establish, expand, and maintain new strategic advantages for the distributors, dealers, and agents that will help your company, as well. When you succeed, there will be plenty of ways for the company and each distributor, dealer, and agent to expand its own value for its stakeholders.*

Your Lesson Three Assignments

1. How can your goals for working with distributors, dealers, and agents be adjusted to encourage adding more value for customers, end users, and other stakeholders?

2. How will compensation and other forms of encouragement need to be changed in order to facilitate such enhanced value creation by and for distributors, dealers, and agents, as well as other stakeholders?

Lesson Four

Stakeholder Benefits for Suppliers and Their Suppliers

Then Jesse said to his son David,
"Take now for your brothers
an ephah of this dried grain
and these ten loaves,
and run to your brothers at the camp.
And carry these ten cheeses
to the captain of their *thousand,*
and see how your brothers fare,
and bring back news of them."

Now Saul and they and
all the men of Israel were
in the Valley of Elah,
fighting with the Philistines.

So David rose early in the morning,
left the sheep with a keeper, and took
the things *and went*
as Jesse had commanded him.

And he came to the camp
as the army was going out
to the fight and shouting for the battle.
For Israel and the Philistines had
drawn up in battle array,
army against army.
And David left his supplies in the hand
of the supply keeper, ran to the army,
and came and greeted his brothers.
Then as he talked with them,
there was the champion,
the Philistine of Gath,
Goliath by name,
coming up from the
armies of the Philistines;
and he spoke according
to the same words.
So David heard them.

— 1 Samuel 17:17-23 (NKJV)

This passage from 1 Samuel 17 (NKJV) describes how David became aware of the opportunity to battle Goliath while delivering supplies to his brothers in Israel's army. However, God had a bigger plan for David that day, to supply not only food, but also victory.

A similar opportunity can exist for working with your suppliers and their suppliers. Instead of just seeing these stakeholders as unchanging cogs in a supply mechanism that needs to be maintained in a smoothly running fashion, you should be aware that suppliers and their suppliers can bring great insights and also apply their skills and experiences to help you accomplish more. Here's the key: Much like David hearing Goliath speak, suppliers and their suppliers need to be told what's going on and to be invited to address the most pertinent issues.

While there are many potential value-improvement triggers, including teaching suppliers how to increase their stakeholder value, more typically increased value is derived in large part by the supplier company providing offerings that make your company (its customer) much more attractive to customers and end users. Such an offering might contain some proprietary element, unique advantage, or powerful appeal to customers, customers' customers, or end users that vastly increases growth, profitability, and other forms of value for the customers, customers' customers, and end users well beyond what the first two complementary 2,000 percent solutions (market expansion and cost reduction) achieve. As a result, the supplier can charge more for the new offering and sell more of it, thus capturing part of the benefits to expand its own value.

Here's an example related to 2,000 percent solutions that's a variation on the one in Lesson Two concerning benefits for customers and customers' customers. If I write a book that tells readers how to make 400 times more profits (as *The 2,000 Percent Squared Solution* does), customers who read and successfully apply the lessons of that book enjoy that many times more profits. In the process, the economic values of their businesses also probably increase by around 400 times.

If instead of doing that, I write a book to show readers how to make at least 160,000 times more profit by providing 400 times more revenues and 400 times negative cost (which occurs when profits exceed 100 percent of total costs by 400 times), I should expect that I will increase sales of such a book by at least 400 times over *The 2,000 Percent Squared Solution* because more people will want to buy it and I should be able to charge much more for it. Even if I charged as much as $10,000 a copy, there should still be a huge demand. Why? The benefit gain is a huge multiple larger than the increased price.

Now, let's imagine that I write another book that explains how to gain 64 million times more cash flow (whimsically titled, perhaps, as *The Unstoppable 2,000 Percent Cubed Solution*). Customers who buy, read, and successfully apply the lessons of this new book will enjoy 64 million times more cash flow. In the process, the economic values of their businesses will probably also increase by around another 400 times over what the first book provides. If I charge 20 times more for the latest book (say, $200,000 a copy), a 20 times value increase is still there for the supplier and customers alike.

It doesn't have to be a product that causes the value increase. It can be a service. Let's call such a service The Billionaire Entrepreneurs' Turnkey Operations. After buying the service, let's assume a company expands the market and it revenues by 400 times and reduces its costs into negative territory by 400 times. As a result, clients who purchase the turnkey service gain 160,000 times more profits. If clients then also learn how to reduce investment intensity so that free cash is 400 times greater, their cash flow also increases by 64 million times. Putting in place such a third complementary improvement will equate to adding another 400 times increase in economic value for clients over the first two complementary solutions. The price of this enhanced service could be 20 times more than the service that only provides 160,000 times more profits, and the benefit would still be well worth the added price in terms of enhancing customer value.

These examples relate to knowledge and skill transfers. A benefit transfer can, of course, be more direct than that. Let's look at a variation on the Lesson Two example of a hot electronic product. We'll call it the Super Phone to reflect its vast superiority over other smartphones. If the supplier only sells the Super Phones through one service provider in a country, say, you in the United States, then anyone who wants a Super Phone is going to buy a service contract from you. Instead of letting you gain all of that benefit, the supplier might seek to retain half of the value added from the service through charging much higher prices to you for the product, which you agree to subsidize for your customers so their value increase isn't affected. In that case, the supplier's value goes up by an additional multiple of what its gain would be from merely producing and selling the Super Phones because of the subsidy you provide to customers. (Let's assume the profits and cash flow from the Super Phone service over the life of the product are at least 40 times greater than from serving just the predecessor product.) If the prices and profits on those plans are large, and tens of millions of people buy, you, as the exclusive carrier who sells the Super Phone, can increase your own organization's value by an additional 20 times.

To isolate the increased value for investors, the supplier company could offer shares in a subsidiary that just sells Super Phones and price its products high enough to gain 50 percent of the normal service profits that you, the sole carrier, would receive without the price premium for the Super Phone.

I believe that you can again see from these examples that the 20 times value enhancement for suppliers will not always be automatic. The supplier will need to create huge amounts increased value to ensure that both it and its customers gain 20 times more value. To be sure this increase occurs, it's good for suppliers to add 400 times more value than what their customers can do for themselves.

What if suppliers have no such ideas or plans? You might help them form valuable partnerships, provide key knowledge and skills, and support their activities in ways that make such huge value improvements possible.

Let's again imagine the potential after such a value improvement occurs. For the supplier and you as the customer to gain 20 times more economic value, that must mean at a minimum that the value of your activities related to the offering is often going to go up by more than 400 times the cost of the offering and the time, effort, and money involved in using it. When that's the case, what are your customers going to do? Well, they are probably going to buy a lot more offerings from you. When that happens, you'll buy a lot more offerings from your suppliers, and their economic values will continue to soar exponentially.

What can suppliers do with that potential? They can earn 20 times more. They can work 96 percent less. They can cut costs by 20 times more. They can invest 20 times as much. And so on. It's up to the supplier. I suspect that most suppliers will want to invest 20 times as much to see if they can add even larger than 400 times increments of value for their customers and capture a great deal of the expanded value improvement for themselves.

What's the key lesson? *By increasing the economic value for suppliers and you, their customer, by 20 times as part the fourth complementary 2,000 percent solution, you can gain from having available more valuable offering benefits and knowledge transfers that provide customers with the choice of increasing benefits in many other dimensions of performance that they prefer. In addition, suppliers can use the value benefits to acquire and develop even more economic benefits by adding more offerings, gaining more from knowledge transfers, or selectively reinvesting in highly valuable activities that will, in turn, add still more value for you and for all of your customers.*

Your Lesson Four Assignments

1. How can your suppliers' offerings be improved in ways that will increase the value of your offerings for your customers, customers' customers, and end users by 400 times?

2. How can your organization transfer operational knowledge in ways that will raise suppliers' value by 20 times?

3. How can your suppliers provide exclusive arrangements with you that will increase their value and yours by 20 times?

4. How can you teach suppliers to increase their value by 20 times, independent of any increased value of offerings, any operational knowledge transfers, or any exclusive arrangements?

5. How can these supplier benefits be transformed into improved relationships so that it will be easier for the suppliers and your company to increase values for other stakeholders by 20 times?

Lesson Five

Stakeholder Benefits for Employees

So then neither he who plants is anything,
nor he who waters,
but God who gives the increase.
Now he who plants and he who waters are one,
and each one will receive his own reward
according to his own labor.
For we are God's fellow workers;
you are God's field, you are *God's building.*

— 1 Corinthians 3:7-9 (NKJV)

These verses from 1 Corinthians 3 (NKJV) precede the Apostle Paul's observation that labor is only fruitful if it is based on Christ and builds God's Kingdom. The example he uses is sharing the Gospel to help lead people to repent and accept Jesus as Lord and Savior. Each of us needs to remember this important lesson, ensuring that we add eternal benefits along with any temporal ones. Otherwise, we might put growing temporal benefits first, thereby reducing or eliminating how many eternal benefits can be generated by God through enhancing our efforts.

One way that the eternal benefits can be increased is by ensuring that the organization gives credit to God for whatever benefit building occurs. In addition, ways should be sought to share the Gospel message while doing so. Employees are usually the stakeholders in the best position to accomplish such sharing. Just compare the witnessing differences between how the Salvation Army operates and what a secular food bank does in terms of building God's Kingdom.

Even if it's not practical to include sharing the Gospel as part of what your organization does officially, be sure to consider ways that temporal resources can be usefully directed for this purpose. For instance, rather than only sponsoring secular events to gain customers, some marketing funds might be applied to multiplying witnessing resources and training.

Let's look now at increasing temporal resources. Increasing stakeholder value by 20 times can do a great deal for employees who receive a significant part of their compensation in company stock options and grants. If an employee, for example, were to receive 10 percent of paid compensation in this form, remain with the firm for many years so that the compensation became fully vested, and continually held the securities so that all potential appreciation was gained, the effect in a company that applied the *Business Basics* and *Advanced Business* methods would be to multiply income over time by 16,000 times what was nominally paid.

In addition, employees are sometimes in a position to know when the organization is about to do even better than in the past because of their often more thorough understanding of effective new offerings, improved business models, and enhanced ways of serving stakeholders. If employees use some of their personal savings to legally make additional security purchases of the company's stock, the wealth increase can be further magnified.

Naturally, the risk of loss can also be great (as employees found who held all of their liquid investments in company stock while working at Enron, WorldCom, and other fraudulently managed enterprises), so wise employees will probably diversify some of their holdings to avoid being too concentrated in their employer's securities.

Employees are usually looking for more in stakeholder benefits than just pay and an opportunity to become wealthy. The biggest employee complaints in the United States about employers usually fall into these categories:

- Lack of respect from supervisors
- Inadequate preparation and insufficient resources for doing a good job
- Overly demanding work environments
- Unrealistic expectations for the employee's performance
- Unpleasant relations with peers

Let me address how the company's enormous success in wealth creation might affect each of these sources of frequent concern and irritation, beginning with lack of respect from supervisors. An organization that performs to the high standards required to add so much stakeholder value will need to have a highly effective staff, low employee turnover so that knowledge builds faster rather than dissipates, and an eye for adding even better talent. All four dimensions of complementary breakthrough performance that we have been considering depend on such staff characteristics. As a result, a well-run company will have taken the time to encourage and prepare supervisors to accord employees the kind of respect that makes them love, rather than dislike, their jobs. Clearly, career advancement and compensation for supervisors should heavily depend on the improvement, success, and retention of the people the supervisor leads. The time, effort, and money involved in performing these activities well are small compared to the potential value improvements that could ensue.

Let's next consider inadequate preparation and insufficient resources for doing a good job. The value-enhancing firm you are creating should be continually evaluating what work should be done by employees, rather than by suppliers or outsourcing organizations. If it will be hard to properly prepare and support an employee, the organization should shift the work to external suppliers that have the right skills and resources. If preparation and resources are needed for employees, funding the expenses with high-value stock can be one way to make the costs easier to bear. As a result, employees should expect to be well prepared and to be provided with at least adequate resources. In fact, the wise supervisor will probably give individual employees wide latitude to take the initiative for meeting their own job-related preparation and resource needs, so that poor performance and frustration don't have a chance to continue.

Your firm might also follow the example of many of the most innovative firms and make the work environment as conducive as possible to excellent performance. Some such firms provide free services for handling employee errands, taking care of children when they aren't in school, and customizing work spaces. When such resources are purchased with the proceeds from selling high-value company stock, these expenditures have a smaller impact on the company's finances while the economic benefits can be enormous.

Unrealistic expectations for an employee's performance could become a problem unless the organization helps all employees to become effective in creating 2,000 percent solutions to improve and speed work. By investing in such skill development, high-value solutions should begin delivering superior results almost as fast as implementation begins. As before, the financial burden will be quite a bit less if paid for by selling high-value company stock, and the benefits generated will also be huge.

Unpleasant relations with peers can be a problem for people who are put in public competition with one another and who lack influence over hiring and with whom they work. Better hiring practices often include extensive evaluations by potential peers and subordinates so that initial compatibility with new hires will be higher. Then, more employees will want to keep the desirable jobs that have been created and properly supported. The corporate culture should make it clear that one of the quickest ways to be fired is by treating peers and subordinates in inappropriate and unpleasant ways.

Of course, if these topics aren't the top issues for employees in your organization, apply the necessary time, effort, and cost to uncover what the top issues are and to then effectively address them.

The only way that such a company could become unpleasant to work for is if the leader doesn't uphold values conducive to establishing and maintaining such an ideal work environment for enabling employees to accomplish what they and the company's stakeholders highly value. Why would leaders risk making such a mistake when there is so much to lose?

What's the key lesson? *By vastly increasing economic value for the firm's shares as well as the aspects of the work environment that employees most value, you will then be able to use low-cost capital to more easily afford selected investments that make the organization an even more attractive place to work. These investments, in turn, will enable far more valuable performance by the organization and increased benefits to all stakeholders that are worth far more than what they cost.*

Your Lesson Five Assignments

1. How can your compensation methods be adjusted to provide the most after-tax income and encourage the longest possible relationship with effective employees?

2. What are the major concerns that would cause valuable employees to look for employment elsewhere?

3. What actions can you take that will improve performance in the areas of employees' greatest concerns?

4. How can the financial burden of acquiring and providing appropriate employee improvements be minimized through using the company's high-value stock?

Lesson Six

Stakeholder Benefits for Employees' Families

And he brought them out and said,
"Sirs, what must I do to be saved?"

So they said,
"Believe on the Lord Jesus Christ,
and you will be saved, you and your household."
Then they spoke the word of the Lord to him
and to all who were in his house.

And he took them the same hour of the night
and washed their *stripes.*
And immediately he and all his family *were baptized.*
Now when he had brought them into his house,
he set food before them; and he rejoiced,
having believed in God with all his household.

— Acts 16:30-34 (NKJV)

Acts 16 (NKJV) describes the initial visit of Paul and Silas to Philippi. While there, the two were arrested, beaten, and imprisoned after Paul commanded an evil spirit to come out of a slave girl who had previously exhibited divining powers. Because she lost her powers, her owners were annoyed that they could no longer profit in this way. While Paul and Silas were praying and singing in the middle of the night, an earthquake jolted the prison, opened all of the doors, and loosened the chains that bound the prisoners. Because the jailer expected to be executed for having lost the prisoners, he prepared to kill himself. Aware of this possibility, Paul called out for the jailer to stop because none of the prisoners had left. Acts 16:30-34 (NKJV) describes the happy events that followed.

These verses remind me that God wants everyone to be saved. When an employee is always busy either working or focusing on what a company needs, the company or a work assignment can become an idol for the employee that interferes with doing God's will. When that happens, the employee's soul is at risk, as well as possibly the souls of some members of the employee's family. Instead, the workplace should be where God's assistance is identified, honored, and properly credited so that His marvelous actions help draw employees, their families, and all other stakeholders closer to Him.

Having addressed some possible spiritual benefits for employees' families, let's now look at other kinds of benefits. Much as company, customer, and supplier stakeholders can receive 20 times increases in value, so can employees who receive a significant part of their compensation in stock options and grants. Consequently, an employee's family is likely to see its wealth increase to very high levels. While many might automatically assume that such a result would only have good effects, there are definite risks to avoid, due to how employees might be changed by seeking or obtaining the wealth. I list a few harmful possibilities below:

- Working more hours in order to gain advancement
- Spending less time with the family due to work responsibilities
- Preoccupation with work while at home
- Less focus on spiritual and moral development due to work pressures

- Frequent moves tied to promotions and new assignments
- Engaging in harmful activities to relieve stress

When an employee is more successful at work, many times leaders assume that the company has also been helpful to the employee and his or her family. In many cases, leaders don't check to see what's really going on with the families. That's a mistake.

While we aren't yet at the point in this lesson for prescribing how to provide value improvements for employees' families, I think it's important to first address how to avoid harming employees' families. More can be done if part of the wealth created for employees is dedicated to directly helping employees' families. How might such resources be directed? Here are a few possibilities:

- Create day-care and after-school-care facilities at work where parents and children can meet during the day while also having continual electronic access to one another.
- Open nearby breakfast, lunch, and after-work facilities where families can enjoyably dine, play, and socialize.
- Provide and subsidize transportation so families can spend more time together, both at work and during work-related travel.
- Offer at-work services that reduce the time employees spend alone doing family and personal errands.
- Subsidize memberships at family-oriented facilities such as YMCAs, swimming pools, tennis clubs, and venues for indoor activities.

As I mention in Lesson Five, employees are naturally looking for more from work than just being well paid, gaining promotions, and becoming wealthy. As that lesson describes, the biggest complaints about employers in the United States usually fall into these categories:

- Lack of respect from supervisors
- Inadequate preparation and insufficient resources for doing a good job

- Overly demanding work environment
- Unrealistic expectations for the employee's performance
- Unpleasant relations with peers

In Lesson Five, I point out how counterproductive it is for such problems to exist and outline some potential ways to reduce or eliminate them. Notice that after such reforms employees' families will benefit from the employee being able to finish work more rapidly, finding the work easier to accomplish, enjoying the work more, feeling affirmed at work, and happily staying with the organization for more years. All such benefits should translate into more family time for the employee that is enjoyed in more pleasant ways.

While it's common to portray families on television as either totally dysfunctional or unbelievably functional, it's more typical for each family to go through occasional severe challenges and to routinely experience some minor problems. When these challenges occur, the employer is too often either unaware of the difficulties or unsympathetic in dealing with them. Here are a few examples of challenges that are somewhat likely to occur and create considerable harm when they do:

- Someone in the family develops a substance abuse problem and isn't able to "kick the habit."
- A child has some serious health issue (such as complications from premature birth, birth defects, autism, juvenile diabetes, leukemia, or a crippling injury).
- A husband's or a wife's parents are incapacitated and need constant, long-term care.
- Severe marital strains arise.
- Husband and wife have difficulties conceiving a child.
- Children develop substantial problems with learning or behavior.
- Someone in the family becomes depressed and needs continual supervision.

Money alone isn't going to solve such problems. The employee has to become more involved. As a result, job responsibilities may need to change, working hours adjusted, and various kinds of support provided. A sympathetic employer can increase value to those who are struggling with the effects of such problems through making helpful work accommodations. I think that providing such assistance is more valuable to a company whose ownership value has grown a lot, due to the employee having the choice in many cases of using personal wealth either to stop working for several years or to retire. With either sort of departure, the organization loses a valuable contributor, and performance will be less than if the employee's family needs are accommodated.

As families shepherd the next generation towards adulthood, there's a lot that employers can do to help ... that they typically don't do now. Such assistance might include tutoring for youngsters having difficulties with school subjects, counseling or mentoring youngsters who are rebelling against their families, internships for those who want to gain experience at a young age, and sponsoring activities that will strengthen family bonds.

As you can see, helping employees' children is one area where implementing the next generation of best practices for adding stakeholder value should be fairly easy to accomplish ... simply because organizations are doing so little now to be helpful.

And guess what? The benefits will be enormous for the stakeholders of the rapidly growing, high-value company.

What's the key lesson? *By vastly increasing the nonfinancial value your organization delivers to employees' families, you will provide a more attractive workplace for hiring and retaining effective employees who will be more joyous, enthusiastic, energized, and at peace. These investments will enable higher company performance that will deliver much more stakeholder value than their cost.*

Your Lesson Six Assignments

1. How can you adjust how you engage with employees to provide more attractive, peaceful, and productive lives for their families and to encourage the longest possible relationship with effective employees?

2. What are the major concerns about their families that would cause valuable employees to look for employment elsewhere, to take a long leave of absence, or to retire?

3. What actions can you take that will improve performance in aspects of family lives that cause your employees to be the most concerned?

4. How can the costs of acquiring and providing the improvements for employees' families be minimized, such as through using the company's high-value stock?

Lesson Seven

Stakeholder Benefits for Partners

When He had stopped speaking,
He said to Simon,
"Launch out into the deep and
let down your nets for a catch."

But Simon answered and said to Him,
"Master, we have toiled all night and
caught nothing; nevertheless at Your word
I will let down the net."

And when they had done this,
they caught a great number of fish,
and their net was breaking.

So they signaled to their *partners*
in the other boat to come and help them.

And they came and filled both the boats,
so that they began to sink.

— Luke 5:4-7 (NKJV)

In Luke 5 (NKJV), we read about Simon Peter, James, and John leaving their fishing businesses to follow Jesus as His disciples. The verses above are preceded by Jesus asking Simon Peter to stop working on his fishing nets and to take Him a little way out in the water so the people could see and hear Him better. Simon Peter did so. In return, Jesus provided a whopping catch, one that overfilled not only Peter's net and boat, but also caused his partners' boat to begin to sink. Such is the abundance that Jesus can bring to those who follow His will.

You may be wondering why these fishermen had partners. Let me suggest one possible reason. Consider that fish tend to swim in schools. Since there was no sonar in Biblical times, there was a certain amount of randomness to finding substantial numbers of fish. If two boats were out, the chances were twice as good that a school would be found. Then, the other boat could join the one making the discovery, also drop its net into the school, and the boats could carry home a larger total catch.

Fishing can also be a lonely occupation. Having partners to discuss the challenges and setbacks with could help make the burden easier to bear.

It takes faith to fish for a living. Many other occupations can provide a steadier, higher income. Notice such faith at work as Simon Peter went out fishing again when Jesus directed him to do so, despite having caught nothing the night before.

As the net began to break, Simon Peter first thought of gaining the material benefit, as evidenced by his signaling to his partners to help with the catch. As the magnitude of what Jesus had provided became more apparent, Simon Peter shifted his attention to the Provider of the catch, rather than the provision. His partners did as well. As a result, Jesus gained four disciples.

We can see in this example the potential for successful partnerships to enrich people both spiritually and materially. In fact, the material benefit may help trigger the spiritual gains by drawing attention to God's infinite grace, love, wisdom, power, kindness, and mercy.

Let's now look at the opportunity to provide more benefits for partners. Just as company, customers', and suppliers' shareholders gain immense wealth from increasing stakeholder value by 20 times, so do partners and their shareholders. Such gains can occur in two forms: increased value for their partnership shares and greater value for their organizations as a result of holding the partnership shares.

As a model for such gains, let's consider an equity stake in a joint venture of some sort. Typically, such ventures allow two organizations to perform as allies in conducting an activity for which neither one has sufficient strategic resources to succeed. For instance, in the early days of its copier business, Xerox shared patents and technological know-how with organizations that had manufacturing and distribution clout in markets where Xerox had little or none.

A good example of this kind of relationship has been Fuji Xerox. Originally, Rank Xerox (a partnership between the UK's Rank Organisation and Xerox Corporation) licensed Fuji (the Japanese film company) to distribute Xerox copiers in Japan through a 50-50 joint venture, Fuji Xerox. Later, Xerox bought Rank, and a closer relationship developed with Fujifilm (Fuji's current name). Fuji Xerox now develops many copier products that Xerox sells outside of Asia. Fujifilm now owns 75 percent of the joint venture, with Xerox holding the remainder.

After Xerox bought Rank, Fujifilm saw its non-copier business lines decline in importance until Fuji Xerox became the parent company's main source of profits. Because of that success, any expansion in the value of the joint venture had a large impact on the value of Fujifilm by increasing the total revenues, profits, and cash flow of the company. In addition, Fujifilm has had the choice (which it has not yet selected) of selling some or all its stake in Fuji Xerox to pay for retiring shares or debt in the parent company. Further, Fujifilm could have offered public shares in Fuji Xerox so that those who were valuing Fujifilm shares could see each day what Fujifilm's shares in Fuji Xerox were worth on the public market. Analysts could then have more easily assigned a value to Fujifilm's other lines of business to establish a minimum value for Fujifilm's shares that would primarily fluctuate with the ownership value in the joint venture's shares.

There's another level at which this relationship has worked. Xerox probably would have had to leave the copier business without help from Fuji Xerox. By the 1980s, the Japanese joint venture was profitably selling its small copiers in Japan at a price that was much lower than what it cost Xerox to make comparable copiers in its Rochester, New York, plants. Xerox chose to learn from the partnership, improving its design and manufacturing skills. Encouraged to do more for Xerox, Fuji Xerox gained opportunities that enhanced its success and added to its expertise.

Such joint ventures can be critical for expanding the value of offerings so that customers and ultimate users gain 20 times more value. As an example, the newest copiers employ digital technology simultaneously creating electronic records of what is copied. Consequently, many of the filing and retrieval costs of handling traditional paper records have been eliminated while great flexibility has been added for working with such records. For instance, by being able to enter, store, retrieve, and print records in more ways, legal proof trails are greatly enhanced for important activities such as patent development and various kinds of legal compliance. If a valuable legal right is retained by the customer or end user that would have otherwise been lost, the economic benefit will be enormous compared to the cost of making copies.

Joint-venture relationships aren't the only way that two organizations can be partners. Another common method is for one of the partners to purchase a significant ownership position in the other or to make a large loan that can be converted into equity. When either type of investment happens in a public company, the value effects can be similar to owning shares in publicly traded joint ventures.

Sometimes partners have no cross-ownership, but their mutual value creation can be substantial for one another, customers, and end users. A good example of such a relationship can be found in the collaboration that Intel and Microsoft have engaged in over the years to establish Intel microprocessors and Microsoft operating systems as the standard for IBM-cloned personal computers. Dubbed "Wintel" by some, the cooperation made such PCs more useful and less expensive than they would otherwise have been. Each company benefited by seeing its revenues, earnings, and cash flows improved by the success of the "partnership" they have shared.

Partnerships can also function as informal exclusivities between customers and their suppliers leading to valuable accommodations being made by both parties to enhance one another's success. For instance, because McDonald's made Martin-Brower its exclusive distributor for supplies, the hamburger chain could expand more rapidly and less expensively, a relationship that also increased value for both companies and their stakeholders.

The main weakness in most partnerships is having partners focused on conflicting goals. Placing more attention on and increasing cooperation in value improvement for all stakeholders can lead to many valuable breakthroughs from working on more useful activities.

At the opposite end of the ownership spectrum are the various "public good" partnerships where people volunteer their time, efforts, and resources to accomplish something of great value that otherwise wouldn't be available, such as occurs with Wikipedia and the Linux computer operating system. Such partnerships create great value for customers and end users while often not adding nearly as much value for suppliers and owners, and that result need not be the case.

Many people have failed to grasp that all of the kinds of partnerships described in this lesson can be employed by a single organization, including attracting volunteers who normally only support nonprofit organizations. Be open to doing more with stakeholders in all of these ways.

What's the key lesson? *Develop cooperative, profitable relationships with partners that are focused on adding 20 times more value for all stakeholders. When you do, there will be plenty of ways for each part-*

ner to expand ownership value for its shareholders and to supply other kinds of value to all of its other stakeholders.

Your Lesson Seven Assignments

1. How can your goals for working with partners be adjusted to encourage adding more value for partners, customers, end users, and other stakeholders?

2. How will compensation and other forms of encouragement need to be changed in order to facilitate such enhanced value creation for other stakeholders?

3. What joint forms of ownership will work best for rewarding stakeholders?

4. How can stakeholders lacking any ownership in the firm obtain opportunities to benefit from expansions of partners' economic values?

5. How can suppliers and owners gain value from public partnerships based on attracting and working with people who volunteer their time, efforts, and resources?

Lesson Eight

Stakeholder Benefits for Company Shareholders

"Go into the village opposite you,
where as you enter you will find a colt tied,
on which no one has ever sat.
Loose it and bring it here.
And if anyone asks you,
'Why are you loosing it?'
thus you shall say to him,
'Because the Lord has need of it.'"

So those who were sent went their way
and found it *just as He had said to them.*

But as they were loosing the colt,
the owners of it said to them,
"Why are you loosing the colt?"

And they said, "The Lord has need of him."

Then they brought him to Jesus.
And they threw their own clothes on the colt,
and they set Jesus on him.

— Luke 19:30-35 (NKJV)

Luke 19 (NKJV) describes the triumphal entry of Jesus into Jerusalem prior to His trials and crucifixion. While some might wonder why He chose to ride on a lowly animal, many Bible students remember that Zechariah 9:9 (NKJV) contains a prophecy that the King would arrive on a donkey's colt. The ensuing events during the rest of His time in and near Jerusalem led to all people gaining the opportunity to accept the free gift of Salvation and enjoy eternal life with God. Could there be any more important spiritual blessings?

As a poor carpenter who had been serving as an itinerant teacher, Jesus didn't own such an animal. As God, He could have simply created a colt. Yet Jesus wanted to bless others by giving them an opportunity to share in this important event. Those He sent to obtain the colt and the owners of the colt gained such blessings by faithfully serving His will.

Unfortunately, many owners fail to remember that God provided everything they have. Also, some forget that whatever they possess still belongs to Him.

Some business owners are narrowly focused on squeezing out the maximum benefit for themselves, often at the expense of other stakeholders. Such owners don't realize that they are usually cutting themselves off from God's intended blessings, as well as benefits that they could gain from enhancing the value of benefits other stakeholders receive.

Even when business owners keep many of their stakeholders in mind, diversion from God's purposes can occur. While it is almost a matter of faith to those who believe in free markets that company shareholders should be generously rewarded, many people have not fully considered how such a focus can affect value for shareholders. Many people might be inclined to simply ask, "Isn't having more value for shareholders better?"

Before addressing these fundamental beliefs, let me observe that implementing the first three complementary 2,000 percent solutions described in *Business Basics* has probably already provided enormous value for company shareholders. After the first solution, the company was 20 times larger. Unless the company's economic fundamentals deteriorated in the process, such an enterprise would often increase shareholder value by 20 times as well. After the second complementary 2,000 percent solution, the company's profits were at least 400 times larger. Having 400 times more profits and growing them rapidly would often equate to a greater than 400 fold gain in a company's shareholder value. With the third complementary 2,000 percent solution, the company's "free cash flow" (cash generated that doesn't need to be reinvested) increased by at least 8,000 times. In most cases, such a company could then expand its activities for share repurchasing, paying cash dividends, and other activities that can boost company shareholder value so that shareholders would have enjoyed at least an 8,000 times gain.

Such an increase means that anyone who had invested $10,000 originally should now own stock worth $80 million. With the next complementary 20 times increase in value that this book describes, the total value goes to $1.6 billion.

I hope you can sufficiently wrap your mind around this example to see that there's an enormous difference between owning $80 million in stock, an amount that many foolish people could lose or spend in a few years, and $1.6 billion, an amount that should keep a family solvent through many generations of foolish decisions ... assuming that decisions for everyone in the family are not concentrated in just one or a few people.

If the $1.6 billion shareholding value increases 5 percent a year, the annual value addition would be $80 million. Continue to compound at this rate for 15 years, and this family's shareholder value goes up by more than another $1.6 billion. Such a family should be well on its way to reasonably permanent wealth.

Investment analysis shows that three major factors can greatly affect the value that company shareholders enjoy:

1. Volatility in the value of holdings
2. The amount of taxes paid when any shares are sold
3. The value of any cash dividends that are paid

Let's separately consider each of these three factors. A typical public company's stock valuation will vary by at least 20 percent from its annual average. I'm sure you will agree that degree of fluctuation is very significant. On the surface, that variation appears to mean plus or minus $320 million at some point during the year for a shareholder with $1.6 billion in stock. If the investor sold at the top and bought back at the bottom, there's the potential to make more than $640 million extra every year by simply trading the stock. Of course, you can reverse that process and potentially lose $640 million the first year and lesser amounts thereafter until little is left. I'm sure you agree that trading such a stock should only be done very cautiously and under ideal circumstances (near-term prices being ridiculously over and under the likely future value of the holdings).

In practice, the trading results could look a lot different than I've just described. For instance, if the company was about to implement a complementary 2,000 percent solution to expand revenues by a second 20 times, the hypothetical investor's ownership value could be going from $1.6 billion to $33.6 billion pretty quickly. Such an investor would be foolish to engage in trading or to be concerned about fluctuations in value: Chances are that the gain will be stratospheric if management continues to do what it's been doing ... simply providing more complementary 2,000 percent solutions that benefit all stakeholders.

It's a rare country that doesn't base taxation for shareholdings on the gains or losses experienced when the stock is sold. While the amount of such taxation may be large or it may be small, in almost all cases the stock is going to be rising in value a lot faster than the interest cost of borrowing by using the stock's value as collateral. When that's the case, shareholders can simply borrow to supply any cash needs they have and still see their financial risk reduced as the holdings go up in value much more rapidly than what they owe the lender. In so doing, shareholders will have whatever cash they need without selling any stock. The tax authorities will receive nothing in the meantime.

As *Business Basics* points out, such enterprises will probably pay out enormous dividends, potentially as large as a multiple of their entire free cash flow. As a result, it's highly likely that dividend payments received will be substantial and rapidly growing. When that's the case, we can expect that such payments will more than cover the daily needs of the shareholder. In our example, even with a large multiple of stock price to earnings, the annual dividend payments to the owner of $33.6 billion in stock should be at least $100 million.

Under such circumstances, we can see that company shareholders have gained something resembling a nearly infinite financial resource in terms of the needs that most people have. Is that circumstance beneficial to company shareholders? You bet! You have put them into a position of having nearly permanent wealth beyond their wildest dreams while taking care of future generations in reasonably similar fashion.

The remaining challenge is to convince shareholders that generously rewarding all stakeholders is in the shareholders' best interests. When shareholder interests cut off stakeholder benefits, shareholders lose because the number and size of company improvements that expand ownership value will be greatly reduced.

What's the key lesson? *By increasing the value of company shares by another 20 times through the fourth complementary 2,000 percent solution, most shareholders will be launched into permanent wealth that can easily be sheltered from dissipation when conservative practices for holding the stock are followed, and investment and spending decisions for the holding are spread among a large group of careful people.*

Your Lesson Eight Assignments

1. How would you manage your shareholdings in a company that is about to put in place the fourth complementary 2,000 percent solution for expanding stakeholder value by 20 times?

2. How would having permanent wealth change the way you lead your life and what advice would you give to family members?

3. How would your behavior change towards those who lack enough resources?

4. How would your motivations change in regard to creating and implementing complementary 2,000 percent solutions?

5. What proof would you want to see as a shareholder to convince you that generously benefiting all stakeholders is in your best interest?

Lesson Nine

Stakeholder Benefits for Lenders and Lessors

"But love your enemies, do good, and lend,
hoping for nothing in return;
and your reward will be great,
and you will be sons of the Most High.
For He is kind to the unthankful and evil.
Therefore be merciful,
just as your Father also is merciful."

— Luke 6:35-36 (NKJV)

These verses from Luke 6 (NKJV) describe what Jesus said about how believers should treat their enemies, as well as the ungrateful, the undeserving, and the unreliable. We are to emulate our Heavenly Father and be merciful to them, even lending to those who we believe will not repay us. Hopefully, your enterprise will pay what is owed to its lenders and make timely payments to lessors. While you may not normally think of lenders and lessors as stakeholders, especially if you don't borrow and lease very much or often, realize that you can provide substantial benefits to such organizations and individuals and that the degree of your faithfulness in paying certainly affects them.

As with company shareholders, a company's lenders have been helped by each of the first three complementary 2,000 percent solutions described in *Business Basics*. Expanding revenues by 20 times potentially increased borrowing needs by 20 times. Reducing costs by 96 percent on a per-unit basis increased company profits by 20 times allowing the company to make interest payments and principal retirement much more easily, thus cutting lenders' risks quite a bit. Shrinking investment intensity reversed the need for so many borrowings by 96 percent, further slicing the risks of not being repaid.

As some of the lessons about eliminating investment intensity in *Business Basics* discuss, it may well be that special borrowings have been used to optimize the entire economic system, thus reversing to some extent any reduced use of borrowings for operations. When it comes to increasing a company's stock price by 20 times, borrowing more money can be very helpful for optimally timing value-building activities, such as share repurchases, acquiring competitors for cash, and obtaining licenses for key technology and patents.

As a company expands its stock price by 20 times through the fourth complementary 2,000 percent solution, the potential effects on existing and new lenders and lessors are primarily two:

1. Lenders and lessors experience less risk of not being repaid as the company's access and capacity improve to raising equity capital through stock sales.
2. Lenders and lessors may enjoy added opportunities to earn more profit by lending and leasing with convertible debt and preferred securities that permit these stakeholders to participate in some of the company's stock-price appreciation in exchange for charging less interest.

In some cases, there will be a third major impact ... becoming the depository for some of the borrower's excess cash. In times when central banks tighten credit, having such deposits enables lenders and lessors to lend and lease more to other borrowers and lessees.

A secondary effect for lenders and lessors can be to gain prestige from serving such a successful organization. In many cases, such prestige can be turned into additional profit by attracting other desirable companies as borrowers or lessees.

As you can see, such a stock-price-improvement program will be entirely positive for a company's lenders and lessors, except if all the company's unusual cash needs are funded by sales or issuances of stock, rather than by borrowings and leases.

I encourage my consulting clients to maintain cordial and mutually profitable relations with lenders and lessors at all times. In practice, it's unlikely for a company to be totally free of debt and not leasing anything. Because corporate tax laws often require paying a great deal to the government for transferring funds from one country to another, even the most liquid companies find it attractive to borrow the cash locally that is needed to operate in a country. In addition, some properties can only be leased because the owners don't want to sell.

Even if no cash is needed, it's always prudent for a company to maintain backup lines of credit for dealing with unusual circumstances and unexpected opportunities. Even if such lines of credit aren't used, there are substantial fees paid for having them that provide good profits to lenders.

How can the value of such mutual benefits translate into increasing lenders' and lessors' value by 20 times? The answers will vary from stakeholder to stakeholder. The biggest impacts will tend to come from participating in the borrower's and lessor's stock-price improvement and receiving large deposits to lend or to use for financing leases to other companies. Since profits from these activities can greatly boost equity value due to earnings growing faster for lenders and lessors, it's possible to expand the value of lenders' and lessors' equity by more than 20 times when a large borrower makes it a policy to find ways to do so.

You may be thinking that there's a win-lose element here. There doesn't have to be. For instance, a borrower or lessee might offer to let the lender or lessor convert a given amount of debt or leases into shares of stock at a value premium to the current stock-price level in exchange for initially paying a lower interest or lease rate. If the borrower or lessee simultaneously purchases an equivalent amount of stock at the current price level and the stock price later greatly increases, all lenders and lessors will gain along with the borrower and lessee. It's a win-win solution. All it takes is having a policy of seeking to add value for the lenders and lessors, as well as the expertise and will to do so.

What's the key lesson? *By increasing the value of company shares by another 20 times as the fourth complementary 2,000 percent solution, company lenders and lessors can benefit in a variety of valuable dimensions from having less risk, to potentially participating in some of the stock-price growth, to earning fees for backup lines of credit, to having low-cost deposits to lend, and to attracting other borrowers and lessees. With care, large borrowers and lessees can plan to deliver such benefits in ways that will expand the value of lenders' and lessors' equity by 20 times as well. This result will be easiest to accomplish at times when the price of lenders' and lessors' shares are very depressed, such as occurred for many lenders and lessors during 2008 and 2009.*

Your Lesson Nine Assignments

1. How can your stock-price-improvement program be made more successful by having friendly, low-cost lending and leasing relationships?

2. What are the ongoing borrowing and liquidity needs that your organization should always meet through having good relations with lenders?

3. Under what circumstances would it make sense to allow lenders and lessors to benefit from some of your company's stock-price appreciation?

4. What strategic role can your excess liquidity play for lenders and lessors through making deposits with them?

5. How can your company help expand lenders' and lessors' stock-price values by 20 times?

Lesson Ten

Stakeholder Benefits for Neighbors

And behold, a certain lawyer stood up
and tested Him, saying,
"Teacher, what shall I do
to inherit eternal life?"

He said to him,
"What is written in the law?
What is your reading of it?"

So he answered and said,
"'You shall love the LORD your God
with all your heart,
with all your soul,
with all your strength,
and with all your mind,'
and 'your neighbor as yourself.'"

And He said to him,
"You have answered rightly;
do this and you will live."

But he, wanting to justify himself,
said to Jesus,
"And who is my neighbor?"

— Luke 10:25-29 (NKJV)

These verses from Luke 10 (NKJV) precede Jesus' telling the parable of the Good Samaritan, which sends the message that anyone with whom we come into contact is to be treated as our neighbor. It's a high standard, but we should remember that God directs our paths so we encounter others for purposes related to advancing His Kingdom. Of course, some business leaders would never think of applying this principle.

Whenever the subject of a company's neighbors arises, I am reminded of two experiences .... both of which involve Tennessee, a mostly rural state in the American South. The first experience occurred about 1978 when I visited a small manufacturer in a remote part of Tennessee. While there, I found that my lungs burned and my eyes wouldn't stop watering. But I didn't see anything that could be causing these reactions.

My host, the corporate development and marketing executive for the client company, pointed across the valley to a large building several miles away. He mentioned that this other company manufactured chemicals and that the invisible pollution from the plant made it very difficult for everyone in his company to breathe and to see. Wow! One company was harming the health of and creating discomfort for its neighbors.

The second example came about 15 years later while learning about the new division of General Motors that made Saturn automobiles. The plant had been sunk so far into the ground in rural Tennessee that you could be a quarter of a mile away and not notice the facility. Clearly, the Saturn people were trying to avoid harm to their neighbors.

However, in neither case did I learn of anyone seeking to increase value by 20 times for a company's neighbors. When I have seen such advances occur, they have mostly been unintended.

A good example of helping without a specific intention to do so can be observed in Anaheim, California, home of Disneyland. This was a lower middle-income suburban community better known for its orange groves than for its economic opportunities when Disneyland opened in 1958. Disney did not buy up very much adjoining land, so neighbors who owned commercially zoned land used for one-story offices based in former residences were able in some cases to sell to someone who wanted to build a fifteen-story hotel. In addition, residences that were located a few blocks away became very valuable for people who loved Disneyland. Residents could buy inexpensive annual passes and walk over to visit every day. While Disneyland brought traffic, it also brought prosperity in the form of greatly increased real estate equity values for almost all of the neighboring landowners.

However, I fear that for every example like Disneyland, there are probably hundreds more like the Tennessee chemical facility.

Why would a company want to enrich its neighbors? Well, we all have neighbors, but we often don't think about what effects they can have on our companies. In fact, neighbors can contribute to company success in many valuable ways. Let me list six possible mutual advantages for neighbors and companies from contributing to making a great neighborhood:

1. If the neighborhood becomes nicer and safer, your own employees and their families may want to reside there. As a result, commutes will be shorter and employees and their families will lead better lives. You may be able to attract better workers. Those who sell their properties to the employees will be able to purchase nicer homes where there is less congestion. I saw this effect occur in Plano, Texas, as companies such as Electronic Data Systems and Frito-Lay moved onto a former

ranch in that suburban community. The offices were surrounded by a parklike buffer zone so that the visual impact was slight on the city and its residents. Due to employees moving to Plano, property values boomed. Former owners reinvested profits to buy gorgeous homes just one town away.

2. If your employees are going to need nearby shopping and services, local businesses are going to boom, and the choices available to nearby residents and other workers will improve. I see this improvement happening all the time in Waltham, Massachusetts, next to where I live, which is home to more square feet of commercial office space than in any other New England community. What was a stagnant former mill town boasting some large pig farms now burgeons with desirable restaurants, stores, and entertainment venues. Employees seek jobs in Waltham because it's a fine place to work and shop. As a result, companies located there are more successful. All of the real estate has increased in value faster than in similar communities without an influx of businesses.

3. In many cases, there are operating cost advantages of locating in dedicated enclaves of associated activities. For instance, companies that provide hub-and-spoke air freight shipping have been able to also locate warehouses, time-sensitive manufacturing facilities, and integrated supply chains into their neighborhoods so that the customers of such operations can obtain offerings much more rapidly. United Parcel Service has made a major business out of managing such facilities for many of its clients located near its hub operations. When such specialized enclaves are utilized and strengthened, a company is more profitable, the value of its and its neighbors' real estate expands, and more customers are attracted.

4. In most cases, local zoning authorities can limit a company's building of facilities and subsequent expansions. When a company's proposed changes are viewed as being positive for neighbors, changes are usually approved much more rapidly and on less costly terms ... simply because of the trust that neighbors will benefit.

5. Some communities have long-standing problems, such as ground and water pollution from prior companies' poor practices, unpleasant smells and appearances from existing buildings, and poorly functioning schools and other public services. A company that moves into such a neighborhood may be able to afford to fix some of those problems by applying some of the funds granted by another governmental authority to locate in this place. When such spending occurs, renewal starts to improve a neighborhood in ways that increase value for neighbors. I have seen this occur to a remarkable degree in the formerly blighted industrial areas around MIT in Cambridge, Massachusetts, as the university bought and developed neighboring land for commercial research activities, leading to everything else that neighbors used being upgraded, as well.

6. Increasing value for neighbors in one community can make it easier a company to move into other communities. Receiving such a welcome is an important benefit for any rapidly expanding organization, especially retailers. Wal-Mart is a counterexample of this point. When Wal-Mart moves into a community, some locally owned retailers start to go out of business and the value of their properties decline. As a result, many communities don't want new Wal-Mart stores and vigorously oppose them.

While this lesson has emphasized land values, neighbors can also gain noneconomic benefits, such as in the Disneyland attendance example. One common economic value benefit occurs when neighbors are sufficiently impressed by well-run companies to purchase company shares. If the value of the company substantially increases, the result is to expand the incomes and net worths of those neighbors who invest in the company.

This investing effect has occurred in a major way in Rochester, New York. For many decades, the town was dominated by Eastman Kodak, the photographic film and camera maker. Almost everyone in town was related to someone who worked there. However, the company declined for many years, and its stock did even worse. People were hurting when Xerox, the first producer of dry copiers using plain paper, went public in the 1960s. Xerox was based in Rochester, and neighbors often bought its soaring shares. Later, when Xerox began to decline, a small company, Paychex (which Carol Coles and I wrote about in *The Ultimate Competitive Advantage*) began to do well, and neighbors bought that stock, instead, creating much new wealth.

What's the key lesson? *By vastly increasing the value your organization delivers for neighbors, you can expect to gain and retain better employees, have more supportive neighbors, experience less opposition to expansion, and benefit from a nicer area in which to work.*

Your Lesson Ten Assignments

1. How can improving value for neighbors deliver more kinds of benefits for them and your organization?

2. What are the major concerns and needs that neighbors have that your help could effectively address?

3. What actions can you take that will improve performance in the areas of neighbors' concerns and needs?

4. How can the costs of acquiring and providing the improvements be minimized through use of the company's high-value stock?

Lesson Eleven

Stakeholder Benefits for Communities

"And do not seek what you should eat
or what you should drink,
nor have an anxious mind.
For all these things
the nations of the world seek after,
and your Father knows
that you need these things.
But seek the kingdom of God, and
all these things shall be added to you.
Do not fear, little flock,
for it is your Father's good pleasure
to give you the kingdom."

— Luke 12:29-32 (NKJV)

These verses from Luke 12 (NKJV) remind us that God will provide for the needs of those who follow Him in seeking to advance His Kingdom. Clearly, one opportunity for which many companies have not done enough is in supporting Christian organizations and activities in the communities that their firms serve. Here is an area where company leaders can make a difference. Those who want to advance in a company often emulate whatever the most senior people do.

When such leaders are actively leading and serving in Christian organizations and activities, many others will do the same.

Creating value for communities is an activity where there is often a lot more lip service (such as informally promising benefits) than practical results. Instead, organizations with jobs that can be brought into or taken away from a community are always being aggressively pursued by government authorities with offers of large subsidized loans, tax forgiveness, and legal exceptions the value of which almost always vastly exceed the value of what the companies ultimately bring to the community. In some cases, taking advantage of a community is unintentional on the company's part. In some other cases, it's a deliberate part of the company's way of doing business.

While at one time company leaders were usually committed to being community improvers, such activities are more often sought today primarily for ego gratification. The closest some companies come to making an investment in some communities where they operate is through sponsorship of a professional sporting event (such as a golf tournament) or buying the naming rights to a local sports stadium.

In Lesson Ten, I describe how many companies also operate in ways that harm the value of neighbor's properties and activities, affecting a portion of the local community. Classic examples in the United States have occurred where companies dumped toxic materials for decades into groundwater, rivers, and streams. Some of these sites will take decades to clean up. The local land is valueless until the remediation is complete. In the meantime, those who come near often have increased risk of becoming ill and dying prematurely.

Even well-meaning leaders often think much more in terms of their responsibilities to shareholders, customers, and lenders than they do to the communities in which they operate. That's often true, in part, because the highly paid leaders reside in different towns that are unaffected by their operations. With such employees leaving behind at 5 p.m. problems that the company has created, the communities in which they operate predictably decline.

Let me contrast such examples with one that I observed in White Plains, New York, part of high-income Westchester County located just north of New York City. For many years, one of the largest employers in the community was General Foods Corporation, then one of the largest companies in the world. Just after World War II, General Foods decided to build a new headquarters on a very visible, prime location near downtown White Plains.

While many companies only build such facilities to serve themselves, the leaders of General Foods were concerned about the effect on the neighborhood and what would happen when they outgrew the building. With the site being located across the street from the largest hospital in the area, the company leaders spent time with the hospital's leaders determining how their new corporate headquarters might be later converted into expansion space for the hospital. Although that eventuality hasn't yet happened, General Foods set a standard followed by many other companies that later came into the community. As a result, large employers are often located on sites that more resemble public parks than commercial facilities, with access to major roads that minimizes the effects on local traffic for those who live and work nearby. Go only a quarter mile from many of these locations, and you would never know that there are high-density commercial uses in the vicinity.

So companies can be sources of and magnets for improvement rather than introducers of decay and death. That's what General Foods did. When that happens, the value of the company's land and buildings is higher, employees better enjoy their work, more people may decide to live nearby (cutting down on commuting time), and the community will have a larger tax base.

If enough companies do this, the community may see its ability to provide public services increase more rapidly than new demands are made for them. This is especially true if the company makes improvements in ways that provide benefits for others in the community. For instance, a company going into a town lacking sewage treatment facilities might build such facilities large enough to provide service for other businesses, homeowners, and the local government.

Adding value isn't limited to making surroundings more attractive and providing new classes of services. Benefits can also relate to upgrading the kind of public services that have a large impact on the value of real estate in local communities, such as schools. A company is likely to be filled with employees whose knowledge and skills can be tremendous resources for the local community when such employees volunteer their time. Companies can encourage such helpfulness. Some companies even pay employees to spend part of their work weeks in service locally. Timberland is a good example of an organization that has done so. The firm has also directed its philanthropy to alleviate social problems in the communities it serves. That's unusual today, when most company foundations spend their money almost solely for gaining marketing advantages.

In recent years, Professor Michael E. Porter of Harvard Business School has been one of several researchers looking at the importance of developing vibrant local communities to provide talent, knowledge, resources, and infrastructure to allow everyone in an industry to prosper. One of his favorite examples is the international flower market located in the Netherlands. This market is so well organized and operated that suppliers and customers from Europe, the Middle East, Africa, and North America bring flowers there to sell even when likely customers may be located in their own country. The advantages of this specialized community outweigh the transportation costs. You see similar benefits occurring in the diamond-cutting industry.

In Lesson Ten, I mention Paychex, a company that has had a beneficial effect on Rochester, New York. Let me expand here on that example. Paychex's founder is Tom Golisano (Carol Coles and I wrote about him in *The Ultimate Competitive Advantage*, Berrett-Koehler, 2003, and he wrote a foreword to that book). As a result of Golisano's success in building Paychex from a three-person operation to a multi-billion-dollar-value enterprise, he became a billionaire. Looking closely at Rochester, he realized that there wasn't a sufficient base in IT education to keep his company strong if it stayed in Rochester.

While many companies would simply pick up and move, Tom Golisano felt that Rochester was a good place for Paychex to be located. He often jokingly referred to how bad the weather is there as one reason why Paychex employees worked so long and hard: There's nothing better to do on most days. Choosing to make a local commitment, he donated hundreds of millions of his own money to upgrade the local high schools and colleges so that IT talent would improve and be more abundant. It's an example that could be followed by any company's leaders who succeed in creating substantial wealth for themselves and their stakeholders.

I believe that value-improving companies will study such examples and seek to exceed best practices in these and other dimensions of performance so that they can enjoy a sounder local foundation for their success: a much more vibrant, desirable, and valuable community in which to operate.

Although the benefits of such changes will often show up in terms of economic values, I believe than even greater blessings will be enjoyed in terms of personal satisfaction from seeing people enjoy better lives and fulfill much more of their potential. Tom Golisano became a sort of local hero in Rochester and he clearly relished that role.

What's the key lesson? *By vastly increasing the value your organization delivers for those who aren't neighbors in the communities in which you operate, you can expect to gain more value for your other stakeholders, have better prepared employees, gain a more supportive political environment, experience less opposition to expansion, and work in a nicer area.*

Your Lesson Eleven Assignments

1. How can improving value for those who aren't neighbors in the communities in which you operate deliver more kinds of benefits for them and for your organization?

2. What are the major concerns and needs of communities where you operate that your company can address?

3. What actions can you take that will improve performance in the areas of the communities' concerns and needs?

4. How can the costs of acquiring and providing the improvements be minimized through use of the company's high-value stock?

Part Two

How Investors Assess Value

For you were bought at a price;
therefore glorify God in your body
and in your spirit, which are God's.

— 1 Corinthians 6:20 (NKJV)

In Part One, you learned about the kinds of value improvements that might be most relevant, mutually helpful, and accessible to provide for various stakeholders. In the process, I'm sure you noticed that advancing the value of the company's shares could be used in a variety of ways to provide economic and noneconomic benefits for almost all types of stakeholders. For this reason, Part Two provides background on how those who value, purchase, and sell assets, operations, businesses, and companies determine the fair price of whatever is bought or sold.

As we consider this information, keep in mind that value is in the eye of the beholder. A collector who admires a certain kind of art that experts consider to be quite bad might pay quite a high price for something that another person wouldn't allow into her or his home. A more common example can be seen while two children are playing. A youngster with a strong desire for something of little economic value may be willing to swap very expensive toys to satisfy his or her desire.

Because you decided to read this book to create value for all stakeholders, rather than to become an expert on valuation, I've kept the lessons in this part to a minimum. In Lesson Twelve, you will learn about the importance of the form in which something is owned or used in determining the price someone will pay. For instance, you've probably observed how someone will pay substantially more for a used item that's been cleaned and made as presentable as possible than for an identical item without such preparations, even if the costs in time, effort, and money are small to make the same improvements.

In Lesson Thirteen, our focus is on price and value volatility. While many investors seek to minimize their exposure to volatility, this lesson introduces the idea that volatility can be a great helper for increasing stakeholder value. We also consider many of the most common factors that cause price shifts.

Lesson Twelve

Valuation Methods

We pay for the water we drink,
And our wood comes at a price.

— Lamentations 5:4 (NKJV)

Water and wood provide perfect examples of how valuations are affected by the form in which something is available. If we drink from a public water fountain, there will be no charge. While there is a charge for the water piped into our homes from a municipal supply, the rate is often quite reasonable. If we order bottled water in large containers to place atop a cooler, that water will be much more costly than piped-in municipal water. However, the price per gallon for the large containers will be much lower than if we purchase the same brand of water in pint bottles. If we purchase the pint bottles at a swank restaurant rather than at a discount store, the price will be much higher. Wood can also range from free (when we obtain fallen branches from our own backyards) to extremely expensive (when obtained from a rare tree in a faraway land that's been processed to look stunning in designer furniture).

In this lesson, we shift to considering economic value forms and the valuation methods most commonly used to determine the price for purchasing or selling an asset, ownership in a business, a business itself, or an entire company. My purpose here is to provide a common perspective for investigating helpful ways to increase value by 20 times for all stakeholders.

I have read books as long as 850 pages describing just a single valuation method for publicly owned companies. As you can see, the challenge to be brief in this lesson is considerable, but must be met, or you will need to keep reading for the next several years.

Let me start with a caution. If you memorized in school that something has only one price and that all rational people will calculate that same price, I'm going to politely disagree with that theory, based on the evidence of what happens on a day-to-day basis in actual transactions.

Perhaps the most important point about valuation is that different ways of valuing an asset, a business, or a company lead to varying answers. That's important to understand because such differences often create opportunities to acquire something at a lower price, make some change, and then either sell it or get credit for it being seen as more valuable through some other valuation form or approach.

Since this point about the effects of different valuation methods may seem abstract, let me give you a practical example. In the early 1980s, valuation multiples of publicly owned companies in the United States were very low. Many companies sold for less than five times a depressed level of earnings. Today, similar companies sell for more than triple that multiple while earnings are near or at record high levels. Short-term interest rates were also very high then. As a result, if you could borrow money long-term, you could afford to pay a 30 percent premium for a public company, operate the firm to generate lots of cash for paying off debt used to fund the purchase (perhaps by selling unneeded operations and cutting unnecessary overheads), and sell the company back to the public five years later for ten times what you paid. Some investors made over 5,000 percent gains on their equity investments at the time (aided by borrowing as much as 99 percent of the total purchase price).

So what value-form shifts have most often been used to generate profits by taking advantage of disparities in valuations? This list of nine ways of shifting from one value form to another isn't exhaustive, but it should help stimulate your thinking:

1. A company, business, operation, or asset is sold to those who want to use just the physical assets in some different way. This purchase might mean buying a paper mill and moving the equipment to a different site where pulp costs are much lower and shipping costs to customers are also less. Changing where the assets are used potentially enhances their value.

2. A company, business, operation, or asset is sold to those who want to use the physical assets in the same way, but can do so more efficiently. An example of this would be a well-run paper company buying a plant from a poorly run firm and operating the equipment to produce more paper at less cost. Operating the facilities better increases their value.

3. A company, business, operation, or asset is sold to a financial buyer who uses the physical assets in the same way, and no more or less efficiently, but who employs a lower-cost form of capital to pay for the purchase and future investments. In this case, the lower-cost capital increases the size of the cash flow created, as well as the value of that cash flow, increasing the price someone would pay for the physical assets with such financing attached.

4. A company, business, operation, or asset is sold to the employees who use the physical assets in the same way, but who are able to operate with lower overhead costs and benefit from a tax subsidy tied to their ownership. In this instance, lowered costs and the tax subsidy increase earnings and cash flow, thereby increasing the value that someone will pay for owning a public part of what the employees bought and continue to own.

5. A company, business, operation, or asset is sold to someone who breaks it up into as many different pieces as can increase value. For instance, the paper mill's equipment might be sold to someone planning to start a new mill in a better location; the land might be sold to someone who wants to develop it for a higher-value purpose; and the building might be demolished in such a way that its old bricks can be salvaged and sold at a high price for use in new buildings.

6. A company, business, or operation is turned into a publicly owned entity by selling stock. The extra costs of being a public company will lower the value unless there is a scarcity of such securities, in which case the price paid could increase in public hands.

7. This is the reverse of the sixth example: A public entity becomes a private one by purchasing all of the outstanding public shares. This shift eliminates the costs of being a public company and permits some tax advantages that increase the entity's value on a cash-flow basis.

8. A public enterprise uses a stock dividend to break itself into public entities that have a higher valuation in total than as one public company. This result might occur where one part of the company is unprofitable and has a lot of liabilities, while other parts of the company are highly valued by public investors.

9. A public enterprise buys back a large percentage of its own stock as a way to increase the per-share financial performance of the remaining shares. The overall enterprise value might not change, but the per-share value could be quite a bit higher.

As you can easily imagine, such transactions can also be performed in differing combinations and sequences across these nine value-transformation categories. Many such transactions are done by so-called private equity firms, earning them as much as multi-billion-dollar profits while making few operational improvements. Such results show that there's a lot of potential financial benefit involved in correctly answering questions about the highest value forms.

While there are probably millions of different ways that people calculate the value of assets, operations, businesses, and companies, the methods employed mostly fall into a few categories. I've listed six of the most common categories below:

1. The prices paid most recently during similar transactions

   Someone looking to buy a public stock would consider the last trade and what offers are on the books to gain an idea at what price the next trade might be. In a private market, such as for homes, realtors would compare properties using characteristics such as location, lot size, square footage, physical condition, and valuable appurtenances ... for instance, a swimming pool ... to estimate comparable values for home buyers and sellers.

2. An estimate of the resale value in another value form

   A person looking to buy a public company and then to sell off the pieces would estimate what the pieces would probably sell for 6–18 months after the purchase had been completed.

3. An estimate of the discounted cash flow of the asset, operation, business, or company

   In this method, projections are made of what will most likely happen to cash flow, and then the future cash is discounted back to the present by employing a combination of current interest rates and an appropriate risk premium.

4. An estimate of the discounted free cash flow of the asset, operation, business, or company

   Here, only the cash is considered and discounted that's not needed to operate what has been purchased.

5. An estimate of the discounted future dividends that will be paid

   From this perspective, cash dividends paid are discounted rather than overall company cash flow or free cash flow.

6. An estimate of the future earnings level and market multiple for a share of publicly traded stock

   In this instance, earnings per share are forecasted and then valued without discount by applying a multiple derived from examining the stock's history and current level, as well as those of its competitors.

The further into the future that estimates are made, the greater the likelihood of the estimates being wrong. In addition, errors become larger for longer-term estimates. As a result, the valuations of rapidly growing companies, businesses, and operations are often greatly overstated, due to people assuming better future performance than will actually occur. Sometimes such errors are based on misinterpreting company actions designed to mislead investors, often called "dressing up for sale," which can be a little like putting new paint on an old house in hopes that no one will notice the needed repairs that should reduce the house's value to a purchaser.

What's the key lesson? *Value can vary from the perspective of the holder versus that of the buyer, as well as from their intentions for taking different actions with a company, business, operation, or asset. Learning how to appreciate the opportunities to buy low and sell high are impor-*

tant aspects of creating breakthrough value improvements that benefit all stakeholders.

Your Lesson Twelve Assignments

1. What are the different ways that your company, business, activity, or assets can be economically valued?

2. How do those economic valuations differ?

3. What value-form shifts would most increase and decrease the valuation of your company, business, activity, or asset?

4. How would making those value-form shifts affect the values of stakeholder benefits?

Lesson Thirteen

Factors That Affect Valuations

According to the number of years
after the Jubilee
you shall buy from your neighbor, and
according to the number of years of crops
he shall sell to you.
According to the multitude of years
you shall increase its price, and
according to the fewer number of years
you shall diminish its price;
for he sells to you according *to*
the number of the years *of the crops.*

— Leviticus 25:15-16 (NKJV)

The idea of adjusting the price of something to reflect your use of it is an old one. In Leviticus 25:15-16 (NKJV), the Israelites are taught how to price agricultural land. In those days, land couldn't be permanently sold by Hebrews. Any "sale" ended at the Jubilee year, which occurred every 50 years. You obviously wouldn't pay the same price to farm the land for one year as you would to farm it for 49 years.

In this lesson, we explore the various ways that valuations are affected. Once again, we'll take a quick, rather than an exhaustive, look at the subject.

Perhaps the most important point about how valuations are affected is that shifts occur quite rapidly so that the level of value identified by any given method is almost always changing, with some values shifting as rapidly as second by second. This point about volatility is important to understand because such fluctuations in values often create opportunities to acquire something at a lower price, then to make an improvement, and either to sell it later or to get credit for what you bought being more valuable because you picked a favorable time to buy.

This observation might not be clear, so let me give you a practical example. If you look at the typical publicly held company, you will see that the stock price will vary over the course of a year by quite a wide margin. It's not unusual for the annual variation to be 30 percent higher and lower than the average daily price. That means you could simply buy such a stock at a 30 percent discount from the average and sell it for a 30 percent premium within 12 months. That's usually an annualized gain of over 100 percent. What's more, you can also make the reverse investment: Sell the stock short (borrow securities and sell them) at a 30 percent premium and later buy it and repay the lender with shares purchased at a 30 percent discount. That's a gain of over 40 percent after paying the usual carrying costs. And with a highly volatile security you might be able to do both kinds of transactions several times in a single year. Think of that!

Obviously, some things about what underlies the security are changing to allow for such wide swings, even if they only occur for short periods of time. What are some factors that can have such large influences on price?

Here is a list of what some of the more significant value influencers have been for common stocks:

- Revenues
    - Revenues per share
    - Revenue growth rate
    - Revenues as a ratio to various performance measures

  - Analyst estimates of each of these performance levels over different time periods in the next few years

- Earnings after tax
  - Earnings per share (total after-tax earnings divided by the average number of shares outstanding)
  - Earnings before taxes and interest costs
  - Earnings before taxes, interest costs, depreciation, and amortization charges
  - Earnings before preferred dividends, taxes, interest costs, depreciation, and amortization charges
  - Per share amounts of the prior three measures that adjust earnings
  - Analyst estimates of each of these performance levels on a per-share basis over different time periods during the next few years

- Cash flow (a wide range of different definitions)
  - Net cash flow (after deducting reinvestments for fixed assets and working capital)
  - Cash-flow measures on a per-share basis over different time periods during the next few years

- Market value of derivative contracts (such as put and call options) for future purchase and sale of commodities, currencies, and operating rights

- Dividends
  - Dividends per share
  - Dividends per share over different time periods during the next few years

- Performance in the preceding dimensions for a specific part of the entire company

- Various balance-sheet ratios, especially related to the level and cost of debt
- Changes in accounting rules that affect the preceding numbers
- The total value of any public shares of larger entities owned by the parent company
- Liquidation or salvage value of the assets independent of their being used to conduct the current businesses

- Value of any brands independent of their use by the current businesses
- Unused tax losses
- Changes in management
- Changes in strategy
- New products and services

- Price increases and decreases
- Application of accounting rules by the firm's auditors
- Large accidents and mistakes (think of substantial oil spills in the Gulf of Mexico)
- Availability of protection for intellectual property (patents, in particular)
- Inflation (many different measures)

- Interest rates (many different measures)
- Changes in government policy that affect inflation and interest rates
- The past price volatility of the company's securities
- Patterns of various "technical" price indicators (based on chart analysis)
- Performance of similar companies in the recent past, current time, or estimated near-term future

- New legislation or regulations that will affect sales, profits, and cash flow
- Transparency of the company's current activities to investors

- Currency values
- Estimates of industry, supplier, and customer buying power, spending, productivity, and pricing trends
- Supply of and demand for the securities

- Borrowing and short-selling rules for the securities
- Presence or absence of an offer to purchase the entire company

As you can easily imagine, many of these value factors are shifting in opposing directions throughout the day, week, month, and year. When the shifts are mostly in the same direction, the effects can be quite dramatic ... such as when a stock rises or falls by 40 percent during a single day.

If we go from looking at valuation for a public security to valuation of a business or part of the company in a private transaction, the time duration under consideration is usually far enough in the future to pass the point for which anyone can hope to accurately assess what will happen. Almost all the same factors are influences, except for the ones about public price action of the company's stock.

What's the key lesson? *Value is continually changing as the factors that affect valuation shift. Consequently, we should expect that future value will be both substantially higher and lower than current value (in any form) in both the near- and longer-term futures. Learning how to appreciate the opportunities that volatility brings to buy low and sell high are important aspects of creating breakthrough value improvements for all stakeholders.*

Your Lesson Thirteen Assignments

1. What are the different ways that your company, business, activity, or assets can be economically valued?

2. How do those economic valuations differ?

3. What shifts in factors affecting valuation methods would most increase and decrease the value of your company, business, activity, or asset?

4. How would those valuation shifts affect benefit values for your various stakeholders?

Part Three

Business Strategies That Add Value

Why do the nations rage,
And the people plot a vain thing?

— Psalm 2:1 (NKJV)

While this verse from the Psalms refers to those who oppose Jesus and God's Kingdom, the verse incidentally describes the limits of many traditional approaches to business strategy. Planning of military campaigns has been the model for much of what companies use today to direct their organizations: Obtaining and retaining customers is the goal, and competing firms are the enemy. As you will see in the next book in the Advanced Business series, *Advanced Business for Innovation,* it's actually much more beneficial to think of competing firms as resources you can use to stimulate useful innovation that will enhance how many benefits can be provided to how many people, rather than as foes. Companies need to redirect strategic-business thinking to include adding value for all stakeholders, rather than ignoring adding such value, leaving it untouched, or even diminishing it.

Consequently, we begin Lesson Fourteen by considering the importance of diagnosing what elements of your organization's performance either enhance or diminish value for each type of stakeholder. The lesson also contains more detailed information about how to make such a diagnosis in terms of influencing shareholder value. This material is supplemented in Part Eight by a more detailed discussion of identifying the optimal program for improving stakeholder value.

Lesson Fifteen spells out accelerating improvement in terms of the value-expanding implications of implementing a number of complementary 2,000 percent solutions and then repeatedly making new ones that improve the same performance areas. The result is to create great flexibility for allocating stakeholder benefits, without annoying anyone by not meeting his or her expectations.

In Lesson Sixteen, I introduce a concept that may be new to you, that of a business model that can be expanded along several dimensions. Such business models serve as growth foundations that are far more robust, sustainable, and valuable than what traditional business models enable.

During Lesson Seventeen, our investigation centers on entering a new business with significant cost and value advantages. The strategy is exemplified by looking at the history of Nucor and how the company reshaped the American steel industry by successfully employing such a strategy.

For Lesson Eighteen, we consider merging two businesses with complementary weaknesses that can be overcome by operating as one company. This lesson considers the possible advantages of the Teva-Cephalon merger in the pharmaceutical industry to demonstrate the potential of such an approach.

Lesson Nineteen points out the advantages of operating in businesses with offerings stakeholders often experience, understand, and like. Such organizations are often able to deliver more value for the same effort and resources due to strong investor preferences for what they do.

In Lesson Twenty, we explore how reducing risk can substantially increase value for stakeholders by making them much more confident about your future success. In so doing, you'll attract more support.

Lesson Twenty-One spells out some of the more important value-improvement advantages of franchising other stakeholders to operate a business under your direction. These advantages include developing a higher value for ownership of an entity, faster growth, lower costs, and sooner creating value for more stakeholders.

During Lesson Twenty-Two, we look at the similar benefits of licensing for accomplishing what franchising does, but without many of the start-up and ongoing costs of franchising. Consequently, you will learn why licensing is often a better strategy than is franchising for smaller organizations.

We wrap up Part Three in Lesson Twenty-Three by examining how a company's location can affect its valuation and describe considerations that could lead a firm to shift its base. This strategy is different from merely changing or adding to where a company's shares are listed and traded.

Lesson Fourteen

Diagnose Value Sensitivities

You shall have a perfect and just weight,
a perfect and just measure,
that your days may be lengthened
in the land which the LORD
your God is giving you.

— Deuteronomy 25:15 (NKJV)

In agrarian Israel during Biblical times, a number of agricultural commodities were bartered and sold. While doing so, it was normal to rely on whoever had a device for measuring the quantities. If such a person had dishonest devices or ways of measuring, unrighteousness occurred. If the measuring device was true and used properly, then righteousness would be the standard. Notice that God also provided that longer life would be enjoyed by those who used accurate measurements. Whether God said this because of supernatural blessings He would provide or because the person was less likely to be killed or injured by someone who was wronged is unclear.

A parallel exists for corporate leaders. If they measure wrongly in trying to provide more stakeholder value, their time in office will probably be shorter than if they do so fairly and accurately. While most such leaders mean to do the right thing, they can easily be mistaken while attempting to do so.

Many company leaders will confidently tell you how their company's performance affects the stock price. If you ask them about how that same performance affects other stakeholders, you may encounter a long silence and some head scratching. If you then check on what the majority of potential investors have to say about the company, you'll usually find that they think the company is horribly misdirected in terms of doing what will advance shareholder value. Conversations with many other current and potential stakeholders will yield similar responses.

How can such huge disagreements occur? Well, company leaders often assume that they know what's best for one and all, without having taken the trouble to check with those who are feeling ignored or offended. Some of such company leaders will defend themselves by carefully explaining how they spend almost all of their time meeting with and listening to stakeholders. These leaders cannot imagine that they don't have a good sense of the pulse of such people.

Similar to how a physician will have trouble taking a pulse without being present in person or by being electronically connected to a sensor that accurately transmits such information, a company leader may be hindered by not receiving candid answers in person to his or her questions. In addition, those who are most disaffected may not even bother to share their views with the company.

The subject of knowing how to improve stakeholder value is important because much of the value gain for all stakeholders comes from making changes that stimulate all stakeholders to take helpful actions: Potential investors buy stock; lenders offer better terms; customers purchase more offerings; end users increase their consumption; suppliers provide more innovative inputs; employees take extra care; employees' families tell everyone they should support the company; and neighbors and communities do the same. By ignoring the possibility that the company doesn't know what will most encourage stakeholders, companies are bound to miss the optimal path for creating more stakeholder value.

Let's look at how to close the gap in understanding what causes increased stakeholder value. In this lesson, we build on the lessons in Part Two that describe different economic value forms: valuation methods most commonly used to determine a price for purchasing or selling an asset, ownership in a business, a business itself, or an entire company; and the factors that have a large impact on those valuation methods.

Perhaps the most important point to share with you is that although hundreds of different methods may be used to determine the value of a given asset, activity, or ownership in a business, a business itself, or an entire company for any given person or organization, a very few factors will have much more influence on those values than any others.

Let me share seven points in terms of shareholder value to open the discussion:

1. Despite a lot of commentary among valuation "purists" that earnings aren't very important for creating economic value, *the equations used to determine value are almost always primarily influenced by either current earnings or projected earnings.* I first became aware of this characteristic over 40 years ago. A friend shared a paper with me based on his DBA dissertation research at Harvard Business School in which he measured the earnings sensitivity of the most popular "value" models. Since then, I've yet to see a commonly used valuation model that isn't primarily driven by earnings or assumptions about earnings.

2. In calculating value, *projected earnings are almost always a bigger factor in value calculations than are current and past earnings.* That's because most methods look at today's value in terms of expected future performance.

3. *Projected earnings are almost always heavily influenced by current and past earnings.* This observation may seem like a misprint, but realize that most valuers don't project future per-

formance from scratch. Many use software programs to create a regression of past performance and then make a few assumptions about that regression to project the future. If, let's say, earnings have been growing at 8 percent a year, the projection might instead use 7 percent a year for five years, and then assume 6 percent growth after that. As you can see, the past growth rate is still the most important factor in determining such numbers.

4. *Projected earnings are notoriously inaccurate.* If you look at prior valuations of soon-to-be bankrupt companies before the legal filing occurred, you'll find most people who valued such companies were estimating profits and cash flow where there would only be losses. As this example suggests, projections can greatly overstate future earnings performance compared to what the reality will be.

5. *Earnings projections usually reflect to some extent the valuer's emotional comfort with the people who provide the information.* Admired executives are assumed to be able to do better, even if past results are based on not-yet-perceived illegal actions and so-called cooked books.

6. *Most people who produce valuations don't understand very much about the rules for making accurate predictions of future performance.* In other words, where pages of projected numbers give the impression of flawless expertise, there is usually at least partial ignorance underlying the preparation of those numbers.

   One of my favorite examples of such partial ignorance in recent years occurred with American mortgage-backed bonds. Their interest payments are based on the actual interest payments made by a group of homeowners on their mortgages. In fraudulent transactions, many people received mortgages who could not afford to make as many as two payments. As a result, soon most of the mortgage holders for a given bond were not making any payments. Yet almost all of these bonds were initially sold at high prices based on assumptions that almost every homeowner in the pool would pay on time and in full. Later investigations showed that many of the highly paid people who valued the bonds never looked into the credit risk or the payment histories of these mortgages. Were they dumb, lazy, or just ignorant? Take your pick.

7. *When asked about why they believed that performance was going to be much better than actually occurred, most valuers will point to an assumption they made that was both unverified and wrong.* In most cases, the stakeholders affected by the valuation had little or no role in setting or influencing those assumptions.

Having been skeptical about the bases of valuations, you may be wondering how you can go about finding your company's sensitivities to various factors that can influence valuations. Let me suggest four methods that should work well for you:

1. Ask someone who does valuations of your company to share the valuation model that she or he uses. Change by 10 percent each of the numbers that are being used by the model to calculate a valuation (one at a time) and write down by what percentage the total valuation changes in each case. The shifts that cause the largest percentage changes in valuation are the ones you are most sensitive to.

2. If you cannot access such a model and the inputs to it, ask someone who does valuations for your kind of asset, activity, business, business ownership, or company where you might find a valuation model you can use that's reasonably similar to what most people use. Chances are that there's either a free or

an inexpensive model available. Conduct the same sort of sensitivity tests as in point 1 above.

3. If neither of those methods turns up a model you can use, do an online search for "valuation models" and include a reference to the type of asset, activity, business, business ownership, or company that you want to evaluate. You will probably find Excel-based models that you can use to create your own valuations and also to measure sensitivities as described in point 1 above.

4. You can also measure how valuation methods have changed over time and what your sensitivities are, if you have enough valuation data points (usually at least 30) over a number of years ... ideally at least fifteen. Let me give you a simple description of a process to use those numbers:

   a. Use some statistical program that allows you to do full-fledged multivariate regressions (I like SPSS, which can be used on a PC and isn't very expensive).
   b. Then apply a full set of standard statistical tests to identify the most robust regressions.
   c. After that, survey those who create valuations for your type of business or activity to ask if and how they use the variables that turned out to be the most important (biggest value influences) in your sensitivity testing.
   d. Take those factors that valuers are actually most often using and focus on enhancing those to improve the future stakeholder value.

While I don't have space here to describe what a parallel process might look like for each type of stakeholder, I'm sure you can imagine that carefully designed interviews conducted by people who aren't known to represent your company can be a great help for determining what factors most influence the behaviors that are helpful for increasing stakeholder value. If the math involved isn't familiar to you, you can probably find a professor or a quality manager in your company who can help you do the necessary work.

What's the key lesson? *Some variables will have a much higher influence than others on your company's valuation and the values your stakeholders receive. Choosing the right variables to emphasize greatly simplifies the task of enhancing stakeholder value. Your strategy for making value improvements for your organization and its stakeholders should focus on enhancing performance in and perceptions of future performance for these variables.*

Your Lesson Fourteen Assignments

1. What are the most important value-influencing variables for your assets, activities, businesses, business ownerships, and companies in terms of benefits for each type of stakeholder?

2. What are the most important value-influencing variables for benefits affecting each of your stakeholders' lives, activities, assets, businesses, business ownerships, and companies?

3. Are there any value-influencing variables to emphasize that will provide the greatest value improvements for your organization, as well as for a large number of your stakeholders?

4. If there aren't any recurring value-influencing variables to emphasize, what strategies will improve the fullest range of the most sensitive value-influencing variables?

Lesson Fifteen

Accelerate Improvement

Therefore David inquired of the LORD,
and He said,

"You shall not go up;
circle around behind them,
and come upon them
in front of the mulberry trees.
And it shall be,
when you hear the sound
of marching in the tops
of the mulberry trees,
then you shall advance quickly.
For then the LORD will
go out before you to strike
the camp of the Philistines."

— 2 Samuel 5:23-24 (NKJV)

As Lesson Thirteen describes, growth in a number of corporate performance measures can translate into a higher price for the company's stock. Such an expansion in stock value can be used to directly enhance value for all stakeholders by allowing them to share in gains from ownership and indirectly by using some of the stock to pay for any costs associated with value improvements.

While some executives have an instinct to seek improvements of all sorts as soon as possible, other executives like to avoid addressing whatever needs improving, while still others wait to make improvements they already know how to implement so that they can easily meet their budget promises without taking very many risks. While either of the latter two approaches can feel as if it makes the executive's job safer, the actual result can be quite the opposite: leaving the leader exposed to justifiable disappointment over not doing what was reasonably achievable. And stakeholders have certainly not benefited to any great extent from such "playing safe."

Let's look at why accelerating improvement is so valuable. The verses from 2 Samuel 5 (NKJV) demonstrate the case in point. David acknowledged that he needed God's help. As He often does, God left an important role for David to play: When David heard the sound of marching in the tops of the mulberry trees, he was to advance quickly. Obviously, David could have chosen to disobey and advance slowly, but surely the results wouldn't have been as good because the Philistines were at maximum disarray then due to God striking their camp. By waiting, the Philistines would have been better able to defend themselves from David and his men. Similarly, your expansion of stakeholder value will be reduced or delayed if you don't accelerate making improvements that God has made available to you. Just consider that God may have other opportunities He wants to present that can only be made available after you grasp the current ones!

Perhaps the most important point to share with you is that valuers expect one of two improvement patterns, either current growth followed by gently decelerating percentage rates of growth or more rapid growth followed by an equally rapid decline. If you deliver accelerating improvement, valuers will usually fail to appreciate that you can keep accomplishing this result longer than other organizations have done. In so doing, you will then have opportunities to use the unexpected improvements to deliver more value for all stakeholders.

Let me share a few general points to open the investigation of value benefits from accelerating growth. In doing so, I want to provide four helpful perspectives on how valuers usually think:

1. *Many valuers assume that growth is constrained by something that cannot be changed.* They think of growing a business as being like the growth of lily pads in a pond. These water-based plants grow very rapidly and soon choke a pond by covering all of the surface area. Whatever the growth rate is, it stays pretty constant until the plants start to run out of either nutrients or surface area. Then, growth suddenly stops. In calculating the value of what you or your stakeholders own, valuers will be looking for such a constraint and will limit their valuations according to where they perceive the constraint.

   As an example, I remember valuers in 1975 trying to determine how many McDonald's restaurants could be built. I don't remember the exact number, but I believe that the estimate then was for reaching 14,000 to 15,000 stores. Today, McDonald's and its franchisees operate more than 35,000 stores and keep adding more. I suspect that the ultimate number will be well over 150,000.

   What happened? Well, the valuers assumed that McDonald's would stay about the same. But it didn't. Some of the innovations that have occurred since then include drive-through windows, a successful breakfast menu, chicken, salads, premium sandwiches, better desserts, and upscale coffees.

   As you can see, even considering the possible consequences of such incremental improvements is difficult for valuers. Imagine how much more trouble valuers have with anticipating the consequences from exponential breakthroughs that they don't see coming.

2. *Most valuers look to new offerings, geographic expansion, and acquisitions as the main drivers of future growth.* As you can easily imagine, each of such changes is normally like taking a single step up a long flight of stairs. As a result, there is rapid initial momentum that quickly dissipates when the new source of growth is fully exploited. After all, once you provide every type of offering in an industry, are available globally, and have acquired all the competitors and related entities you can, it would seem as if there wouldn't be much room left for rapid growth. Such companies mostly innovate by cutting costs by taking advantage of their increased size. Seldom do they focus on the kind of breakthrough operational changes that make larger and longer-term growth possible.

3. *Valuers almost always consider an organization's history in estimating the rate of future growth and improvements.* The more rapidly an organization is growing, typically the more slowly it makes improvements in areas that aren't necessary for creating more near-term growth. For instance, Apple is expanding through providing a wide array of mobile electronic devices tied to its software and applications libraries. Although I have not studied the company in detail, as a valuer I would assume that helping customers access more valuable exclusive content (such as older movies converted into 3-D images that could be displayed on Apple's mobile devices) would probably do far more than simply offering sleeker, better-styled devices that use a little faster chip, provide a slightly brighter display, contain batteries that last somewhat longer, and feature new components that improve some aspect of visual or sound quality a little.

   As a result, I can assure you that valuers are estimating Apple's future improvements around its historic pattern of introducing new portable devices, rather than including the benefits of anything else, even if Apple is actually working hard at improving other fundamental aspects of what it provides or does.

4. *Valuers rarely consider potential improvements unless management makes a strong case that such improvements are being sought and that credible progress is being made.* In other words, valuers are skeptical about possible new sources of expansion. Can you imagine how someone who has never seen a 2,000 percent solution might respond to the idea that an organization might create a regular stream of them affecting all aspects of what the firm does?

In addressing these four valuer perspectives, *let me note that the right 2,000 percent solutions can accelerate value improvement for quite a long time.* That's true, in part, because complementary 2,000 percent solutions (such as increasing revenues by 20 times, decreasing offering costs by 96 percent, reducing investment intensity by 96 percent, and increasing value by 20 times) equally multiply some form of benefits for stakeholders. That statement is also true in part because complementary 2,000 percent solutions can be added in most cases faster than the full gain is realized from past solutions, due to positive secondary and tertiary effects from applying any given solution.

I've put together a little display of growth effects from 2,000 percent solutions below that demonstrates what I've described in the preceding paragraph about how growth rates can accelerate following such solutions. The table below describes the individual growth effects on the entire organization of seven different solutions and four further 2,000 percent solutions being introduced in the first four solution areas, as well as the cumulative annual effects of all the solutions on the entire organization's growth over five years:

	Year 1	Year 2	Year 3	Year 4	Year 5
Solution 1	20%	35%	45%	500%	2,000%
Solution 2	5%	25%	80%	200%	2,000%
Solution 3	5%	60%	230%	550%	2,000%
Solution 4	60%	90%	217%	400%	1,300%
Solution 5	0%	5%	60%	529%	1,400%
Solution 6	0%	0%	10%	55%	230%
Solution 7	0%	0%	0%	30%	70%
Further 1*	0%	0%	0%	0%	400%
Further 2*	0%	0%	0%	0%	100%
Further 3*	0%	0%	0%	0%	100%
Further 4*	0%	0%	0%	0%	1,200%
TOTAL	90%	215%	642%	2,264%	10,800%

*Assuming the further solution in an area provides benefits 20 times faster than the first solution did, the typical result identified by The 400 Year Project.

If I were to add 10 more years of new and further solutions to this table, annual growth would continue to accelerate because the growth impact of the further solutions in the earlier solution areas would keep expanding exponentially. So even if the rate of developing initial and further solutions in the same areas declined, the total company growth rate could easily accelerate for 15 years. That's unheard of in business history. Think of how exciting it will be to accomplish this result!

Another aspect of these valuer perspectives can be appreciated by looking at how business leaders typically behave. *Most business leaders long ago learned to negotiate for delivering the least amount of improvement that owners and their superiors will accept.* As a result, a leader might seek to grow value at 10 percent a year.

If a great breakthrough was developed, such a leader would typically slow down the implementation of the improvement so that the string of 10 percent annual improvements could be extended for as many years as possible. This behavior is called "satisficing," a term coined by Herbert Simon to capture the typical attempt to minimally satisfy others. Simon argued that human beings lack an ability to conceive of a "maximizing" outcome. What do you think of Simon's argument?

Instead, I believe that such behavior is connected to a combination of fear (not expecting to ever make another big improvement) and laziness (not wanting to do enough work to match the earlier large improvement).

With knowledge of and successful experience with the 2,000 percent solution development processes, the psychology totally changes. Each complementary solution makes it easier to locate and implement a much more valuable solution. Each solution can also make each earlier solution up to 20 times more valuable in terms of stakeholder benefits. As a result, most people will be eager to get on with seeking the next breakthrough. The psychology is more like taking a first bite of something you love, triggering a desire to eat as much as you can.

Consider that those leaders who persist in operating with the satisficing mentality should love 2,000 percent solutions. Such leaders could string out the gains from four complementary 2,000 percent solutions into being able to expand volume and value by 10 percent a year for several lifetimes. All they would have to do is be sure that most of the staff learned how to make 2,000 percent solutions and worked on the right ones. How could a little leadership effort ever pay off better in terms of creating exponential benefits?

An important lesson from these observations is that the competitive advantages an organization can gain from working hard on complementary 2,000 percent solutions are so substantial that the bulk of the benefits will be hidden from valuers and competitors until many years after the actual solutions have been developed and are being implemented.

The lesson I would like you to draw from this thinking about valuers is that *owners and managers should seriously consider develop-*

ing a long-term strategy of increasing the rate of exponential growth to permit greater flexibility in unexpectedly delivering more value to end users, customers, employees, owners, and other stakeholders.

If you are curious about what such a strategy is and how it might be accomplished, you'll find specific guidance in the remaining Part Three lessons, as well as in the discussions of which 2,000 percent solutions to seek in Part Four. You can also supplement these materials by reading and applying *The 2,000 Percent Solution*, *The 2,000 Percent Solution Workbook*, *The 2,000 Percent Squared Solution*, and *Business Basics*.

What's the key lesson? *When the full force of numerous, complementary 2,000 percent solutions is in place, you can overwhelm expectations to the upside by such a wide margin as to dramatically tilt the customer, competitor, and valuation landscapes in your favor. The resulting value gains will soar long into the future as stakeholder value improvements accelerate and appreciation for what you are doing gradually sinks in with valuers.*

Your Lesson Fifteen Assignments

1. Consider which combinations of complementary 2,000 percent solutions and further solutions to the same problems or opportunity areas will most accelerate value growth for all stakeholders.

2. Develop a 15-year plan to provide a continually accelerating rate of growth and growth in value.

3. Evaluate how the 15-year plan could be improved to create even more customer value, greater advantage over competitors, and larger benefits for owners by tilting the landscape in your favor.

4. Investigate how all stakeholders will be affected.

5. Modify the plan to reflect what you learn about tilting the landscape and the impact on stakeholders so you can create more benefits in both dimensions.

6. Monitor the plan's implementation to see where adjustments need to be made based on the results that are achieved.

Lesson Sixteen

Establish a Business Model That Is Expandable in Several Dimensions

"Enlarge the place of your tent,
And let them stretch out
the curtains of your dwellings;
Do not spare;
Lengthen your cords,
And strengthen your stakes."

— Isaiah 54:2 (NKJV)

This verse from Isaiah 54 (NKJV) is often cited as an example of what God wants each of his believers to do in preparation for increasing His Kingdom. A business model that's expandable in several dimensions provides opportunities for a corporate leader to do something comparable for stakeholders.

Before discussing an expandable business model, let's first define a few terms. A *business model* has seven elements: the "who," "what," "when," "where," "why," "how," and "how much" of serving customers and adding value for stakeholders. If you want to explore the aspects of this definition in more depth, please consult *The Ultimate Competitive Advantage* by Carol Coles and me.

An expandable dimension can be part of any of these seven elements, but the dimension has to enable a business to develop or improve an advantage versus competitors in accomplishing some valuable new tasks for stakeholders. A business model can be greatly enhanced by improving performance in any one of the seven dimensions listed above. *However, an expandable business model improves the performance of at least four of the seven dimensions.*

Here's an example to clarify these concepts. Sir Richard Branson has established more than 100 businesses under the Virgin brand, enterprises that range from bridal wear to cellular telephone service to an airline. His businesses have usually been reasonably successful. Whenever he develops a new offering, Sir Richard changes "what" is provided from the standard to something that some customers or end users prefer. In most cases, the ways of providing the offering are different from prior ones, an adjustment of "how" a business is conducted. Many of the customers and other stakeholders are different, often affecting "who" is involved. Price points are different, usually lower, causing shifts in "how much" is charged. The geographic markets are sometimes different, affecting "where" the business is conducted. New and existing customers try the new offerings due to confidence built by having had good experiences with other Virgin offerings. Because of the overall brand strength and Sir Richard's reputation, this approach for expanding a business model into new dimensions can be continued for many more years.

Consider a different example. Amazon.com entered the book retailing business by putting book wholesalers' lists online, enabling the purchase of special-order books to seem almost like buying in-stock books. Based on the profits from this lucrative business, Amazon.com was able to expand into selling branded items in a large number of consumer-goods categories. From there, the company began to attract more visitors to its Web site by building an active online community, especially through reader "reviews." The company then became a book publisher for people who wanted to self-publish. To lower costs and improve service, Amazon.com put print-on-demand equipment in all of its warehouses, making these books immediately available to ship at a small additional production expense over mass printing. After that, the company developed the Kindle, an electronic format for reading that many people prefer to physical books, and Amazon.com became the world's largest publisher and seller of e-books. Now, its book-related profits mostly come from selling e-books, which can be purchased for immediate download. Encouraged by this success, Amazon.com now seeks to do the same thing with movies via streaming video. The company has clearly shown skill in converting physical businesses into electronic, online ones and building a huge, appreciative audience. Such a process can be repeated indefinitely, changing all seven elements of the business model by expanding into new dimensions. It shouldn't surprise us that today's market capitalization for the firm is one of the largest in the world, with a price/earnings ratio at a stratospheric level.

To a casual observer, such a dimension-stretching strategy involving business models may only seem appropriate for market-expanding breakthroughs. While such strategies are certainly great for market expansion, I want you to realize that the approach is even more useful for developing and implementing solutions that greatly expand value for all stakeholders.

Let me explain. As I've mentioned before, investors pay very high prices when they believe that growth in revenues and profits can continue for a long time at a high rate. That's why some people bought private shares in the social networking site Facebook at an enterprise equity value of over $50 billion before the company went public.

An expandable business model that operates along several dimensions is ideal for encouraging such enthusiasm. Different investors will be persuaded by the various ways that the organization can grow, assigning much value for what the company isn't doing yet, but which it certainly can be counted on to accomplish. In the case of Facebook, the anticipated opportunity was selling substantial advertising to be displayed on mobile devices, something that wasn't accomplished for two years after being widely anticipated.

Establishing such an expandable business model requires developing some core business skills that relate to the opportunities, attracting an ever-increasing number of enthusiastic customers, and organizing innovative activities that can be accomplished simultaneously by many different people. If you want to see a contrast between an expandable business model with several dimensions and one that doesn't expand, just compare Apple with Microsoft as they were in 2010. I'm sure you'll agree that Steve Jobs had created an expandable business model then for Apple while Microsoft had not. The latter's forays into other business models have almost always been flops.

What's the key lesson? *By establishing a business model that is expandable in several dimensions, the potential is exponentially enhanced to succeed in market expansion, cost-cutting, investment reductions, and value improvements for stakeholders. The most substantial increases will come in stakeholder benefits, due to having more resources to apply for this purpose and making the likelihood of long-term growth and profitability easier for stakeholders to appreciate and support.*

Lesson Sixteen Assignments

1. Examine your business model to determine whether it is expandable or not, and, if it is, along what dimensions.

2. Consider how you could make your business model more expandable along more dimensions.

3. Evaluate how credible such expansions would be to potential investors and stakeholders.

4. Determine how you can increase effectiveness and credibility for expanding your business model along several dimensions.

Lesson Seventeen

Enter a New Business with Significant Cost and Value Advantages

"Enter by the narrow gate;
for wide is *the gate and*
broad is *the way that leads to destruction,*
and there are many who go in by it.
Because narrow is *the gate and*
difficult is *the way which leads to life,*
and there are few who find it."

— Matthew 7:13-14 (NKJV)

These verses from Matthew 7 (NKJV) contain the words of Jesus describing how difficult it is for some people to choose Salvation by repenting their sins and following Him, rather than conforming to the world's ideas of what should be done. In doing so, Jesus reminds us that much of what people believe is quite wrong. For instance, almost every corporate leader sees entering a new business area as a solution for everything from lacking enough growth to finding new customers. Unfortunately, most companies enter new businesses in ways that usually leave the firm weaker and more vulnerable, without adding appreciable lasting value for any stakeholders.

Despite this sorry track record, entering a new business is a way of improving stakeholder value that most people feel they completely understand, seek opportunities to invest in, and are willing to pay unusually high prices to accomplish. In doing so, despite the obvious stakeholder value advantages of starting with significant cost and value advantages over competitors, few company leaders seek such opportunities when looking for new businesses to enter.

Let me help you understand the sources of such illogical behavior. I begin by explaining what I mean by cost and value advantages:

- By cost advantages, I mean that it costs all stakeholders at least 20 percent less (including the price paid for the offering) to use this new offering than whatever offering they have been using.
- By value advantage, I mean that stakeholders obtain at least 25 percent more of at least one highly esteemed quality than they do now while receiving no less of any other benefits provided by the offering that they currently use.

Here's an example of cost and value advantages in entering a new business: American steelmaking leader Nucor originally decided to manufacture because domestic producers charged Nucor too much and the quality of imported steel wasn't good enough to be used for constructing steel joists. Because Nucor didn't need very much steel, the company chose to buy an electric arc furnace suitable for melting scrap steel rather than building a much larger blast furnace for combining basic materials. Traditionally, steel made from scrap was also of poor quality due to the variability of the input. However, under the leadership of the company's metallurgist, CEO Ken Iverson, Nucor began to make higher-quality steel from scrap than others could at lower cost than blast-furnace producers.

Since then, the company has continually found ways to use still-lower quality, less expensive scrap while producing ever higher-quality finished steel products and selling them at lower prices than producers who use blast furnaces or continuous casting technology.

As a result, the number of steel markets in which Nucor competes has greatly expanded. In the course of making these improvements, Nucor has also learned how to create steel that's superior to any alternative sources, regardless of the production method. At the time when such superior results began to occur, Nucor was, in fact, producing with both major cost and value advantages over all of its competitors.

Such methods work well strategically because new entrants can only serve a small part of the market. As a consequence, the prices that the highest-cost producers charge continue to prevail, creating a so-called price umbrella under which the low-cost producer can charge lower than market prices while gaining an unusually high profit margin (after-tax profits as a percentage of the selling price). Market share changes hands mainly due to shifts in capacity from the old technology (or business methods) to expansions of the newer, more efficient ones.

This process of capacity adjustment under a price umbrella continues until almost all of the old capacity and methods have been replaced either by the new entrants, or similar or better changes are made by the original producers. At about that time, the price drops to a much lower level that is appealing to those using the new methods, but uneconomical for using any of the prior methods and technologies. Those who don't adjust shut down their operations rather than lose more money. Market share gains slow at this point for the advantaged entrants until new ways of securing even more cost and value advantages are introduced.

The Nucor example may not be easy for you to follow. If so, consider instead how consumer electronics have evolved for storing and playing music, listening to radio programs, watching television shows, playing electronic games, enhancing high-tech effects such as through making 3D images available from screens, and cellular telephones. If you adjust prices for what else could be bought with that amount of money at the time (measuring in constant purchasing power), you see that each new generation of consumer electronics has cost less for the same functions and has performed these functions better ... and often provided new functions that users highly valued at no net cost in terms of purchasing power.

The low-priced end of the different national markets for vehicles has often operated the same way. New entrants brought lower prices for vehicles with better quality and reliability, greater fuel economy, and fewer unwanted emissions.

So far this lesson sounds like a standard business strategy review, doesn't it? You are probably wondering what the connection is to adding more stakeholder value. Let's now look narrowly at just that element.

First, realize that such strategies provide enormous growth potential, something that investors love because of the size of the annual percentage gains and how long they can continue. For instance, when PepsiCo bought Frito-Lay, its salty snack business that had many superior product benefits and lower costs due to direct-to-store delivery, in 1965, the business was only selling $180 million worth of snacks a year. Fifty years later, the business was selling more than $11 billion worth of snacks for a total growth of 63 times, a 9 percent compound annual rate of sales growth, which is all but unheard of in a packaged-food business for time periods longer than five years.

Second, such strategies normally lead to faster earnings than sales growth, something that causes many investors to add a premium to what they would normally pay for outstanding growth prospects. In addition, more resources are generated to add stakeholder value.

Third, such strategies are rarely derailed in the short term. As a result, the pathway causes investors to gain an unusual amount of confidence that the high rate of growth will continue in the future. When feeling more confident, investors will pay more. Stakeholders who can contribute to increasing the success also share in that confidence and increase their support.

Fourth, the contrast is dramatic between how well the innovator does and how poorly the stalled organizations are performing, causing investors to perceive management performance as being much better than it really is. Much of what investors see as superior management is actually more akin to gravity. If you push a rock off the top of a tall building, it will keep falling until it hits something solid or the ground. The initial push was all that it took for the rock to travel. This kind of strategy creates a similar effect.

Fifth, it's hard for management to get it wrong. If they just keep repeating what they've been doing in adding more value and reducing costs, these efforts will probably be enough to succeed ... at least until the next business model innovation by a major industry entrant or competitor.

Sixth, by accomplishing such results in a new business area, it's easier to create an attractive value structure around the new success. Since what's happening in that business doesn't have much effect on the rest of the company, there are also fewer discouraging delays caused by internal squabbles over what to do next. Investors and stakeholders cheer and rush to climb on the bandwagon of proven success.

I could go on, but I'm sure you get the idea.

Naturally, while making such headway, there's plenty of room to identify and provide new value to other stakeholders, funded by the ever-expanding profit margins and cash flows that seem to defy gravity.

What's the key lesson? *By entering a new business with substantial cost and value advantages, you can improve eventual business performance and also cause value perceptions to be higher and more stable, leading to faster share value growth. By doing so, you protect your ability to reward stakeholders who can add further gains to your economic performance.*

Your Lesson Seventeen Assignments

1. Find five new businesses that you can enter with substantial cost and value advantages.

2. Determine which of these businesses has the greatest long-term growth potential.

3. Consider which one of these businesses would most limit competitors from responding.

4. Investigate how stakeholders and investors think about the value potential for them of each business.

5. Focus on the business that provides the greatest benefits along these dimensions and is easiest to manage.

6. Determine how you can demonstrate to investors that you can perform well in this new business.

7. Identify how you can expand benefits for all stakeholders in ways that will further enhance and extend the existing benefits.

Lesson Eighteen

Merge with Strategically Complementary Businesses to Overcome Weaknesses in Both

For in fact the body is not one member but many.
If the foot should say,
"Because I am not a hand, I am not of the body,"
is it therefore not of the body?
And if the ear should say,
"Because I am not an eye, I am not of the body,"
is it therefore not of the body?
If the whole body were *an eye,*
where would be *the hearing?*
If the whole were *hearing,*
where would be *the smelling?*
But now God has set the members,
each one of them,
in the body just as He pleased.
And if they were all one member,
where would *the body* be?
But now indeed there are *many members,*

yet one body.
And the eye cannot say to the hand,
"I have no need of you";
nor again the head to the feet,
"I have no need of you."
No, much rather, those members of the body
which seem to be weaker are necessary.

— 1 Corinthians 12:14-22 (NKJV)

1 Corinthians 12 (NKJV) reminds us that complementary capabilities in the body can only be combined to create uniquely valuable results in a whole person. The same point holds true for combining organizations with weaknesses whose capabilities complement one another. While many organizations would rather fight than combine, unless there is a legal prohibition to doing so, making the right combination can be remarkably effective for enhancing combined effectiveness and stakeholder value.

Here's an example of making such a combination to consider. When Teva Pharmaceuticals announced the friendly acquisition of Cephalon in 2011, both stocks rose at a time when the overall equity markets were declining. You may remember that Carol Coles and I wrote about Cephalon in *The Ultimate Competitive Advantage.* A decade before, Cephalon was a small biotechnology firm specialized in making human pharmaceuticals. It had developed only one patented treatment and was looking to gain approval for more uses of that product. With sales of $200 million at the time, the firm faced a cost of $200 million each to develop any other biotechnology-based pharmaceuticals. Raising enough cash to engage in several such endeavors, while maintaining sufficient earnings and cash flow to attract equity investors, was going to be an issue.

The company hoped to prosper by working on opportunities that were a bit smaller than the largest pharmaceutical companies sought. In addition, Cephalon had developed a specialist sales force for neurologists that allowed it to become the marketing agent for foreign firms that did not have their own U.S. sales forces and needed to influence neurologists. The CEO's big concern at the time was that development costs were expected to expand geometrically as new therapies required simultaneous innovations in genes, proteins, and enzymes, a dauntingly difficult and expensive prospect.

Despite those challenges Cephalon did well in many dimensions. In the prior decade, its revenues expanded by 14 times, and, despite heavy investing in new product development, its profits in 2010 were more than double what its revenues had been in 2001.

Cephalon experienced a lingering problem. Investors grew to be less and less confident about the firm's future. As a result, the stock traded in a range from about $40 to $80 a share from 2001 through 2010. During that time, Cephalon went from being a premium-priced enterprise to one that traded at both a discount to the average of the stock market and to similar firms in its own industry. Why? When compared to its current sales and profits, the pipeline of new products didn't look all that promising by the end of 2010.

The firm's balance sheet also wasn't in as good a shape as it should have been. The billion dollars of cash was approximately equaled by its borrowings. Cephalon was going to need much more money to pay for additional pharmaceutical developments, several billion dollars more. And its portfolio of approved drugs it sold was going to soon begin losing patent protections. How would the huge profit-reducing development expenses be paid without destroying the company's stock-market value?

Others thought about the same challenge, and a much smaller and less profitable firm, Canadian-based Valeant Pharmaceuticals (formerly known as Biovail), made a hostile bid for Cephalon. Valeant was a very debt-laden company, so combining with them would just increase the risk that Cephalon wouldn't be able to acquire enough low-cost capital to continue as a pharmaceutical industry innovator.

Cephalon began hunting for a more appropriate partner and possibly found one in Israel-based Teva Pharmaceuticals, a much larger generic drug maker with relatively little debt compared to its assets, strong cash flows, and good marketing strength in many product categories. Firms such as Teva prosper by offering lower-priced versions of established pharmaceuticals after the patents expire. As a result, such firms don't have to spend nearly as much on research and development or to gain regulatory approvals for their products. However, their profit margins are much thinner.

Teva had also done well in the prior decade, especially in stock-price growth. Its share price expanded from about $15 in 2001 to around $47 at the time the deal with Cephalon was announced. In addition, earnings had more than tripled during the immediately prior two years. Fast growth was expected to continue in 2011 through 2013, due to many pharmaceuticals becoming open to generic competition for the first time.

Why did Cephalon and Teva decide to combine? While the behind-the-scenes talks will probably never be fully revealed, some security analyst reports provide hints.

Cephalon could anticipate these nine possibilities:

1. Teva would be interested in potentially earning high profit margins from future biotechnology-based, patented pharmaceutical products.

2. Teva could afford to pay for the necessary research and development expenses for Cephalon's program without harming its balance sheet or unduly depressing earnings.

3. Because there weren't going to be very many major branded pharmaceuticals coming off patent for a few years beginning in 2014, Teva was facing the potential for experiencing a medium-term reduction in its revenue and profit growth.

4. Teva could pay a premium price compared to the Valeant offer and still see its earnings per share improve in 2011 and 2012.

5. Teva had enough unused debt capacity so that the firm could make an all-cash offer, something that Valeant could not match.

6. If Teva's stock continued to rise, Teva could sell shares later and use the proceeds to retire the debt incurred for the purchase, making the Cephalon investment less costly than initially.

7. With access to Teva's higher stock-price multiple and more debt capacity, Cephalon could afford to conduct more pharmaceutical development than it could as a stand-alone firm.

8. Teva probably couldn't find a more attractive company to buy for these purposes, resulting in a single-minded focus on the possibility of acquiring Cephalon.

9. As an Israel-based company, there was little risk that Teva might be taken over unless it wanted to be.

Teva, for its part, could anticipate these nine possibilities:

1. Cephalon would provide a technology platform for product development that Teva could not easily duplicate on its own.

2. Over a period of the next several decades, Cephalon's new products could potentially provide much larger profits than what Teva could earn from generic drugs.

3. Cephalon's product sales would be higher because of Teva's marketing clout.

4. When Cephalon's products come off patent, the combined firm could gain a higher market share of the branded and generic versions, providing more profits.

5. Cephalon could add to its development portfolio by attracting more opportunities from larger firms interested in seeing what the combined Teva/Cephalon sales teams could do.

6. Cephalon could expand its capacity to develop more pharmaceuticals because of its past successes and good industry reputation, as long as someone paid the costs.

7. Some Cephalon investors would ultimately be attracted into Teva stock, helping boost Teva's multiple.

8. Teva might sell for a higher multiple by adding a biotechnology capability and a portfolio of branded products, rather than just being a generic drug company.

9. By paying cash for Cephalon, there was no risk of having angry employee shareholders threatening to undermine management if Teva's stock didn't do well in the near term.

Teva could anticipate that some or all of three new doors might open for the combined companies:

1. Other biotechnology companies that needed consistent funding and strong sales forces would consider friendly purchases of their firms by Teva.

2. If it gained a higher multiple for its stock, Teva might be able to make future complementary acquisitions for stock.

3. Other generic drug makers might want to join Teva via stock acquisition in hopes of gaining a higher multiple for their stock due to any expansion in Teva's multiple because of entering biotechnology.

Of course, much more time will have to pass before we will be able to determine what parts of this logic are valid. I emphasize that point because in most mergers the purchasers and the sellers argue for many unique, valuable advantages being brought to the transaction. Such arguments more often prove to be based in wishful thinking rather than in reality.

Let me give you an example of mistaken thinking about perceived merger advantages from the early 1980s. I wrote a letter then to the CEO and largest shareholder of a global engineering firm describing attractive acquisition opportunities for his company. I had in mind that the firm would purchase another global engineering firm with different, but complementary, skills.

The CEO wrote back to say that he loved the concepts in my letter. He shared with me that his firm was about to announce a merger that would implement all of the points I had made. Two weeks later, the engineering firm bought a coal-mining company based in Appalachia. No merger could have been further away from the principles described in my letter or in this lesson.

It turned out that the CEO had become excited by the idea of taking the excess cash flow from the engineering firm and using it to expand existing coal mines. What he didn't realize is that this coal business would lose money for each of the next 20 years. The result for shareholder value was like carrying an expensive dead weight.

The case history I've shared in this lesson may provide more information than you want to know, but I decided to go into such detail because you may not have been aware of a complementary merger where strategic enhancements actually alleviated major weaknesses.

Even where the potential for complementing the other organization is good (as was probably the case here), you still need to implement well. Both the former Teva and Cephalon businesses will need to be highly productive in grasping opportunities for this merger to work well. And, of course, any new activities will also need to be successful. Remember that even good strategy can be totally tripped up by poor execution.

So what should you look for? It's actually pretty simple. Consider these four points:

1. Each of the two organizations should be able to grow sales, profits, and cash flow much faster when together than they could apart ... regardless of future industry conditions.

2. Many new, large opportunities will open up that would not be able to be engaged without the merger.

3. Parts of the two organizations will be able to enhance the performance of their counterparts in the other organization.

4. Investors will be willing to pay a higher price for the acquiring company's shares than the two organizations would have enjoyed in total if independent of one another.

Whether enough opportunity is grasped is a function of factors such as these four:

1. How easy the changes are to implement
2. How risky the businesses are
3. How much can go wrong in implementation
4. How large the potential benefits are compared to the risks

My advice is to only consider situations where the likely potential benefits exceed the total risks by a factor of at least four to one ... and will increase overall stakeholder value by at least 30 percent within two years.

What's the key lesson? *By merging with strategically complementary businesses and implementing the new directions well, you will increase profits, profitability, cash, and cash flow, and gain and retain a higher multiple value of equity for your economic performance. If you can also use the improved results and the extra value premium to create* *some other strategic and economic advantages, you can be well on your way to expanding value by 20 times more than would otherwise be the case for all stakeholders.*

Your Lesson Eighteen Assignments

1. Identify your company's strategic weaknesses that reduce by a large amount the potential to expand stakeholder value.

2. Also identify your company's strategic strengths that might increase by a large percentage the stakeholder value of another business or company.

3. Evaluate all other businesses and companies to determine if any of them complement your company's strengths and weaknesses in ways that would substantially improve the stakeholder value provided by the combined entities.

4. Test your thinking with industry experts and by confidentially creating a description of joint value-improvement opportunities.

5. Confidentially approach the complementary organization on a friendly basis to determine if there is any interest in turning the potential into reality.

6. If rejected, keep your value-improvement information up-to-date in case the other organization's leaders change their minds.

Lesson Nineteen

Focus on Businesses With Offerings Stakeholders Regularly Experience And Like

Love suffers long and *is kind;*
love does not envy;
love does not parade itself,
is not puffed up;
does not behave rudely,
does not seek its own,
is not provoked, thinks no evil;
does not rejoice in iniquity,
but rejoices in the truth;
bears all things, believes all things,
hopes all things, endures all things.

— 1 Corinthians 13:4-7 (NKJV)

1 Corinthians 13 (NKJV) reminds us of love's influence and power. While stakeholders are never going to love a business, its offerings,

or its benefits as much as they love God or another person, familiarity and liking can combine to create feelings that help build patience and understanding. If you doubt that observation, think about how you might feel if some slight delay occurred in receiving your favorite dessert on your birthday. While you would undoubtedly prefer for the dessert not to be delayed, you could be more patient by knowing what a treat was coming. If the delay were explained in terms of some familiar issue, such as the need to get an important ingredient (such as hot fudge for a sundae) to the ideal temperature, you would understand and possibly even approve of the delay.

As we focus on businesses with offerings that stakeholders regularly experience, let me begin by providing some examples of businesses with offerings that many stakeholders *don't* regularly experience. What is out of sight is often out of mind. Thus, those businesses providing low-profile offerings to their customers and end users that aren't often noticed or thought of by the rest of society may well fit into this category.

Mention treadle pumps, and most people have no idea what you are talking about. Yet, these simple gadgets (that typically resemble a primitive, wooden stair-stepper exercise machine) allow poor farmers where water is scarce to inexpensively lift water from underground to irrigate fields by using their own leg muscles, serving as a low-cost alternative to the gasoline-powered and electric pumps that they cannot afford to buy and operate. While a treadle pump seems like an obsolete technology, efficient, low-cost ones are essential devices for helping many poor farmers to become sufficiently more productive so that they can eventually afford to apply more of the "green revolution" techniques that can further increase crops.

When something strikes people as probably being unpleasant, that impression will keep many people blissfully ignorant of any related business activities and opportunities. Let's stick with farming. While many people will tell you that they prefer and often prepare and eat organic food, few really know what's involved to produce the food. Organic plants are usually fertilized with animal droppings, a source of nutrients that few people want to come anywhere near. If a supplier found a great way to collect, process, improve, and distribute such droppings, most people still wouldn't want to come within smelling distance of learning about the process.

While many people think in terms of segregation keeping apart people of different ethnic or national origins, it's more likely today that income differences cause such separations. If you go into poor neighborhoods in the United States, you won't find Coach, Saks Fifth Avenue, and Tiffany's. Instead, you may find Family Dollar Stores. Unless you are a poor person who must shop at low-priced chains, chances are good that you won't even know that such stores exist, how to identify an effective store of this type, and whether such a chain is improving or not.

I don't want to make this aspect of the subject seem to be all about wealth. Technical details can be barriers, too. Many people either don't know much about math or science, or they seek to avoid such learning. So a new method for remotely inspecting pipes in nuclear facilities that relies on mathematical formulas will escape the attention of many people.

In looking at the opposite circumstance, where stakeholders can't seem to contain their enthusiasm, I'm often struck by what seems to be excess interest. I well remember going to a party attended by pension fund and mutual fund managers about the time that Starbucks was becoming available in most American cities. These multimillionaires couldn't stop talking about how "cheap" the $4 beverages were and how good they were compared to what was usually available for $2 at the local doughnut-shop chain. Of course, the average person at the time thought that $4 was way too much to pay for $0.30 worth of ingredients. Such a high profit-contribution margin didn't deter the multimillionaires from buying huge amounts of Starbucks stock at price-earnings multiples over 70 times. Because advertising for high-priced consumer goods and services is very visible to virtually anyone in nations where access to television is common, a high percentage of investor-preferred companies will come from those who provide such offerings.

If you can also add the "spice" of exciting new offerings involving gadgets that stakeholders love, security prices can go through the roof. At the time of this writing, Amazon.com's stock was selling at over 340 times projected earnings per share while Microsoft (without the Kindle cachet) was selling at 15 times projected earnings per share. While the differences between two such companies will rarely translate into a 20 times multiple difference in stock price, the absolute dollars can be huge. The premium over Microsoft's multiple in Amazon.com's case adds up to over $130 billion at the time of this writing.

One of my favorite examples of both unpopularity and popularity is Priceline.com, the discount-travel booking site. When the company was new, the stock had a tremendous overvaluation during the dot-com boom. When almost all such stocks fell out of favor, few thought that Priceline.com would survive. That's because most of its bookings then were for very undesirable airline flights (low-price flights that might start at 3 a.m., require five stops, and take 14 hours to cover 2,000 miles). Since most stakeholders wouldn't consider traveling that way, they wouldn't invest in Priceline.com. The price of the shares dropped from over $900 to less than $10.

But the stakeholders mostly missed that Priceline.com could also save you $200 a night on a beautiful hotel room. Gradually, people figured that out, and the stock climbed recently to over $1,100 a share as business boomed. Priceline.com also began offering standard hotel reservations at discount prices. The company's shares now trade at 26 times trailing earnings and will probably trade higher than that at some point as more stakeholders realize this site can save them thousands of travel dollars a year, while allowing them to stay in more beautiful accommodations.

As an example of Priceline.com's superior purchasing options, my wife, daughter, and I stayed at one of the top three hotels in Connecticut for only $50 the night before my younger son's wedding. Everyone else paid at least $175 at a noisy place ten miles away with the "wedding-party discount." No one else thought to book on Priceline.com.

Naturally, it doesn't make sense to engage in an unattractive business opportunity just because stakeholders will pay a lot more for performance in such an area. But when all other factors are reasonably similar, engage in the opportunities that will thrill stakeholders, and your company, too, will gain more value that can be made available for all stakeholders.

What's the key lesson? *By focusing on businesses with offerings stakeholders regularly experience and like, you will be credited with a higher value for the benefits you provide. If you can also use that premium to create some other strategic and economic advantages, you can be well on your way to expanding value by 20 times more than would otherwise be the case for all stakeholders.*

Your Lesson Nineteen Assignments

1. Examine your business opportunities to consider whether you can expand into offerings that stakeholders regularly experience and like much better than what you do now.

2. Consider how you could shift your business model to make that new focus more successful.

3. Evaluate how appealing such expansions would be to potential investors and your stakeholders.

4. Identify the steps you can take to substantially increase effectiveness and appeal for expanding your business into offerings that stakeholders regularly experience and like.

Lesson Twenty

Reduce Risks That Make Stakeholders Squirm

So the three broke through the camp of the Philistines,
drew water from the well of Bethlehem
that was *by the gate, and took* it
and brought it *to David.*

Nevertheless David would not drink it,
but poured it out to the LORD.

And he said,
"Far be it from me, O my God, that I should do this!
Shall I drink the blood of these men
who have put *their lives* in jeopardy?
For at the risk of their lives they brought it."

Therefore he would not drink it.

— 1 Chronicles 11:18-19 (NKJV)

One person's uncomfortable risk, such as rock climbing, can be another person's greatest joy. We see such a contrast in 1 Chronicles 11:18-19 (NKJV). When King David casually mentioned how nice it would be to have a drink of water from a well that the Philistines controlled, his three mightiest warriors risked their lives to bring water to him from that source. Appalled by what had just happened, David poured out the water, instead, as an offering to God, and then compared drinking such water himself to being like drinking the warriors' blood.

Similar excessive risk-taking can feel just as uncomfortable when stakeholders realize what was involved in providing them with benefits. When the riskiness is too high, they, too, will reject, rather than embrace, the benefits. The potential value to them can thus be lost.

Although we have addressed some specific risks in the past and how to turn such risks into advantages, in this lesson we consider all other risks that may cause discomfort. The 2011 nuclear crisis in Japan that followed the earthquake and tsunami reminds me of this issue.

Immediately after the event, many so-called experts opined that the downside risk of the reactor-core cooling problems wasn't really so bad, except for whoever owns the plants. However, it's clear that many investors and other stakeholders disagreed ... having done as much as possible to distance themselves from risks due to the nuclear plant.

The investors and stakeholders who fled had it right. Today, with hindsight, we know that the radioactivity released during this incident will probably take decades to properly contain.

Before going deeper into this topic, let me just observe that my prayers and sympathy have always been with the Japanese people who have struggled with such determination to deal with a bad situation. In no way am I making any judgments about the people involved, nor do I feel anything other than deep concern and a sincere desire for a safe resolution. I'm sure you join me in such prayers, concerns, and desires. I continue to be saddened by the loss of life, the injuries, and the suffering that have affected so many people in Japan during and in the aftermath of the earthquake and tsunami, as I'm sure you are.

You may be wondering about my choice of the word "squirm" in this lesson's title. I am using that word in the sense of "to show or to feel distress." I mean to reference occasions when stakeholders are so concerned that their bodies visibly change due to strong emotions afflicting them.

Psychologists have shown that some circumstances can cause much greater negative emotional responses than others. For instance, few people get excited about the notion that tens of thousands of drivers and passengers die in vehicle accidents every year in the United States. Most people won't give the risk a thought even while driving during dangerous conditions.

In contrast, the loss of about 3,000 lives during the attacks on the World Trade towers in New York City and on the Pentagon in Washington, D.C. haunts the sleep and disturbs the peace of tens of millions of Americans while traveling by air, even though the event occurred well over a decade ago. I know I'm still bothered by what happened. You may be, as well.

Managements make decisions all the time to accept some types of and certain degrees of risk. All risks cannot be eliminated, and the costs to reduce certain risks can sometimes be more than anyone would want to spend. Having made decisions about what risks to take, most management teams become rigidly committed to the original decision.

When stakeholders challenge a particular decision due to the risk exposure, most management teams focus on explaining their thinking in logical terms. That approach is usually a big mistake. Instead, managements should be continually checking to see what risks make stakeholders acutely uncomfortable, avoiding such risks as much as possible, and reducing whatever remaining discomfort-inducing risks that cannot be eliminated.

In doing so, management teams need to treat emotional reactions as important considerations to address, just as other things outside their control (from the weather to earthquakes) have to be dealt with when they arise.

In commenting on such risks, I'm not talking about just putting a good face on a bad situation for stakeholders. That's what investment banks did in packaging worthless U.S. home mortgages into bundles of ownership that rating agencies labeled as "safe." That's a lot like discovering mildew in the walls of a building and slapping a new coat of paint on the exteriors, while the mildew is left to grow in place.

Instead, I'm talking about addressing the actual risk to fundamentally reduce it. Let me share some information that may shock you. In the 1980s, one of my clients was a well-known company (not the one that designed the damaged Japanese nuclear facilities) that serviced nuclear reactors. During client meetings, it often came up that many of the nuclear reactors in Japan were likely to fail if there was ever a large earthquake in or near Japan. I once asked what could be done. The comment was made that only by decommissioning the plants and replacing them with either safer nuclear technology or nonnuclear plants could the risk be reduced to manageable levels. Everyone in the discussions recognized that such steps were unlikely to occur until a large earthquake struck and extensive harm occurred.

Only time will tell what the long-term reaction will be to the design of those nuclear plants in Japan. I suspect it will be, however, quite different from the attitude prior to 2011.

Many management teams will correctly point to huge difficulties involved in reducing risk, describing how much money will be lost, how bad earnings will be, how much weaker the balance sheet will be, and so forth. In doing so, a management team will often be addressing measures that affect their own bonuses, the results that they have been asked to produce for the company's owners. There's sure to be some self-interested defensiveness, as well.

However, experience teaches that getting rid of such "unacceptable" risks often creates enormous rewards in terms of increased value. While such risks are in place, most existing and potential stakeholders either shun the opportunity to invest or participate tepidly due to feeling awfully uncomfortable. When the "decks are cleared" so that no future problems can be expected from the discomforting source, those who are stakeholders will increase their commitment and many potential stakeholders will commit for the first time. After such big "write-offs" to discontinue and deal with risky activities, for instance, many stock prices soar in a few days more than they normally would in a decade.

To find out what risks have value implications, you need to talk to those who are (and easily could become) your stakeholders. Take what they have to say seriously. Don't argue. Listen and ask about what changes stakeholders (and potential stakeholders) want.

You may feel that you have better ideas than stakeholders do for getting rid of the risks. Don't assume that stakeholders (and potential stakeholders) will agree. Check out the "solutions" you prefer with stakeholders (and potential stakeholders) to find out what they will do in response. Be prepared to be surprised by so-called irrational preferences for no, or little, risk in certain areas. Then, deal with any risk in the ways that stakeholders (and potential stakeholders) prefer.

What's the key lesson? *By reducing risks that make stakeholders squirm, you will gain a higher value for your performance. If you can also use that premium to create some other strategic and economic advantages, you can be well on your way to expanding stakeholder value by 20 times more than would otherwise be the case.*

Your Lesson Twenty Assignments

1. Examine your current businesses and business opportunities to learn what risks make current and potential stakeholders squirm.

2. Consider how you could shift your business model and activities to reduce those risks.

3. Evaluate how making such risk reductions would affect the comfort and behavior of current and potential stakeholders.

Lesson Twenty-One

Be a Franchisor

So Joseph found favor in his sight,
and served him.
Then he made him overseer of his house,
and all that *he had he put under his authority.*

— Genesis 39:4 (NKJV)

Let me begin this lesson by explaining what franchising is. Imagine that an individual or a company develops a way of doing business that others would benefit from duplicating to operate on their own. The developer, the franchisor, decides to grant the right to engage in such duplications and operations, a franchise, in exchange for a fee, typically charged as a percentage of revenues, to a franchisee. Well-known examples include fast food (McDonald's, Kentucky Fried Chicken, and Pizza Hut), automotive services (AAMCO and Midas), hearing aids (Miracle-Ear), and retail (Circle K, GNC, Pearle Vision, and Radio Shack). In such a relationship, each party has to do its part. The franchisor needs to enhance the business and find ways for franchisees to help one another, such as through cooperative advertising. The franchisees must provide the offerings effectively and conduct business in ways approved of by the franchisor.

Although franchisees are certainly not slaves, as Joseph was, they need to do things properly. As they do, the franchisor may reward them by allowing them to open more franchise operations. Such a mutually cooperative relationship is somewhat like that of Joseph with his master, Potiphar, the captain of Pharaoh's guard, before Potiphar's wife falsely accused Joseph of sexually mistreating her.

For many businesses, becoming a franchisor can have a very large positive impact on providing stakeholder value in the following six ways:

1. Providing the opportunity to have a very high-value entity or asset
2. Accelerating growth
3. Adding ways to shift more value to stakeholders
4. Sooner serving and involving more stakeholders
5. Reducing costs more rapidly
6. Eliminating many investments and expenses

I address each of these points separately in the lesson to help you understand what the opportunities are.

We first examine how *franchising can provide an opportunity to have a very high-value entity or asset.* As mentioned in earlier lessons, one of the most effective and simplest ways to add much value for all stakeholders is to provide opportunities for them to own some of an extremely high-value entity or asset before the biggest portion of its value increase takes place. Franchising can provide the opportunity to provide and increase such an asset or entity value expansion. Here's why:

- Franchising can be done solely in terms of receiving royalty payments, so that franchisees invest their own capital or borrow from arms-length lenders to provide for any fixed assets or working funds that are needed to operate.
- While first franchising, such a royalty-receiving entity tends to lose money, due to start-up costs associated with developing a franchise system, marketing the offering, and putting in a supervisory system. As a consequence, the initial valuation of

such an entity or asset is usually very low. When the entity or asset grows to a significant size, the shift from losing money to high profitability is rapid and dramatic, causing value to grow even more quickly than profits and cash flow do.

- A fully mature franchising operation can have almost no fixed assets, require little working capital, and provide significant free-cash-flow growth. As a result, those who place a high value on discounted free cash flows are strongly attracted to such assets and entities.
- The royalty portion of a franchised business entity is often worth more than the entire entity. As a result, value-form arbitrage is available to shift assets into forms that maximize their value, while the free cash flow is held in a form that maximizes its value. As a result, the combined approach may well create more value in total than a combined entity would enjoy in the public or private markets.

Franchising can also be used to accelerate growth. In businesses that require numerous small operating entities (such as fast-food restaurants or specialty retailers), there is a tremendous amount of work involved in locating sites, building and preparing facilities, locating and training managers and employees, and attracting customers. A small organization that operates all of such units must grow more slowly than a franchised one, or risk making a huge mess out of its expansion.

By contrast, a franchised operation has to do a lot less to support each site. Most of the burden falls on the single-unit franchisee. If that person has significant experience in a related activity, the start-up can be quite rapid and smooth.

As a consequence, an organization that might be overwhelmed by establishing 5 new locations could be able to properly support franchise expansion of 25 outlets during the same period of time. Such more rapid growth may lower risk by allowing the organization to reach the minimum scale of operations more rapidly in a given city or town. As a result, costs are lower for each location, more advertising is done than would otherwise be affordable, and the excitement involved with customers discovering these units is considerably higher.

As we know, faster growth is good for valuation, so such results will accelerate the value growth of whatever entities and assets are established.

Franchising can also add ways to shift more value to stakeholders. A franchisor can decide to do more for franchisees than to just collect royalties. Each time another value form is added, there are more ways for stakeholders to participate. Here are some examples of value forms that could be created:

- Royalty-receiving asset or entity
- Product-producing asset or entity
- Land-owning assets or entities
- Equipment-owning assets or entities
- Distributor-owning assets or entities
- Management-company assets or entities
- Service-related assets or entities

Let me use Coca-Cola as an example to explain how such value forms might be structured if this long-established company were being formed today. Rather than only selling syrup at a high price to geographical franchisees, each franchisee might also be expected to pay a 5 percent of revenues royalty on all products licensed from the product-developing and -producing entity. The Coca-Cola system lacks such an entity now.

In addition, there could be a separate unit that sells the syrup to franchisees who add water and carbonation to create packaged and fountain versions of the beverages. The profits from selling the syrup would be captured in a second type of asset or entity. This second part would be somewhat similar to the parent company of Coca-Cola today.

The franchisor could require each franchisee to buy and lease any needed land from a landowning entity. As a result, there would be an opportunity to enjoy capital gains on any value increases in the land while reducing how much money each franchisee had to invest in order to operate. Such an entity could be financed almost totally with nonrecourse debt without harming the credit of either the franchisor or the franchisees.

The franchisor could also require franchisees to buy and lease any needed equipment and vehicles from a leasing entity. The entities and assets could be held in such a way as to maximize tax savings and to again provide access to low-cost, nonrecourse debt financing that wouldn't affect the credit or borrowing capacity of the franchisor or franchisees.

Distribution is often difficult and relatively unprofitable for such entities. Rather than have the local bottler be tied into operating a costly delivery fleet of trucks, these important, but low-value, operations could be owned and operated separately from the local franchises. As a result, the local franchises would be a lot more valuable.

Separate from any of these assets or entities, management companies could be established that would have a high value based on requiring few assets and having the potential to rapidly grow free cash flow.

In some cases, services could be more efficiently provided by a specialized entity. An example might be restocking vending machines with beverages. Several franchisees might combine to have one asset or entity to provide such services for all of them in a larger geographical area.

By slicing and dicing into many assets and entities, each stakeholder could be provided with more choices and ways to participate in value expansion, enabling more stakeholders to be accommodated and more gains to be experienced.

Franchising can also make it possible to sooner serve and involve more stakeholders. While at first blush the growth of a franchised operation mostly seems to expand revenues and customers served, the expansion of how many stakeholders are affected is actually much greater. That's mostly because there will be so many more owners of various entities and thereby more people affected who live in the communities served by the much more rapidly expanding franchising enterprise.

Here's a brief example to illustrate that point. If a company-only operation established 5 locations, the total number of owners might be 5, the number of employees might be 100, the number of customers might be 4,000, and the number of community residents affected might be 40,000. In a franchise operation adding 25 locations, the total number of owners might be 125, the number of employees might be 500, the number of customers might be 20,000, and the number of community residents affected might be 200,000.

Franchising can also help reduce costs more rapidly. Most costs decline due to either scale effects (spreading fixed and semifixed costs over more revenues) or experience (learning how to perform more effectively). Since a franchise-based system is going to expand more rapidly, such scale and learning effects occur sooner and are larger.

Such effects will often be experienced in a specific geographic market. For instance, the optimal advertising in a market with 25 units operating might only need to be twice the level of what a market of 5 units operating could afford at most. As a result, the cost of advertising on a per-unit basis goes down by 60 percent while effectiveness increases. Similar efficiencies would show up in many overhead-type costs. If having twice the advertising increased sales per unit, that result would also create lower costs by spreading fixed and semifixed costs on a per-unit basis over more unit volume.

Franchising is also beneficial for eliminating the need for many expenses and investments. In the kind of multiple-unit operation I've been describing, many investments relate to supervision. A multiple-unit operation would typically need an extra layer of management and support for every 10 units. But a franchised operation where each unit is separately owned by capable, experienced people would only need an extra layer of management and support for every 40 units.

On a small scale, an operator might have to provide dedicated distribution using its own trucks. With larger scale, an existing distributor who services many similar organizations may be able to handle the distribution on a more cost- and investment-effective basis.

What's the key lesson? *By using franchising, you can expand value faster and have more ways to reward stakeholders with value increases.*

Your Lesson Twenty-One Assignments

1. Determine ways that franchising could enhance the performance of your entities and assets for stakeholders.

2. Evaluate how various franchising structures could cause more value improvement for the most desirable entities.

3. Consider the size of the potential benefits from such changed actions compared to the net worths of those whom you would like to encourage.

4. Provide incentives for those stakeholders who can help the most to increase valuable behavior and see how well the incentives work.

5. Adjust incentives to encourage even more valuable behavior changes.

6. Expand successful programs if the advantages are large and appear to be sustainable.

Lesson Twenty-Two

Be a Licensor

But Paul said,
"I am a Jew from Tarsus, in Cilicia,
a citizen of no mean city; and I implore you,
permit me to speak to the people."

So when he had given him permission,
Paul stood on the stairs and
motioned with his hand to the people.
And when there was a great silence,
he spoke to them *in the Hebrew language,*

— Acts 21:39-40 (NKJV)

Acts 21:39-40 (NKJV) helps us to understand how licensing works in practice. After being attacked in the Temple, Paul wanted access to a platform and protection to speak in Jerusalem. The head of the Roman guard that had rescued Paul gave him permission to do so, and Paul gave his testimony in Acts 22 (NKJV). Without the permission and protection of the Roman soldiers, Paul could not have gotten his message across. This circumstance is much like an owner of a mailing list licensing it for one-time use by someone with a message to share.

Licensing by a company or an individual is normally associated with granting permission to use intellectual property, a brand, a design, a business program, or access to customers. In doing so, the licensor exercises relatively limited control over the use of what is licensed. For example, I often license books created by The 400 Year Project for use by those who want to make translations of and market them. When I do so, I ask the licensee to make a good translation, but I retain no power to change the translation. I usually lack sufficient knowledge of the other language to be able to tell what's going on. It would also cost me far more than any royalties that might be generated to check on the translation. If the licensee does ineffective marketing, I have no recourse. If I learned that the licensed rights were being abused in some way, my main remedy would be to cancel the license.

I chose licensing as the next strategy to consider because the opportunity shares many qualities in common with franchising (the preceding lesson's topic) for stakeholder-value enhancement. In fact, franchising often involves issuing licenses for brands and intellectual property. In this lesson, however, we look at licensing in the absence of a franchising relationship. One reason for doing so is that many smaller businesses cannot afford to become franchisors. However, for them the opportunity to license others can have a very large positive impact on valuation in the following six ways:

1. Providing the opportunity to have a very high-value entity or asset
2. Accelerating growth
3. Adding ways to shift more value to stakeholders
4. Sooner serving and involving more stakeholders
5. Reducing costs more rapidly
6. Eliminating many investments

I address each of these points separately so that you will be sure to understand what the opportunities are.

Before doing so, let me share a little more information to help you understand some of the important differences between licensing and franchising. In franchising, there's usually a closer link between franchisor and franchisee such that the franchisor tries to control almost everything that the franchisee does so that customers will be able to tell little difference between franchisor and franchised operations, as well as among franchisees. Think of fast-food restaurant chains such as McDonald's and Kentucky Fried Chicken as examples of this kind of franchising. Almost every element of what a franchisee has to do is prescribed by the franchisor in detailed rules, specialized equipment, and careful training. The franchisee gains some advantages in brand value, coordination of marketing and distribution, and a continuing stream of business-model improvements. In some cases, the franchisee also receives an exclusive territory that serves to reduce competition from the franchisor and other franchisees.

Because the burdens of what the franchisor has to do are very great, many smaller organizations either find that it's not worth the time, money, effort, and trouble to franchise or that they don't have adequate resources to do so. In such cases, the smaller organization may choose, instead, to employ licensing for its valuable patents, trademarks, service marks, copyrights, know-how, or trade secrets that others would like to use.

In most instances, identities of a company and its offerings can be turned into trademarks, service marks, or copyrights quickly, with little effort, and with predictable expense that is often affordable. For a modest cost, know-how and trade secrets can be protected through contract agreements. Only patents are expensive to create, to protect against rival applicants, and to defend against infringers. Consequently, all but the smallest companies can afford to create enough protection to be able to consider licensing some of its valuable knowledge or other forms of intellectual property.

Companies can offer either exclusive or nonexclusive licenses. People will obviously pay more for an exclusive license, but in such cases it's very important to obtain performance guarantees in terms of minimum license payments. Otherwise, someone might buy an exclusive license and simply sit on it, doing nothing. Any such requirements are obviously subject to a negotiated agreement.

Okay, let's look at how *licensing can help increase stakeholder value by 20 times by providing the opportunity to have a very high-value entity or asset*. Here's why:

- Licensing can be done solely in terms of establishing royalty payments, so that licensees invest their own capital or borrow from arms-length lenders to provide for any fixed assets or working funds that are needed to operate.
- While first licensing, such a royalty-receiving entity tends to lose a little money due to start-up costs involved with developing legal protections for intellectual property, marketing the licenses, and negotiating license agreements. As a consequence, the initial valuation of such an entity or asset is usually very low compared to what it will be later after substantial licensing income is being received. When the entity or asset grows to a large size, the shift from losing a little money to enjoying substantial profits is rapid and dramatic, causing value to grow even more quickly than profits and cash flow do.
- A fully mature licensing operation can have almost no fixed assets, require little working capital, and provide lots of free-cash-flow growth. As a result, those who place a high value on discounted free cash flow are strongly attracted to such assets and entities.
- The licensing portion of a business entity is often worth more than the entire business. As a result, value-form arbitrage is available to hold assets in forms that maximize their value while the free cash flow is held in a form that maximizes its value. Consequently, the combined approach may well create more value in total than a combined entity would enjoy in the public markets.

Let's look next at how *licensing can accelerate growth*. In businesses that require numerous operating entities around the world (such as providing local manufacturing, service, or training), there is a tremendous amount of work involved in setting up organizations, obtaining approvals to operate, designing a marketing approach, putting distribution in place, creating awareness, establishing credibility, and building trust. A small organization must grow rather more slowly or risk making a huge mess out of its global expansion.

By contrast, a licensor has to do a lot less to support each licensee. Most of the burden falls on the licensee, who will usually have established knowledge, credibility, customers, and influence in the key market segments. If that person or company has sufficient experience in a related activity, such a new licensee will often do better than what the licensor would accomplish in the same territory.

As a consequence, a licensor organization that might be overwhelmed by establishing 5 new international locations could be able to support effective licensee expansions in 50 countries during the same period of time.

As we know, faster growth is good for valuation, so such results would accelerate the value growth of whatever entities and assets are established.

Now, let's consider how *licensing can add ways to shift more value to stakeholders.* A licensor can decide to do more for licensees than to just collect royalties. Each time another value form is added, there are more ways for stakeholders to participate through ownership. Here are some examples of value forms that can be created:

- Royalty-receiving asset or entity
- Product-producing asset or entity
- Land-owning assets or entities
- Equipment-owning assets or entities
- Distributor-owning assets or entities
- Management-company assets or entities
- Service-related assets or entities

Let me use Xerox as an example to explain how some of such value forms might be established if this company were being formed today. Rather than only selling royalty-based licenses to make and market products, each licensee might also be expected to pay an additional 5 percent of revenues towards international marketing to stimulate demand for services that use Xerox products. No such marketing entity exists within the Xerox licensing system now, and services based on Xerox technology have grown much more slowly than otherwise might have occurred.

In addition, there could be a unit that sells the products from the most effective manufacturing licensees to distributors. No such separate unit exists today.

Xerox could require each licensee to buy and lease any needed land from a landowning entity. As a result, there would be an opportunity to enjoy capital gains on any value increases in the land while reducing how much money each licensee had to invest in order to operate. Such an entity could be financed almost totally with nonrecourse debt without harming the credit of either the licensor or the licensees.

Xerox could also require licensees to buy and lease any needed production and distribution equipment and vehicles from a leasing entity. The entities and assets could be held in such a way as to maximize tax savings and to again provide access to low-cost, nonrecourse debt financing that wouldn't affect the credit or borrowing capacity of the licensor or licensees.

Separate from any of these assets or entities, management companies could be established that would have a high value based on requiring few assets and having the potential to rapidly grow free cash flow.

In some cases, services could be more efficiently provided by a specialized entity. An example might be setting up and operating copy centers in large companies. Several licensees might combine to have one asset or entity that provides such services for all of them in a larger geographical area.

By segmenting into so many assets and entities, each stakeholder could be provided with more choices and ways to participate in value expansion so that more gains could be experienced and more stakeholders accommodated.

Before leaving this subject, let me note that in some countries caution must be taken in making such requirements of licensees. Laws may interpret such arrangements as amounting to franchising, thus bringing back in many of the costs that a small organization is seeking to avoid.

Licensing also makes it possible to sooner serve and involve more stakeholders. While at first blush the growth of a licensed operation mostly seems to expand revenues and customers served, the expansion in how many stakeholders are affected is actually much greater. That's primarily because there will be so many more owners of various entities and people affected who live in the communities served by the much more rapidly expanding licensing enterprise.

Here's a brief example to illustrate that point. If a company-only operation were establishing 5 locations, the total owners might be 5, the number of employees might be 100, the number of customers might be 4,000, and the number of community residents affected might be 40,000. Realize that licensees are often larger organizations than a small licensor. Consequently, in a licensing-focused operation where licensees add 50 locations, the total owners might be 500, the number of employees might be 2,000, the number of customers might be 60,000, and the number of community residents affected might be 1,000,000, simply through combined scale effects that make it attractive to involve more people.

Licensing provides the opportunity to reduce costs more rapidly. Most costs decline with either scale effects (spreading fixed and semifixed costs over more volume) or experience (learning how to perform more effectively). Since a license-based system is going to expand more rapidly, such scale and learning effects become significant sooner.

Such effects will often be experienced in a given geography. For instance, the advertising in a market with 50 service units might only need to be twice the level of what a market of 5 units operating could afford. As a result, the cost of advertising on a per-unit basis goes down by 80 percent. Similar efficiencies would show up in many overhead costs. If having twice the advertising increased sales per unit, that would also create lower costs by spreading fixed and semifixed costs on a per-unit basis over more unit volume, as well.

Licensing eliminates the need for making many investments. In the kind of multiple-unit operation I've been describing, many investments relate to supervision. A multiple-unit operation will typically need an extra layer of management and support for every 10 units. But a licensed operation where each unit is separately owned and operated by different people will only need an extra layer of management and support for every 100 units.

What's the key lesson? *By using licensing, you can expand value faster and have more ways to reward all stakeholders through value increases than would otherwise occur.*

Your Lesson Twenty-Two Assignments

1. Determine ways that licensing could enhance the performance of your entities and assets for stakeholders.

2. Evaluate how various licensing structures could cause more value improvement for the most attractive entities.

3. Consider the size of the potential benefits from such changed actions compared to the net worths of those whom you would like to encourage.

4. Provide incentives for those stakeholders who can help improve value the most and see how well the incentives work.

5. Adjust incentives to encourage even more valuable behavior changes.

6. If the advantages are large and appear to be sustainable, expand the successful programs.

Lesson Twenty-Three

Be Based Where Owners Will Pay the Most

For those who say such things
declare plainly that they seek a homeland.
And truly if they had called to mind
that country *from which they had come out,*
they would have had opportunity to return.
But now they desire a better,
that is, a heavenly country.
Therefore God is not ashamed
to be called their God,
for He has prepared a city for them.

— Hebrews 11:14-16 (NKJV)

You may be puzzled by the choice of topic for this lesson. What could the location of a company's home have to do with what owners will pay for shares in it? *Perhaps the most important point for you to understand is that valuers in some country will set a higher value on your enterprise and those of your stakeholders than valuers in any other country. When you pick the right base in that country, you establish a permanent premium value that cannot be matched by those who are located and valued elsewhere.*

Hebrews 11:14-16 (NKJV) provides a good perspective on the issue of where to be located. God wants us to focus on our future residence with Him in heaven, not where we happen to live now or previously lived. We should always want the best that He provides. In the case of businesses, He has provided some locales that are much more favorable for valuation than others. And in noting this, I'm not just talking about grants and tax incentives to move to a certain legal jurisdiction.

Let me share a few general points to open the discussion. *Valuers reflect a perspective that's unique to their country.* There are good reasons for valuers to do so. The currency value of that country is different relative to all other currencies (except where there is a currency union, such as with the Euro). Interest rates in that country are often unique. Government policies, including taxation on investment gains, are different, too. Alternative investments are looked at differently, as well. In some nations, for instance, major classes of owners, such as pension funds, can only own domestic companies. Valuers are also more attracted to what's visibly doing well in their country.

Valuers are also affected by accounting rules that cause different reported results, depending on where the company is based. Such rules often cause adjustments in financial results. As an example, when the domestic currency rises in value, that currency value change increases the value of local assets and earnings while reducing the value of assets and earnings outside the country. In some cases, local laws cause other accounting adjustments so that earnings and cash flow are increased or decreased versus being based in some other country.

Valuers have different philosophies of how to estimate value from one country to another. As a consequence, your performance will be assessed differently, even with identical fact situations, in one country versus another.

Valuers have different dominant investment styles from one country to another. If business performance is good, the buy-and-hold investment style will be most conducive to an extremely high valuation.

Many times the duration of holding relates to local taxes on owners, especially whether taxes are based on current quotes (the excise-tax model) or on the difference between the selling and purchase price when a security is sold (the capital-gains-tax model).

Questions of national pride come into play. An organization that people in a country are proud of will be valued more highly than one in which they do not take any particular pride. Thus, Disney gets a premium in the United States due to its cultural heritage and visibility there, while Euro Disney didn't get a premium in France due to having no connection to mainstream French culture. A great small vineyard, by contrast, from which some of the best wines have always been made might have a spectacular value in France while a similar vineyard in Costa Rica might receive no premium because wine isn't a major part of the Central American nation's identity.

Styles of investing cycle differently from country to country. As an example, around 1990, Japanese valuers became convinced that real estate would always appreciate, no matter how high its value was. Since then, the value of property there has fallen dramatically. Yet real estate values are still unusually high. Despite this evidence, homeowners in the United States were thinking like the Japanese when they overpaid for homes in 2005.

The economic cycle and its effect on values differ from country to country. Favor for one type of investment follows another type in different sequences from one nation to another. Thus, domestic semiconductor shares might be trading at 70 times earnings in one nation while another nation's domestic semiconductor companies might sell at only 13 times earnings.

Export-oriented businesses often receive much more favorable treatment in some nations than in others, such that local valuers will pay more for the most effective exporters. This is true in part due to tax policy, which may increase earnings and cash flow for some companies versus others in the local economy, as well as economic tariff barriers and other forms of protection for big exporters in serving their local market.

In some countries, you will be the "only game in town," providing you a premium value because investors want to invest in your type of business and cannot easily do so in any other way. This factor is often the case for pension assets in smaller countries.

Now, it's also important to keep in mind that not every business can be appropriately centered in another country to gain such a premium. A copper mine in Chile cannot be moved to New Zealand. A biotechnology company isn't going to be able to attract and retain the right workforce in Zimbabwe. But many businesses can be moved, and many businesses already have substantial beachheads in more than one nation that can be expanded to become the company's new home base. In other cases, acquisitions and divestitures can shift focus from one locale to another.

There may also be legal and cultural constraints. A few years ago, American companies correctly appreciated that Bermuda was a better base for valuation than the United States was. But the American Congress was so incensed that it put substantial penalties on those who sought to go to Bermuda, and the opportunity quickly ended.

Many people confuse the opportunity described in this lesson with where they should list their shares for trading. That's a different subject. Typically, value will follow whatever country has the most trading volume. Adding new exchanges won't shift value in such cases except where a local subsidiary operation is taken partially public solely in that country. When that happens, some of the premium for that nation will stick to the parent company's valuation. The effect is similar to arbitrage. Simply sharing information about how local operations are doing doesn't have the same effect either.

Owners and managers should evaluate and act on what they learn about how valuation for the company and its stakeholders will be affected by being based in one country versus another.

What's the key lesson? *By picking the right home country for your business through considering how valuers will assess and pay for your* *performance differently from one locale to another, you can permanently increase the value your owners and other stakeholders enjoy.*

Your Lesson Twenty-Three Assignments

1. Determine in which countries your business could be based so that you would receive a higher valuation.

2. Look at how such valuations would be relatively higher or lower than one another from country to country in different circumstances and cycles.

3. Identify if there are any places where under all circumstances a premium would be gained and retained.

4. Consider if partially public local operations would add any significant value benefits.

5. Test your ideas about shifting with valuers in the country where you are and the one you may move to.

6. Move if the advantages are large and sustainable.

Part Four

Operating Methods That Increase Value

Moreover I will make a covenant of peace with them,
and it shall be an everlasting covenant with them;
I will establish them and multiply them, and
I will set My sanctuary in their midst forevermore.

— Ezekiel 37:26 (NKJV)

Having considered strategies for value improvement that should work in all circumstances, we now turn to a handful of operating methods that can also substantially increase value. Some may wonder where the line should be drawn between value-improving business strategies and operating methods. To me, strategies give us both a direction and a primary means of following it. Operating methods, although essential to maintaining value, are seldom game changers. However, I have seen three distinct types of operating methods that have had, on occasion, such large value impacts.

Let's consider the subject of strategy and operating methods in the context of Ezekiel 37:26 (NKJV). In this verse, God is stating part of His plan for the Israelites. Our Heavenly Father was looking forward to the strategy of having His only Son, Jesus, come to the Earth in humble circumstances to die for the past, present, and future sins of all mankind. In the context of that grand plan, it's hard to imagine that any operating methods could have made a difference. Yet, through specific actions that Jesus took, such as resurrecting Lazarus from the dead, some of His disciples came to faith that He was the Messiah, the Anointed One, of whom the Old Testament prophesies. Those actions surely count as operating methods that increased the value of our Heavenly Father's strategy.

Similarly, some operating methods can make profound and lasting improvements to the value of a business. For instance, one of my students found a way to inexpensively expand the capacity of a large fertilizer plant by 60 percent. The effect was to more than quadruple the value of the plant. In this part, we address how to find such opportunities, what sorts of issues to consider, and what means to use in overcoming seemingly insurmountable obstacles.

We begin in Lesson Twenty-Four by examining how 2,000 percent solutions (ways of accomplishing 20 times more with the same or less time, effort, and resources, or accomplishing the same results with 1/21 the time, effort, and resources) can greatly increase value. Our discussion centers on the notion of working on the right 2,000 percent solutions. Suggestions are included for what sequences of such solutions might work best for three typical kinds of businesses.

Lesson Twenty-Five focuses on the importance of checking your ideas about the optimal choice of and order for strategic and operational 2,000 percent solutions and actions. You'll learn a process for making such evaluations. This information is an important foundation for the lessons in Part Eight that describe in more detail how to develop the optimal value-improvement program for your company.

In Lesson Twenty-Six, we discuss tracking perceptions of your company's future growth, profit, and cash flow. When those perceptions dip, find out why. If these are misperceptions, use communications to change the views. If the concerns are valid, this lesson describes how demonstrating changed operating methods can make a difference. Be vigilant!

Lesson Twenty-Four

How 2,000 Percent Solutions Affect Value

Now may He who supplies seed to the sower,
and bread for food, supply and multiply
the seed you have sown *and*
increase the fruits of your righteousness,
while you are *enriched in everything*
for all liberality, which causes thanksgiving
through us to God.

— 2 Corinthians 9:10-11 (NKJV)

God intends to multiply all good things, whether they are the results of righteous actions or simply the harvests that He uses to feed us. Yet many people seldom notice such multiplication, despite the natural world abounding in it. For instance, just a handful of the right kind of seeds properly watered, fed, nurtured, harvested, and their seeds later planted, as well, with the process continuing from crop to crop, can feed large numbers of people for many decades. Although many people feel that such opportunities are few and far between, my experience has been that the potential to create such large multiplications is usually easier to achieve in our own lives than in the natural world. Why? Due to being informed and empowered by the Holy Spirit, we can pick better targets and move faster.

Despite the obvious advantages of being able to make such fruitfulness occur, few people who feel that they need more bother to learn how to accomplish such multiplication. It's as if they were hungry in the middle of a supermarket while holding a fistful of hundred-dollar bills. All they have to do is pick out the food, take it to the register, hand over some money, prepare the food, and eat.

While becoming competent in making 2,000 percent solutions requires more effort than buying and preparing food in the supermarket example, learning is minor compared to the size of the benefit. Few people require more than 80 hours for gaining the necessary skill. What's 80 hours compared to the potential to generate in a few months the equivalent of several centuries' worth of benefits produced in the same old ways?

Okay, let's talk about the role of 2,000 percent solutions in creating more value. *Perhaps the most important point to share with you is that 2,000 percent solutions with better goals create vastly more value than other such solutions do. If you care about improving value, pick the best solutions to work on and do so in the optimal order.*

Let me share seven points:

1. *Simply expanding revenues by 20 times will not, by itself, necessarily increase value.* The exceptions to that observation mostly occur in the following circumstances:
   (a) You are in a new industry where no one is yet profitable and revenues are used as a surrogate for estimating future profits (such as how cellular-telephone-service providers and Internet-based businesses were valued in the 1990s).
   (b) Your operation could be consolidated by a new owner into an existing one to make the revenues much more valuable in terms of profits, cash flow, and dividends.
   (c) Your below-scale enterprise or operation leaps above the minimum scale to become much more attractive in terms of the percentage of revenues that provide profits,

cash flow, and dividends. This shift will be true of many small businesses when they reach medium or large size.

(d) Your profits grow in line with the revenue increases, causing profits rather than revenues to account for your improvement.

2. *Decreasing costs by 96 percent to serve a customer or end user will usually yield a more than 20 times increase in value:*
   (a) Such a change will normally increase profits, cash flow, and dividends by more than 20 times.
   (b) Some of the cost decreases can be applied either to attracting more customers who will be highly profitable or to adding revenues from existing, profitable customers.

3. *Decreasing by 96 percent the fixed assets and working capital needed to serve a customer or end user will usually yield a more than 20 times increase in value:*
   (a) Such a change will normally increase cash flow and the ability to pay dividends by more than 20 times.
   (b) Some of the decreased investment intensity will permit faster growth, further accelerating profit, cash flow, and dividend expansion.

4. *Increasing value for noncustomer stakeholders by 20 times has no direct impact on the organization, unless those value improvements translate into changed behavior that expands the organization's profits, cash flow, and dividends.*

5. *Increasing by 20 times the economic value received by customers and end users at the same or a lower price, cost, time, and effort may have more impact on value for an organization and its stakeholders than any other 2,000 percent solution:*
   (a) This change potentially allows for rapid expansion in revenues, profits, cash flow, and dividends for all stakeholders, as current and potential customers and end us-

ers greatly increase their consumption at the current or lower price level.

(b) If the market is above average in elasticity for increased economic value, the results for revenues, profits, cash flow, and dividends can be a large multiple of 20 times.

(c) The increased performance experienced by other stakeholders is likely to create multiplied benefits for the organization and its stakeholders in terms of reduced costs, less investment intensity, lower cost of capital, and greater access to key people and critical physical resources.

6. *In most instances, the smaller the unit that is benefited by any particular 2,000 percent solution, the less the value impact will be:*
   (a) The primary exception will be if the unit is engaged in activities that investors value much more highly than other units in the same company, organization, business, or operation.
   (b) A secondary exception will be when a smaller unit is more sensitive to the value aspects from the improvement than either the entire company is or some larger unit or subunit.

7. *Improvements that accelerate the rate of expanding earnings, cash flow, and dividends over more years will create a larger increase in value.*
   (a) Potential investors will assume that the improvements will continue in the future and pay a premium for what hasn't happened yet.
   (b) The ultimate base that is created will usually be larger than what can be generated by a quick burst of improvements whose benefits don't continue to multiply.

From those seven observations, you can see that *the optimal order of 2,000 percent solutions may not be the same as first expanding revenues by 20 times, then reducing all costs to serve a customer or end user by 96 per-*

cent, followed by reducing investment intensity by 96 percent, and then making selected changes to increase value by 20 times. Let's explore the question of the right order for engaging in 2,000 percent solutions that improve value through considering some hypothetical examples of various types of businesses.

For the first example, let's consider a typical investment-intensive manufacturing business. Such an organization needs $1 million in net assets for every $2 million in revenues. Obtaining the first million is going to be difficult for most start-ups. Growing by 20 times will then require adding another $10 million in investments. I'm sure you see the point. For such an enterprise, reducing investment intensity is probably the right first 2,000 percent solution. The investment needed in the beginning drops from $1 million to merely $40 thousand. To grow revenues by 20 times then requires only adding $800 thousand, a small amount compared to the cash flow that will be generated from adding the $20 million in revenues.

Let's look at a typical distribution business as the second example. Such organizations usually don't require much investment compared to revenues ($200 thousand in net investment might be enough for $2 million in revenues), but they usually have small margins (profits divided by revenues). If you start by reducing costs to serve a customer by 96 percent, you create explosive value improvements because profits, cash flow, and dividends grow so much and so rapidly. With such a healthier base, growing the business is very affordable, bringing more value to benefits.

As the third example, let's consider an organization that's very profitable, has a great cash flow, and pays enormous dividends ... but is very small. If this organization focuses on anything other than revenue growth, the value expansions will not be nearly as substantial.

The lesson I would like you to draw from these examples is that *each organization has to consider the value sensitivity of various 2,000 percent solutions for its organization and stakeholders in order to determine the optimal order for creating and implementing 2,000 percent solutions.* In doing so, it may also be the case that repeating a 2,000 percent solution (to create a 2,000 percent squared solution in the same activity) may be more valuable than moving on to make a complementary 2,000 percent solution in a different performance dimension.

What's the key lesson? *The most attractive 2,000 percent solutions to develop and the optimal order for expanding the value of an organization and its stakeholders will vary quite widely from one business to the next. One of the most important strategy decisions that an organization makes is selecting the right breakthroughs to work on and the best sequence for accomplishing them.*

Your Lesson Twenty-Four Assignments

1. What are the relative values of improvements for your organization and stakeholders from the different ways that your company, business, activity, or assets can be developed by creating and applying 2,000 percent solutions?

2. How do the sequences of accomplishing these activities differ in their effects on your organization's valuation and the values received by your stakeholders?

3. Are there substantially more attractive value opportunities to repeat making breakthroughs in one performance area before starting work on a different type of performance improvement?

4. Can you create any 2,000 percent solutions that will expand multiple dimensions of value for your organization and its stakeholders without making additional breakthroughs?

5. What happens to value when you work first in the areas described in your answer to question 4?

Lesson Twenty-Five

How to Pick 2,000 Percent Solutions That Improve Value

Now this is the confidence that we have in Him,
that if we ask anything according to His will,
He hears us.

— 1 John 5:14 (NKJV)

Perhaps the most important point to share with you about this lesson is that your subjective opinion doesn't matter much in determining the right 2,000 percent solutions to engage in to create vastly more value than less helpful ones. If you care about improving value, you need to be sure that you find out what others think about which 2,000 percent solutions to develop and in what order from among those whose opinions affect your valuation.

In previous lessons, I've written about how some corporate leaders are highly confident, but mistaken, in thinking that they know what stakeholders would like them to do. In 1 John 5:14 (NKJV), the Bible teaches us that God is always willing to listen to us when we ask for what is in accord with His will. Similarly, when corporate leaders describe plans to accomplish what valuers and stakeholders most desire to be done, these individuals are going to listen carefully and closely.

While it's obvious that leaders should check their understanding of what valuers and stakeholders would like to see, accomplishing this task is much easier said than done. Among the many complications are legal restrictions in many nations on selectively disclosing plans about publicly traded companies. If such rules apply in your country, you'll have to use intermediaries to gain the information in ways that disguise your identity as sponsor.

In this lesson, we look at some ways to be sure that you pick the right 2,000 percent solutions for expanding value. Let me share seven points as openers:

1. If you think your business is worth $100 *billion* and no one else thinks it is worth more than $1 *million*, your business is going to be worth no more than $1 *million*. I share that point because *almost all owners greatly overestimate how much their businesses are worth. In addition, almost all owners favor making changes designed to create more value that won't succeed in doing so, even if the desired results are accomplished.*

2. *Don't take casual comments about value very seriously.* Many people speak very loosely while describing the value they would pay or assign to an asset, a business, a company, or some other kind of resource. Such comments are often used simply to gain someone's attention, rather than to indicate a serious assessment of the actual circumstance. Here's an example of what I mean. When I was new to working on corporate acquisitions for Heublein, I was amazed to receive a string of letters from sellers' agents describing businesses that they had for sale at very low prices. In some cases, these were businesses that we had tried to interest the owners in selling with no success. Whenever I followed up with an indication of interest to an agent, there would be a long delay. Eventually, I would be

told that the owner had changed his or her mind. After this happened a few times, I realized that these letters were probably designed to attract me as bait for the agents to get a seller as a client. The agents might have been taking my indication of interest and telling the owners that I wanted to buy the businesses and would pay a high price for them. When the owners decided they didn't want to sell (which most already had so determined), the reply I received simply meant that the agent had heard from the owners, not that the owners had ever hired the agent. The representations by the agents were likely all smoke and mirrors, lacking any reality.

3. *In most circumstances, one person's opinion (or view) about value won't be very important in determining what the value actually is.* The only exception is if that one person is the buyer who will pay the highest price compared to everyone else in the world. Let me give you an example. I was asked by a company's owners for help in selling the firm to its employees. Due to tax advantages involved in such a sale, the owners hoped to gain the highest possible price. The owners miscalculated. The company had very severe environmental liabilities that would be turned from *potential* expenditures into *actual* expenditures upon any sale of the whole company. The employees knew that very well and deducted the estimated cost of those expenditures from their offer. The result was a price that was not very appealing to the owners. The owners next asked a small firm that did no research on the company to conduct an auction, and the small firm found buyers for each part of the company who would pay as though there were no such severe environmental liabilities. In addition, the small firm would first buy the entire company, incurring the entire legal liability without being compensated enough by the fee for taking on that expense. The firm accepted the liability anyway. Why would anyone do that? I suspect the buyers simply made mis-

takes in considering the liabilities. There's evidence for that view in the many studies showing that only a small percentage of acquired businesses ever provide enough earnings and cash flow to justify their purchase prices.

4. *If you are bidding to buy an asset, a business, or a company, and you cannot identify who is making a mistake in the transaction by undercharging or overpaying, the person who is making a mistake is you, and the others are simply enjoying your dangerous walk toward financial quicksand.* As I mentioned during the auction example, buyers usually overpay. There are many reasons, including ignorance, overestimating how much they can improve something, and getting caught up in the excitement of trying to "bag" a business (not unlike the emotional fever that causes some hunters to track their prey for days, even when they don't need to kill what they are hunting).

5. *Carefully calculated and beautifully documented valuations are usually wrong.* Most people think you can just hire a valuation expert, provide the requested information, and the value will be correctly calculated in such a way as to command respect from all and sundry. The problem with that view is that no two "experts" and "buyers" calculate value in the same way. All the documentation does is to make it clearer to anyone who reads it what they don't like about the valuation.

6. *Transactions count more than words, but transactions can still be way off the mark.* Some of my favorite examples of this observation occurred during the early days of the leveraged buyout boom in the 1980s. The new owners would offer a premium of 30 to 40 percent over the public share price, buy the company at that price, offer the same management team substantial bonuses to double cash-flow generation, and resell the business at triple the price within two to three years. Clearly,

there was something wrong with both the stock-price transactions on a daily basis and in the price paid to take the company private. In almost every case, these businesses had been operated to maximize earnings-per-share by investing money at very low returns to eke out a few more pennies of earnings. When the companies stopped doing that, they became rich sources of cash flow ... on only slightly lower earnings.

7. As the last example demonstrates, *many valuations are higher or lower than they otherwise would be because of the decisions that owners and managers have made about how to operate the business.* Change those decisions, and you change the value.

I believe that you can see from those seven observations that *accurate methods for picking the right 2,000 percent solutions and their optimal order are critical to correctly expanding value.* Keeping in mind that assets, businesses, and companies have varying valuations at different times, in alternate forms, when operated in other ways, financed from other kinds of sources, and with new owners, there are eleven selection methods that can help. Here they are:

1. Estimate the value of the asset, business, and company in its highest value forms, operated optimally to emphasize its appeal in each value form.

2. Use what you learn to assume combinations of value-improvement moves (such as selling some assets that investors who like the business don't care for but other investors who like the assets do).

3. Test sensitivities of the highest value forms and value-improvement moves to the major 2,000 percent solution options that you have.

4. Consider how the order of implementing the more attractive 2,000 percent solutions affects the apparent values now, in a year, and beyond that.

5. Determine the time frame in which you want to optimize value.

6. Select the value-improvement moves you are willing to do.

7. Determine the easiest-to-accomplish 2,000 percent solutions you want to make in their proper order for apparent value enhancement during your time frame.

8. Write a description of what you plan to do and ask in a legally appropriate way those who could affect the value in your preferred form how they would evaluate the value of the plan you have put together now, after you have been doing it for a year, and after you succeed. Ask them also to tell you how confident they are of your success.

9. Adjust your plan based on the feedback you receive.

10. Begin implementation and adjust the plan to reflect the success you have with the 2,000 percent solutions.

11. Update what you did in step 8 and repeat steps 9 and 10 until you reach the valuation you want.

The lesson I would like you to draw from this process is that each organization has to consider the value sensitivity of various value forms, value-improvement methods, 2,000 percent solutions, and the order of 2,000 percent solutions for its organization and its stakeholders in terms of "theoretical impacts" as well as value makers' reactions to what is planned in order to determine the optimal order for creating and implementing 2,000 percent solutions.

What's the key lesson? *Choosing the right 2,000 percent solutions to develop in the best order for creating the optimal value for an organization and its stakeholders requires careful consideration of the highest* *value forms, other value-improvement methods, and the views of those whose actions can help determine value.*

<u>Your Lesson Twenty-Five Assignments</u>

1. What are the highest value forms for your company, businesses, activities, and assets?

2. What are the best value-improvement actions you can take for putting your company, businesses, activities, and assets in their highest value forms?

3. How can 2,000 percent solutions make those results much more valuable?

4. What order of 2,000 percent solutions makes the most sense for the value-improvement time frame you have in mind?

5. Are there substantial value-improvement opportunities to repeat making breakthroughs in one area of performance before starting to work on a different performance improvement?

6. Can you create any 2,000 percent solutions that will expand multiple dimensions of value for your organization and its stakeholders without making additional breakthroughs?

7. How do those who can affect value in any of these forms assess what you have in mind in terms of value influences and credibility?

Lesson Twenty-Six

Demonstrate How to Overcome Apparent Growth And Profit Limitations

But God demonstrates His own love toward us,
in that while we were still sinners,
Christ died for us.

— Romans 5:8 (NKJV)

One of the first expressions I learned that has stayed with me is, "I'm from Missouri." People who say that are expressing that they need proof of something, not that they had once lived in St. Louis. I often think of that expression while reading the Bible's verses about various doubters.

Those people who don't believe in God are often confident in saying that they see no evidence that God exists. Those people who believe that God does exist, but don't like Him, may point out events in the world that they don't like. Yet the Bible tells us about miraculous events witnessed by large numbers of people demonstrating that our Heavenly Father sent His Son, Jesus, to the Earth to be a witness, as well as a sacrifice to remit our sins. What more evidence could anyone want? Well, for many, even their own eyes weren't enough. Thomas, one of disciples, doubted those who had already met and spoken with the risen Jesus after His Resurrection.

If God's demonstrations aren't enough to satisfy many people, imagine how much more difficult it will be for your company to persuade doubters that apparently impermeable limits to revenue and profit growth can be overcome. Obviously, there's no proof quite like what you can directly experience. Even Thomas believed after he saw and was invited to put his finger in the holes where Jesus had been nailed to the cross and punctured by a spear.

Some business leaders delay demonstrating how to overcome apparent limitations on revenue and profit growth because they see no near-term profit or cash-flow benefits to doing so. Few consider that such actions are extremely helpful for increasing stakeholder value.

Let me explain what I mean by apparent limits on revenue and profit growth. Here are some examples:

- A software company has already obtained as a customer every company that could use its current applications.
- A luxury goods maker's offerings have come to be viewed by most wealthy people as less stylish than those of its most effective competitors.
- A restaurant chain is seeing revenues in its newly opened locations fall well below results at its other restaurants.
- An author's latest book has far fewer sales than his or her prior books.
- A retailer has lost exclusive distribution rights to a "hot" item that accounts for a high percentage of the retailer's sales and profits.
- Unemployment is growing among those who are a company's key customers, and spending for such offerings is rapidly declining among those who are still employed.

What these circumstances have in common is presenting either evidence of or increased risk of growth rates being curtailed in the present or the near future. If you recall our lessons about how valuations are made, such a shift in expected growth would cause many investors to reduce the amount they would pay for assets, businesses, or securities associated with such lower expected economic performance.

In these cases, future earnings and cash flow would be forecast at lower levels due to reduced sales expectations. Factors that are independent of expected growth can also reduce profit and cash-flow forecasts. Here are a few examples:

- The cost of a major raw material ingredient has started going up very rapidly, much more quickly than the offering's price.
- A competitor has just cut prices for a company's main offering, creating the likelihood that everyone else in the industry will have to reduce prices as well.
- The country to which most of the products are exported has just installed a large import duty.
- Exports of an important raw material have been embargoed due to shortages and prices are expected to triple.

I'm sure that even better examples occurred to you while you read the ones I provided.

Companies need to monitor current and potential investors' perceptions of future growth, profits, and cash flow. Whenever an organization realizes that such perceptions are becoming less optimistic, the important next step is to determine why. In many cases, the reason won't be apparent and questions need to be asked. In the course of such investigations, don't be surprised if you find that the perceptions are based on some investors' misunderstandings and errors. Naturally, investor-relations activities should be able to overcome any false views.

Let's turn our attention to the circumstances where the concerns are valid, and there's no existing information or evidence to change anyone's views. In such instances, I strongly urge you to assess what could be done to accelerate revenue, profit, or cash-flow growth, despite whatever factors are in play. Then, put in place programs to determine which methods will be most effective in overcoming the negative circumstances involved. As Carol Coles and I point out in *The Irresistible Growth Enterprise* (Stylus, 2000), the best solution is often to choose a strategy that turns any irresistible forces (ones outside your ability to direct) into helpful influences, regardless of how the forces act.

While it's beyond the scope of this lesson to address all the ways that solutions can be found, let me address a few possible approaches for dealing with the issues in the examples I earlier referenced.

- A software company has already obtained as a customer every company that could use its current applications.

  Such a supplier has a number of possible opportunities including developing software that serves other applications for the same customers, acquiring a company that already has such complementary software, licensing the rights to offer outstanding complementary software, and adding totally new software (in whatever way) that will permit serving new customers.

- A luxury goods maker's offerings have come to be viewed by most wealthy people as less stylish than those of its most effective competitors.

  The most obvious place to begin is by learning how important a factor it is for style to be improved. If it is important, a second line could be brought out that's more up-to-date in style for wealthy people while redirecting existing offerings to those who aren't quite as well off but like the style. An acquisition could also be made of a line of goods that is more attractive to wealthy people.

- A restaurant chain is seeing revenues in its newly opened locations fall well below results at its other restaurants.

The challenge here is to find out what the source of the problem is. This is such an unusual circumstance that there is no obvious place to start, but certainly the site-location process should be reviewed to see if the new real estate is targeting different customers from those who traditionally have been the core of the chain's success. Also check whether the new units are closer to existing units than newer units have been previously. If any changes have been made in facilities, those should be evaluated. It may also be that hiring of managers and employees has changed so that in-store performance isn't as good. Surveys in the new restaurants should be compared with results from older restaurants to see if customers perceive anything different. Such surveys should also include people who aren't customers to see if there's some difference in how they perceive or experience the appeal of visiting the restaurants. Regardless of what the problem is, there are undoubtedly opportunities to upgrade the quality of sites, facilities, staffing, offerings, and in-restaurant experience. With enough of the right changes, new stores can quickly become higher performers than the existing operations have been.

- An author's latest book has far fewer sales than his or her prior books.

Authors have problems when they shift their subjects and styles. These possibilities should be checked out. In addition, pricing may have changed. Right now, many publishers are annoying readers by charging too much for Kindle versions of books. When that happens, many readers boycott such a book. Reviews are important, too. Did reviewers like the latest offering? Unless the author has lost the ability to write due to stroke or illness, causes should be identified and the sources of the reduced sales can be addressed through the author's next book.

- A retailer has lost exclusive distribution rights to a "hot" item that accounts for a high percentage of the retailer's sales and profits.

  Obviously, the retailer can also go out and locate new items for which it will have exclusive distribution. With more experience than anyone else in selling the "hot" item, the retailer may also be able provide better stocking and more appealing in-store displays to make most people choose to buy there. If the "hot" item is still expanding its sales, volume can continue to expand just as fast as or faster than before by applying superior execution. More marketing could help. A modest price reduction could help to steer cost-conscious customers to their stores.

- Unemployment is growing among those who are a company's key customers, and spending for such offerings is rapidly declining among those who are still employed.

  A solution in this instance could be as simple as upgrading the value of a company's offerings. A good approach can be to make the offerings more durable so that they will last longer, creating an effective reduction in the cost per use. Even during times of economic stress, spending increases for some types of goods. If the circumstance is expected to last for a long time, the company can also look into adding items of special appeal to its target customers in such an environment.

- The cost of a major raw material ingredient has started going up very rapidly, much more quickly than the offering's price.

  The most attractive solution is to find substitute materials that are not subject to so much price inflation. If that's not possible, consider redesigns that totally eliminate the need for any such materials. Look for new suppliers who will make price concessions because of the volume you offer them.

- A competitor has just cut prices for a company's main offering, creating the likelihood that everyone else in the industry will have to reduce prices as well.

  Sometimes such a price cut won't be followed. Don't jump on the bandwagon too quickly. Also, check into why the competitor did that. It may be that it's only a temporary event. However, if the price cut is a large and lasting one, you'll have to meet it. But in doing so, investigate how volume can be increased enough to offset any profit-margin pressure. One way to do this is to offer volume discounts so that customers will buy enough more in each transaction to provide cost savings that more than offset the lower price. Also, explore how you can add more value for customers in ways that don't increase your own costs so that there will be a preference for your offerings that will allow you to sustain a premium price over competitors.

- The country to which most of the products are exported has just installed a large import duty.

  The solution is similar to the case of an increased price for a major raw material. In addition, you can contact the country to see if an exemption can be created for your industry or company.

- Exports of an important raw material have been embargoed due to shortages and prices are expected to triple.

  Here, it's important to understand how price elastic the demand for your offerings is. Purchases for something like gasoline don't shrink very much when prices are much higher because many people having few alternatives to driving. If your offering is price sensitive, you won't be able to recover all of the cost increase. If the problem is long term, your best bet could be to purchase a supplier of the raw material so that the profits you earn in selling to others help offset some of the cost pressure on your profit margin. Otherwise, check to see if you can change the formulation to use a lower-cost material that provides other benefits.

What's the key lesson? *By demonstrating how to overcome apparent limits on growth and greater profits, you can improve eventual business performance while stabilizing value due to increasing confidence that revenue and profit growth will be solid. By so doing, you protect your ability to reward stakeholders who can add further gains to your economic performance before considering the effects of such limit-breaking solutions.*

Your Lesson Twenty-Six Assignments

1. Put in place ways to monitor investors' perceptions of your future revenue and profit growth prospects.

2. Whenever perceptions of future performance dip, pinpoint the basis of those concerns.

3. Check the validity of the concerns. If they aren't valid, explain to investors why they aren't.

4. If the concerns are valid, identify the best methods to overcome the apparent limits and begin testing them.

5. Favor solutions that allow you to prosper even if forces outside your control begin to operate in unexpected ways.

6. Demonstrate irrefutable proof to investors that you can perform well.

Part Five

Human-Resources Practices for Growing Value

Moreover I will make a covenant of peace with them,
and it shall be an everlasting covenant with them;
I will establish them and multiply them, and
I will set My sanctuary in their midst forevermore.

— Ezekiel 37:26 (NKJV)

The people in your organization want to succeed, both personally and as a group. While your colleagues' actions may sometimes cause unintentional harm or not be effective enough, it's rare that they won't be trying to do the right things. With such goodwill in place, you can experience something much like the promise God made to the Israelites in Ezekiel 37:26 (NKJV) for enjoying peaceful expansion. With God's help to lead you, you can then show them how to be more fruitful.

While there are many helpful methods for encouraging people to accomplish more, only certain ones are likely to make large value improvements in an ongoing fashion. In this part, we consider the most effective of such practices.

Lesson Twenty-Seven investigates how changing value forms can improve the effectiveness of executives and managers in making value improvements. Some might compare such real-life shifts to the helpfulness of the simulations that pilots and nuclear power plant operators use to hone their skills for dealing with new and challenging circumstances. With an ideal frequency of shifting value forms, about every three to four years, you'll enjoy more value improvement from the initiatives and efforts that your executives and managers undertake than you can by doing anything else, other than teaching and encouraging them to add the right complementary 2,000 percent solutions.

Almost every organization says that it wants to gain skills and knowledge ahead of competitors. Yet few organizations manage to accomplish this desirable goal. Lesson Twenty-Eight explains the large value potential of doing so through "wowing" investors and other key influencers of value with superior skills and knowledge. With this understanding, your organization can make such improvements a higher priority. Simply developing advanced skill in creating 2,000 percent solutions will be sufficient in many industries.

Many firms pretend that senior executives can do no wrong. Consequently, many organizations struggle under the dual weight of making actual errors then discouraging everyone else in the firm from fixing the errors. In Lesson Twenty-Nine, we discuss the greater value in seeking out mistakes and remedying them just as soon as possible. Clearly, such a change requires a top-down and bottom-up culture adjustment. Doing so will provide more benefits to stakeholders in economic terms, while reducing the stresses associated with having to pretend that all is well ... when it isn't.

Lesson Thirty is a natural follow up to Lesson Twenty-Nine. Sometimes mistakes cannot be overcome and opportunities fully grasped until leaders are put into more appropriate roles, ones to which they are better attuned and more appropriately skilled for what needs to be done. Such changes increase confidence that all will be well, encouraging all stakeholders to be helpful. Increasing the sense of more good things to come can often expand value in ways that makes it easier to accomplish such results.

Lesson Twenty-Seven

Change Value Forms to Stimulate Management

Behold, I tell you a mystery: We shall not all sleep, but we shall all be changed –

– 1 Corinthians 15:51 (NKJV)

In 1 Corinthians 15:51 (NKJV), the Apostle Paul wrote about the transformation of our human bodies into glorified, immortal ones that will occur at the sound of the last trumpet. That transformation is certainly one of the most profound changes that believers in and followers of Jesus Christ can expect to experience. While this wonderful event is certainly inspiring, I'm sure God also wants us to transform ourselves in simpler ways in the meantime, such as by changing how we think and act to be more like His Son, Jesus.

I've always been fascinated by the concept of how substantial changes can occur quite quickly based on appropriate human actions without Divine help. Naturally, I was fascinated to observe such changes among my clients whose businesses changed value forms, such as when one public company went through a leveraged buyout and become a private firm that needed to quickly pay off much debt. Another sleepy business that had been buried in a middling conglomerate went public, and the leaders suddenly became quite entrepreneurial. I could add other examples, but it wasn't long before I concluded that value-form changes could make helpful impacts on the people who led the businesses.

Most organizations don't even consider changing value forms as a strategy for stimulating value enhancement through refocusing company leaders ... and miss great opportunities to become more successful in operational, as well as in value, terms. This strategy is also consistent with having a very high-value entity or asset for stakeholders to participate with or in through ownership or ownership-related incentives. In total, I see the following seven potential benefits from changing value forms to stimulate management:

1. Providing the opportunity to have a very high-value entity or asset
2. Accelerating growth
3. Adding ways to shift more value to stakeholders
4. Sooner serving and involving more stakeholders
5. Cutting costs more rapidly and extensively
6. Eliminating many investments
7. Enhancing credibility with investors

I briefly address each of these points near the end of the lesson, but first let me summarize why such a strategy works. The basic idea is to shift a company's operating structure and financial context into a higher value form about every three to four years.

You may not see any potential benefit from making such frequent shifts, other than whatever comes from gaining a higher value form. Let me explain the basis for gaining additional value through management stimulation.

Industrial experimenters have long been interested in whether making changes in work environments can affect productivity. The often-misquoted Hawthorne experiments of Elton Mayo first led many to believe that making changes is always good, regardless of what the changes are. While many today would argue with drawing this conclusion from these experiments, it's clear that industrial-engineering solutions providing better methods of operating can lift productivity in quick, major ways, which can later be improved further, but more slowly.

What does this observation mean? People can learn to produce more, even after making a great breakthrough. But you already knew that from watching children master new tasks and your own experiences with learning.

Let's consider, instead, the results of another sort of change. In the late 1970s, Carol Coles and I became interested in what would happen if publicly owned companies sold 10 to 19 percent of their most valuable businesses to the public. Our hypothesis was that such an offering would make the worth of the most valuable business more transparent due to public-market pricing, as well as make it easier to appreciate what the rest of the company was worth. We believed that some investors would then begin to buy and sell the two securities in a form of arbitrage, such that the parent company's stock would be lifted closer to the company's public breakup value without actually breaking the company apart.

Several clients followed our advice and made such offerings. We called such transactions partial-public offerings (or PPOs). Being conscientious researchers, we measured everything we could about the companies and the various units before and after the PPOs.

While we were not surprised when this form of value arbitrage turned out to work well to increase parent company stock prices, many others were. However, we didn't expect by how much the newly public businesses accelerated revenue, profit, and cash-flow growth during the subsequent three years. Even after we adjusted for what competitors did during the same time periods, it was clear that some new factor was significantly boosting operating performance.

Interviews with the executives and managers who operated the newly public businesses suggested that a substantial part of the performance improvement resulted from their increased desire to make a good impression, due to the greater visibility of their unit's financial performance. In some cases, new types of compensation were more closely based on the business's performance, further contributing to improvement.

We continued to measure all such partially public units, and the above-trend operating improvements persisted. Curious about where else such operating improvements might be found, we also looked at leveraged buyouts (LBOs in common parlance – going from being public to private, while taking on a boatload of debt) where the same management team continued to operate the business (as occurred in the case of the early partial-public offerings).

While our LBO study sample was smaller and less representative due to many organizations not having reported information about their performance while privately held, we found some cases that could be measured. Again, operating performance greatly improved in the first three to four years, but mostly in terms of free cash flow (the amount of cash flow that isn't reinvested into the business). This finding made sense because LBOs require cash to pay substantial interest costs and make principal repayments for reducing debt to less costly levels. Management incentives in such cases heavily ran to improving this performance measure, as well.

Separately, much research has been done to determine the operating effects experienced by businesses that have become owned by employee trusts in the United States (called ESOPs). While taking such an ownership percentage too high seemed to backfire due to increasing employees' ability to advance their conflicting interests of keep-their jobs and making money as owners in ways that caused bad decisions, at lower percentages of employee ownership a similar stimulation of revenue, profit, and cash-flow growth occurred.

To us, it seemed that we were measuring the same effect: Changing value forms meant providing new incentives for management (or management and employees in the case of ESOPs) to perform in different ways. Management learned faster and made fewer mistakes, and such businesses greatly improved their operating performances in their new value forms.

While I have seen no research measuring this phenomenon following other value-form shifts, my hypothesis is that the same kinds of operating improvements would occur again if the value forms for a business or activity and management incentives were shifted about every three to four years. We also know from the research described in *The Ultimate Competitive Advantage* that most management teams can successfully make business-model innovations with such frequency. Making value-form shifts could also increase management awareness of the need for, the benefits from, and ways to implement new business models.

If you would like to go into this subject in greater detail, just send me your comments and questions to askdonmitchell@yahoo.com/, and I'll be glad to address your concerns and issues.

Here are several of the more obvious value-form shifts that may be attractive to make for improving operating performance to increase value even faster:

- Take a high-value publicly owned subsidiary private, after experiencing a substantial profit stumble.
- Take an LBO partially public when interest rates on the organization's debt are expected to rise much more than originally anticipated.
- Put risky assets into cash-flow-improving value forms when cash flow is more reliable to produce than performance in terms of any other value-influencing dimensions.
- Remove businesses and assets from cash-flow-oriented structures when cash-flow growth is more desirable and available than steady cash flow.
- Discipline a management team that has been using too much cash to grow by shifting into an LBO structure requiring much more cash for large debt repayments and high interest costs.
- Shift structures whenever changed tax rules make it more attractive to own a business or an asset in a different value form.

- Shift value forms to provide opportunities for new stakeholders to participate in substantial value appreciation.
- Change into a new value form when a government grant makes it far easier than previously to operate a business or asset to optimize a different aspect of its performance.

Let's look briefly at how such arrangements can help increase stakeholder value by 20 times through stimulating better management performance. As Lesson Thirty-Two discusses in detail, one of the most effective and simplest ways to add substantial value for all stakeholders is by providing opportunities to own some of an extremely high-value entity or asset before the biggest portion of value enhancement occurs. Shifting value forms more frequently can help increase business performance, enhance the gains that stakeholders receive, and permit more opportunities for new stakeholders to participate.

When faster growth is desired, an organization can shift into value forms that encourage this kind of performance. By alternating between growth- and cash-flow-emphasizing value forms, growth and the cash needed to pay for growth will be more available.

The increased frequency of value-form shifts permits new stakeholders to get in on the ground floor every three to four years for a period of rapid value growth. If the number of stakeholders is growing rapidly, this flexibility is essential to richly reward newer stakeholders. By growing faster, more rapidly expanding cash flow, and providing more ground-floor opportunities to reward stakeholders, this condition is met.

Each value-form shift encourages cutting costs in healthy, sustainable ways. By changing the rationale and incentives for doing so more frequently, the total amount of cost reductions should become greater.

More value-form shifts will provide a lower cost of capital and reduced need for cash investments, due to high-value securities being used more often to acquire what's needed in ways that also reduce the need for near-term operating investments.

With more frequent shifts in value forms, investors have more ways to be rewarded and benefit. As a result, it will be more attractive for investors to make a long-term commitment to such an enterprise.

What's the key lesson? *By establishing a company that frequently shifts value forms for the whole enterprise, as well as for portions of its businesses, assets, and activities, you can improve business performance faster, causing stakeholder value to expand still more rapidly, while having more ways to reward all stakeholders through value increases than would otherwise occur.*

Your Lesson Twenty-Seven Assignments

1. Determine ways that more frequently shifting value forms could enhance the operating performance of your entities and assets for stakeholders.

2. Evaluate how various value forms could cause more value improvement for the most valuable operations and assets.

3. Consider the size of the potential benefits from such changed actions compared to the net worths of those whom you would like to encourage.

4. Provide incentives for those stakeholders who can help the most and see how well the incentives work.

5. Adjust incentives to encourage even more valuable behavior changes.

6. If the advantages are large and appear to be sustainable, expand the successful programs.

Lesson Twenty-Eight

Add Critical Skills and Knowledge before Competitors

But also for this very reason, giving all diligence,
add to your faith virtue, to virtue knowledge,
to knowledge self-control,
to self-control perseverance,
to perseverance godliness,
to godliness brotherly kindness,
and to brotherly kindness love.
For if these things are yours and abound,
you *will be neither barren nor unfruitful*
in the knowledge of our Lord Jesus Christ.

— 2 Peter 1:5-8 (NKJV)

These verses from 2 Peter 1:5-8 (NKJV) provide a remarkably succinct, but thorough, description of how to combine a righteous approach to life with useful knowledge and the good practices for being fruitful. Clearly, we can all seek to improve with "all diligence" in these regards. Similarly, adding critical skills and knowledge ahead of competitors can lead to secular advantages, much as working on the qualities mentioned in 2 Peter 1 helps with expanding fruitfulness for the Lord.

This strategy came to mind when one of my students described his remarkable success in building a major company by being the first in that part of Asia to develop technical skills for solving important materials problems for major companies. That success brought to mind the many technically focused companies that became the market leaders and gained a premium valuation through being pioneers in expanding beneficial knowledge in their industries.

An example of gaining such knowledge and skill advantages can be seen in the long rivalry between NVIDIA and ATI in producing graphics semiconductors for electronic games. NVIDIA voluntarily adopted the discipline of producing a major upgrade in cutting-edge graphics every six months. ATI didn't try to match that improvement pace, but simply followed NVIDIA to produce decent graphics at lower prices for the larger market segments.

In many industries, such a strategy would work quite well because "good enough at a lower price" is what many people want. In electronic games, that approach was less successful for ATI. The dedicated game players who account for almost the whole market always want something better, and they don't mind paying a large premium. Many of the biggest spending end users are single males in their late twenties and thirties who can easily afford to indulge their preferences. Eventually, ATI stopped trying to be an independent company and was acquired by Advanced Micro Devices in 2006.

NVIDIA found other markets where better graphics were worth a premium price, such as advanced scientific applications and theatrical films with special effects, and developed cutting-edge knowledge and expertise in those markets, as well.

Some might mistake my comments by concluding that I'm solely focused on research and development (R&D) activities. R&D is just part of what I'm addressing. Twelve of the other potential areas for gaining and expanding on important skill and knowledge advantages include:

1. Business-model innovation
2. Identifying customer needs with greater potential impact
3. Gaining more trust at less expense

4. Attracting end users to try offerings
5. Helping customers to gain more benefit from their purchases and usage
6. Simplifying operations
7. Speeding up the provision of benefits
8. Adding excitement to being involved with the organization
9. Accessing more knowledge through global contests
10. Performing difficult activities with fewer mistakes
11. Creating more stakeholder value
12. Teaching stakeholders how to make more breakthroughs

Okay, you probably don't disagree with anything I've written so far, but you may be wondering what the connection is from each of these skill and knowledge areas to increasing stakeholder value by 20 times .... other than by simply improving operating performance. To explain the answer, let me start by asking you a question. Have you ever attended a theatrical performance, a music concert, a dinner, or an athletic contest where something so amazingly good happened that you couldn't stop talking about it?

If the answer is yes, how did that experience change your behavior? Chances are that you didn't want to settle for anything less in the future ... and that you were anxious to return.

Let me share the story of one of my children and the Broadway musical *Cats*. If you have never seen the show, let me explain that it has music written by Andrew Lloyd Webber to lyrics from T.S. Eliot's poetry in *Old Possum's Book of Practical Cats* (Harcourt, 1982). There's no real plot, just a loosely linked series of songs by actors and actresses dressed up as cats in a back-alley setting.

From quite a young age, my child had an interest in *Cats*. At first, the darkness and the performers dressed as cats creeping all around the audience and stage were frightening. But eventually, this youth's courage increased, coming to prefer being right in the middle of the action. Having tried out many different seats, one preferred seat was identified. If that seat wasn't available, there was no interest in seeing the show. Grandparents generously provided tickets. I lost track of how many times my youngster saw the show.

During all those years, there was no interest in attending any other Broadway shows ... or in sitting in any different seats.

Investors are much the same way. If you can show them something that just "wows" them, they keep coming back for more. Companies that have powerful knowledge and skill advantages often learn to put on compelling shows that throw the spotlight on their biggest advantages. Think of Steve Jobs up on a stage and how he introduced the latest electronic gear from Apple. It was high drama. And the value of the company's stock expanded due to the excitement.

Much as a magician can make the Statue of Liberty "disappear" or an elephant "appear" from "nowhere," people enjoy the experience of seeing something amazing. They can learn to derive some of their sense of self-worth from being a shareholder in a company that provides such amazing moments, compulsively using the company's offerings and being evangelists for the offerings and the stock.

When such identifications occur, estimates of future company performance may reach unusually optimistic levels ... supporting a higher stock-price multiple. Obviously, such inflated valuations create a favorable environment for rewarding the company's stakeholders.

What's the key lesson? *By adding critical skills and knowledge before competitors do, you will increase profits, profitability, cash, and cash flow, as well as gain and retain a higher value multiple for your economic performance. If you can also use that extra premium to create some other strategic and economic advantages, you can be well on your way to expanding value by 20 times more than would otherwise be the case.*

Your Lesson Twenty-Eight Assignments

1. Research your stakeholders to locate areas where skill and knowledge advantages will create the most substantial strategic

improvements in market expansion, reducing costs, eliminating investments, and expanding valuation.

2. Determine what skill and knowledge levels competitors have now and will probably have in the next few years.

3. Design ways to gain large, valuable skill and knowledge advantages in these strategic activities.

4. Consider what the effects of such advantages will be on stakeholders and valuation.

5. Explore what new strategic options such advantages open up, especially for making strategic and operating improvements.

6. Look for ways to "wow" stakeholders with the results of having applied the skill and knowledge advantages.

Lesson Twenty-Nine

Quickly Identify and Remedy Harmful Errors

Whoever loves instruction loves knowledge,
But he who hates correction is *stupid.*

— Proverbs 12:1 (NKJV)

We hardly need to read Proverbs 12:1 (NKJV) to realize that having others show us our mistakes is essential to gaining knowledge and becoming more effective. Yet many business leaders would go to any lengths to avoid gaining any of such valuable input.

Stakeholders know that everyone makes mistakes. Most stakeholders also realize that few people are quick to correct errors. After identifying companies that act in such desirable ways, stakeholders will do more to support such an organization, causing its value to expand more than would otherwise occur.

When stakeholders see, instead, that leaders are "married" to wrong directions, stakeholders realize that the consequences include missed opportunities, unnecessary costs, and harm to stakeholders. Let me discuss such a situation in the context of the 2010 battle between disgruntled shareholders led by hedge-fund operator Elliott Management and the board of directors of Iron Mountain.

You may remember Iron Mountain from Carol Coles' and my discussion of it in *The Ultimate Competitive Advantage*. The company has long led its industry (storage of business documents) with innovative new services and ways of operating.

Early in the twenty-first century, the company decided to expand beyond its traditional business of storing records and began to also offer data-processing storage. Unlike records storage, data-processing storage requires substantial technology investments and continuing high levels of expenses. Many of such investments represent fixed costs that are incurred regardless of how many customers receive services or what the revenues are. Since 2004, the company struggled to make money in the new service area and took multi-hundred-million dollar charges to write off technology investments. The CEO who championed this new business area resigned a few years later, and the firm's former long-time CEO, Richard Reese, returned to lead the company. Soon thereafter, Iron Mountain announced that it would pay out over $2.2 billion in dividends to shareholders during the subsequent two years, add two new members to the board to appease investors, look into what to do with the unsuccessful business, increase its international expansion, and consider whether to convert some or all of the firm into a Real Estate Investment Trust (REIT) as a way to increase the after-tax value of cash dividends to investors. As a result, Elliott Management agreed not to wage a proxy contest seeking to elect four dissidents to the company's board of directors.

Although the press release announcing the agreement didn't mention it, undoubtedly Iron Mountain spent tens of millions of dollars for legal, accounting, consulting, and investment banking services to deal with issues it should have been working on without any prodding from investors. What a waste!

What happened? Iron Mountain made a change that didn't work, providing a service that required competing directly with some of the world's top information-technology firms. Iron Mountain had previously only bumped heads with smaller, less talented firms. This time it was playing with the big boys and girls in a sandbox where it had almost no advantages and few competencies.

Organizations make similar mistakes all the time. When quickly addressed, costs of any errors can be contained. However, if an organization's leaders choose to keep making the same mistake, year after year, resources, time, and attention are drained away from other opportunities that obviously look better to shareholders.

While in office, the Iron Mountain CEO who resigned had staked his credibility and reputation on plans for the failed new business area. When that happens, a lot of CEOs aren't willing to do anything other than to defend and to sustain their past decisions. When such support protects an error, such CEO behavior usually compounds the mistake by precluding many ways to fix it while the organization follows a direction that makes matters worse.

I wish I could say that it's rare for company leaders to fall in love with their mistakes ... but I wouldn't be telling the truth. In fact, it's hard for an organization to appreciate a mistake ... and even harder to later admit it has made one. A major advantage of changing CEOs every so often is that the new one will often get rid of the mistakes that the last one was overly attached to.

Successful investors often take the opposite approach: They soon sell a stock after having made a mistake in buying it. Professional investors also have four occasions a year that encourage them to do so, just before they report their investing results for the latest three months. While a company can often use accounting rules to disguise its problems, professional investors have no such way to hide.

Disclosure requirements for public firms in the United States make it easy for investors to quickly learn where a company is losing money, when any problems worsen, and the leaders' answers provided to pointed questions in open forums about what's being done to eliminate the problems. If investors don't like what they see and hear, they will sell their shares to organizations that intend to make money by forcing management either to fix the ongoing problems or to resign.

In private companies, I've often seen similar dynamics within families that own an organization. Some family members won't like to see money being wasted, and they will pointedly demand that it be stopped. Those who manage the business are often offended that mere "owners" might challenge what they are doing.

A better approach is one that Acacia Research's long-time CEO, Paul R. Ryan, favored: Look carefully at everything a company is doing daily as though you had just been appointed as the new CEO that morning and had the benefit of 20-20 hindsight into what's been working and what hasn't. If something isn't up-to-snuff, deal with it by noon ... even if that means deciding to sell or exit the activity.

There's a simple point here for improving stakeholder value: Everyone makes mistakes, but only a few people work hard to identify and to remedy the errors as soon as possible. Such people attract more investors who stay invested.

Accounting rules often favor management decisiveness when dealing with problems. In many cases, an organization is able to immediately change its reported results (sometimes even including large adjustments to prior years) when it decides to stop doing something. At the same time, it's often the case that such a decision can instantly reduce the company's tax bill.

Here's an example under American accounting rules. If you decide to sell a business, it becomes a "discontinued operation" and the results (usually losses) aren't included in your past, current, and future results from "continuing" operations. It's like having a mulligan (a "do-over," another chance to hit a better shot) for every shot taken during a game of golf. Although not permitted by the rules of golf, something like a mulligan is permitted in accounting for business results. It's a wise leader who makes such do-overs early and often whenever something goes seriously wrong.

Notice that your earnings "score" immediately improves due to making the announcement, even if it takes several years to sell or to shut down the business. Such consequences are even better for eliminating shareholder pain from mistakes than selling a losing stock before the end of a quarter. Why? You also get to upgrade reported results (earnings per share, in this instance), while the professional investors still have to show the poor results from the prior quarter, even after making trades to hide the sources of their mistakes.

Prior to 1985, investors were skeptical of company managements that needed to take such mulligans. Such skepticism gradually evaporated so that by about 1995 investors were, instead, mainly skeptical of managements that didn't take lots of write-offs to discontinue failed operations and to sell unsuccessful businesses.

However, management desires to avoid embarrassment continue to retard taking the right steps. If someone once told everyone who would listen what a brilliant stroke it was to enter the XYZ business, naturally many of such people feel uncomfortable later describing that action as a major and expensive mistake. Who was the "dummy" who got us into that business, after all?

Students of the Old Testament can find in Saul, Israel's first king, a prime example of such behavior. Saul ignored God's instructions and did things his own way. When the results didn't work out, Saul was full of explanations for why he was in the right. Saul wouldn't fix the mistakes, causing lots of problems, first for the prophet Samuel and later for the future king David.

Don't be like that. Seek to find and eliminate whatever is causing harm. See if you can fix it. If you can't, admit the mistake, improve matters as best you can, and move on. Otherwise, you just compound the error and reduce the organization's value by more and for a longer period of time. Learn, too, to be humble and low-key in describing new activities, so you won't feel so awkward in dealing with them if they don't turn out well.

If you, as leader, do this, you'll also encourage everyone else in the organization to ferret out and remedy harmful errors as soon as possible. Just imagine how much value that would add!

What's the key lesson? *Learn to quickly identify and remedy harmful errors so that profits, profitability, cash, and cash flow can increase, and your company can gain and retain a higher equity value for its economic performance. If you can also use the improved results and* *the extra value premium to create other strategic and economic advantages, you will be further ahead in expanding value by 20 times more than would otherwise be the case.*

Your Lesson Twenty-Nine Assignments

1. Locate all the places where performance has been declining or unsatisfactory for at least two years.

2. See what has been done to improve matters.

3. Quickly determine what can be salvaged from the situation.

4. Announce a deadline for changing directions to doing something better.

5. If you should exit what you have been doing, as soon as possible announce that you will do so. Explain that a mistake has occurred, apologize, and carefully describe what you intend to do about it.

6. Seek all the benefits you can gain from applying accounting and tax rules.

7. Search for other mistakes that executives and managers have not disclosed.

8. Encourage executives and managers to reveal such problems and to take fast action.

Lesson Thirty

Put Leaders in More Appropriate Roles

Then the leaders of the fathers' houses,
leaders of the tribes of Israel,
the captains of thousands and of hundreds,
with the officers over the king's work,
offered willingly.

— 1 Chronicles 29:6 (NKJV)

King Solomon was appointed by God to build the Temple in Jerusalem. Solomon got this assignment, in part, because God decided that his father, King David, was not the right person to do the task. This is just one of many examples of how God looked deep into the hearts of His people to select the right ones for advancing His Kingdom. This verse from 1 Chronicles 29:6 (NKJV) describes the beginning of Solomon's building project, during which he asked the hereditary and military leaders of the tribes of Israel, and his own officers to consecrate the Temple project with their gifts. While God could clearly have provided whatever was needed for His Temple, in making this request Solomon was checking on the hearts of Israel's leaders and encouraging them to be properly engaged in supporting the project and worshiping in the Temple thereafter. Similarly, human-resources practices that place leaders into more appropriate roles can add value for a business.

I was reminded of this issue in 2011 when Cisco Systems announced that it would be leaving a number of businesses, cutting costs by one billion dollars, and reorganizing its management structure. Let me provide some background concerning the implications of such a shift.

When there's lots of demand for offerings, companies emphasize expanding capacity to provide the current offerings, as well as developing new offerings. When the demand is light, some companies shift to becoming leaner and reducing costs so that they can compete more easily with low-cost competitors. As you can imagine, the kind of leaders who are outstanding in leading capacity expansion and offering development are often quite different from those who are superb in becoming low-cost competitors.

Of course, depending on what industry you are in, the issues could be quite different. A medical-device maker of implants such as Medtronic that is greatly harmed by expensive product recalls might decide to improve processes and implant procedures to reduce errors that could endanger patients.

In changed circumstances, unseasoned company leaders will simply aim to jettison the current leaders ... knowing that investors will suspend judgment about how the new leaders will perform for a period of time (often 12 to 24 months). Some cynical company leaders would regularly fire almost every leader in the company, if necessary, in an effort to appear "indispensable," even though an objective observer might begin to wonder about a conflict of interest.

In most companies, more than one type of leadership is going to be needed over time. Realizing that, staff realignments offer opportunities to keep the best people by refocusing them into their most potentially productive near-, medium-, and long-term activities.

After such realignments, those who can "hit the ground running" can be placed into roles where such quick insights and action are appropriate and more will be accomplished. Where causes are murky, those who "like to get the bottom of things" can be expected to root around in dark corners until they uncover the "rotten apples" that are spoiling the barrel.

As you can see, successful reassignments are often psychologically based. Competence plays a role, too. Those who know how to financially analyze a business will often make faster initial progress in reducing unnecessary spending. But when innovation is essential, those who have an accurate technology vision of where the market is going and a keen sense of the requirements for new offerings can clearly add a lot of value.

Now consider investors. Each one will have a somewhat different agenda for what needs to be done to make an organization much more valuable. When an organization engages highly competent and psychologically well-attuned leaders to work on a variety of important tasks, chances are that any given investor will see "champions" of his or her ideal strategy for improving the company. If these company leaders are accessible to investors, almost all investors will initially perceive that all will be well ... and that the company's shares are a "bargain" compared to future business performance.

In essence, investors are being given a chance to look at the company in a way that provides a glimpse filtered through the flattering lens of their perspective, an image they admire and find appealing.

But that's not the end of putting leaders in more appropriate roles as a way to enhance value: There's also the opportunity to streamline the organizational structure. In so doing, reporting relationships can be shifted so that preferences for ways of operating can be further increased. People who like cost reductions want to see them accomplished quickly, so such leaders should be given more authority and freed from much bureaucracy in performing their tasks. Products that have been ignored ... but offer high potential ... may see organizations restructured around the idea of giving these offerings more attention. Think of such changes as being like the pedestals on which marble heads and busts are often displayed in museums. Such pedestals put at eye level what would otherwise be on the floor or hidden on an obscure shelf so that more attention is received.

Beyond that, the company's CEO is always in the spotlight. Some investors are hopeful that the CEO will thrive. Others are skeptical that will occur. By placing people into different roles, investors get a clearer sense of who might be a good successor to the CEO.

In any event, putting leaders in more appropriate roles is also a good leading indicator for investors of whether the organization will be stalled ... or filled with stallbusters.

Make such appointments well ... and at a time when you aren't having problems (Cisco was about 18 months late), and you can gain a premium ... a good step towards a 20 times increase in stakeholder value.

Think, too, of other stakeholders. Newly placed leaders are often more visible to stakeholders who aren't investors. Customers may receive fresh hope that long-standing complaints will be finally addressed. The actions of more effective leaders may give end users reasons to increase their loyalty. Employees and their families can gain more security and confidence. And on it goes in terms of increasing value for all stakeholders. If you would like a metaphor, imagine how good it would feel if your house were on fire and a fire truck arrived before too much damage had been done. You as the homeowner, as well as your neighbors who are threatened by the fire, would feel equally relieved ... and much value will be saved from damage.

What's the key lesson? *By putting leaders in more appropriate roles, you will increase profits, profitability, cash, and cash flow, as well as gain and retain a higher multiple value of equity for your economic performance. In addition, you will give investors a sense that such improvements are coming long before they arrive, adding a premium to the organization's value that can be good for all stakeholders. If you can also use the improved results and the extra value premium to create some* *other strategic and economic advantages, you can be well on your way to expanding value by 20 times more than would otherwise be the case.*

Your Lesson Thirty Assignments

1. Identify your company's strategic weaknesses that hold down potential value by large amounts.

2. Also identify your company's strategic strengths that might increase the value of your organization by a large percentage.

3. Evaluate those in your organization to see how well they match up against overcoming the weaknesses that are holding down value and building the strengths that could increase value even more.

4. Consider how well the organizational structure is designed for overcoming such weaknesses and building such strengths.

5. Look for those who can provide any missing talent.

6. Put in a new organizational structure and place leaders where their perspectives and competences best match what needs to be done.

7. Let investors and other stakeholders meet the new leaders and learn about the new roles and intentions.

8. Provide regular progress reports.

Part Six

Financial Techniques for Boosting Value

So it was, at that time,
when the chest was brought to
the king's official by the hand of the Levites, and
when they saw that there was *much money,*
that the king's scribe and the high priest's officer
came and emptied the chest, and
took it and returned it to its place.
Thus they did day by day, and
gathered money in abundance.
The king and Jehoiada gave it to those
who did the work of the service
of the house of the LORD*; and they hired*
masons and carpenters to repair
the house of the LORD*, and*
also those who worked in iron and bronze
to restore the house of the LORD*.*
So the workmen labored, and
the work was completed by them;
they restored the house of God
to its original condition and reinforced it.

— 2 Chronicles 24:11-13 (NKJV)

The verses in 2 Chronicles 24 (NKJV) describe Joash becoming king of Israel and then acting on his desire to repair the Temple. Knowing that collecting the money and then applying it was a task assigned by God to the priests and the Levites, King Joash first reminded them to do their duty. When the chief priest, Jehoiada, and the Levites were slow to respond, Joash took matters into his own hands and directed Jehoiada to construct a box for collecting the needed funds and to place it outside the entrance to the Temple. Joash next issued a decree reminding one and all to bring to the Temple the collection that Moses had required of Israel for the Tabernacle. Everyone immediately complied, enough funds were collected, and the Temple was repaired. Presumably, the spiritual values of Israel were enhanced, increasing the priority given to following God and being uplifted by worshiping in the restored Temple.

Similarly, good financing practices by companies can fall by the wayside when those who are in charge fail to do their duty. In addition, some people lack sufficient knowledge, imagination, or connection to the Holy Spirit to conceive of how best to finance a company's important tasks. In such cases, financial officers may only describe reasons why financing isn't possible, rather than just obtaining the money on favorable terms.

While the ability to raise money by financing is primarily determined by the underlying strengths and performance of a company's businesses, failing to take full advantage of such strengths and performance through optimal financing techniques will limit how much value can be created for stakeholders. In this part of *Advanced Business*, we consider seven financial techniques for providing much more stakeholder value.

Lesson Thirty-One sets the stage by explaining and demonstrating how cross-ownership by stakeholders can expand value by providing incentives for performing more helpfully to those who can make the greatest value-enhancement contributions. Encouraging such ownership should enhance benefits for all stakeholders.

Lesson Thirty-Two examines and illustrates how financing with advance payments from customers can both increase value and provide more opportunities for stakeholders to participate in value expansion. When such expansions are tied to increasing helpful performance by stakeholders, value improvement will be even greater.

Our Lesson Thirty-Three investigation demonstrates how eliminating or reducing taxes for the company and all of its stakeholders is highly beneficial for creating more stakeholder rewards and increasing ways of participating in substantial value expansions. These benefits are similar to the ones identified in Lesson Thirty-Two and build on insights from Lesson Thirty-One.

Lesson Thirty-Four considers using volatility in prices and values to accelerate the rate of value improvement while increasing benefits for all stakeholders. The lesson contains a detailed example of the share-repurchasing opportunities for public companies. Private and public companies can advantageously make acquisitions and divestitures in a similar fashion.

The opportunity to use futures contracts to gain advantages from all kinds of price volatility is the centerpiece of Lesson Thirty-Five. Privately held firms will be especially attracted to using this method for creating value.

Lesson Thirty-Six expands the ways of gaining advantages from volatility by describing how convertible securities can be custom designed to provide more value to the company and all of its stakeholders. We also consider some of the possible implications of an environment in which interest rates rise substantially.

Our final lesson in this part, Lesson Thirty-Seven, considers how to benefit from the attractiveness of securities that pay high dividends during low interest-rate environments. The lesson's key point applies to companies that have already implemented three complementary 2,000 percent solutions or an excellent solution. Such firms should be able to pay out much more cash in dividends than other firms, while still growing very rapidly. For dividend-hungry investors, the combination is likely to attract a price premium that can benefit any stakeholders who already own the security before such dividend increases are made.

Lesson Thirty-One

Employ Valuable Cross-Ownership among Stakeholders

"... I will make them one nation in the land,
on the mountains of Israel;
and one king shall be king over them all;
they shall no longer be two nations,
nor shall they ever be divided
into two kingdoms again."

— Ezekiel 37:22 (NKJV)

This lesson looks at how cross-ownership by stakeholders of assets, activities, portions of a business, an entire business, or the whole company can also increase value for other stakeholders. Here are seven points about such cross-ownership for your consideration:

1. *Asset valuers look separately at any equity stakes connected with an asset and adjust total value accordingly.*

   Here's an example. Imagine that the asset is real estate owned by a trust. Part of the value of any real estate is determined by its use. If a tenant company obtained a long-term lease at a time when it couldn't initially afford to pay all of the rent in cash, the tenant might have negotiated with the trust to pay part of the rent in its company's stock. If this stock was not sold by the trust and later greatly increased in value, the stock in the trust might eventually become worth quite a bit more than the real estate. If more payments in stock were expected and the value attributed to the cash equivalent of the payments was less than the discounted future market value of the shares, the value of the trust's ownership would also increase by the discounted value of the expected differential.

2. *Valuers of the portions of a business will look separately at any equity stakes that are associated with partial ownership of another business and adjust values for the portions of a business accordingly.*

   Let's assume that a portion of a business supplies another company that has paid for a portion of what it purchases with warrants to acquire its shares in the future at a fixed price that is well below today's market price for such shares. Valuers will look at the differential between the current and expected future value of these warrants and will add the discounted value of these value enhancements to the value of whatever partial ownership of the customer that the portion of the business already holds.

3. *Valuers of businesses will look separately at any equity stakes that are associated with ownership of a whole business and adjust business values accordingly when equity stakes are split.*

   This kind of valuation is done all the time. Consider a company that owns two businesses, one of which is part of the other. Let's assume the smaller business that is part of the larger one is worth nothing, and the larger one is worth a great deal. If the worthless business is to be simply given away or shut down, valuers will stop paying attention to the smaller business. Just as soon as plans are announced to give away or shut down the worthless business, the larger one will be credited for its full value, less any liabilities and debt that the overall company has.

4. *Valuers of companies will look separately at any equity stakes that are associated with ownership of a whole company and adjust company values accordingly.*

   Let's imagine that you are looking at a large international company, such as Coca-Cola. This firm owns 100 percent of many whole companies, typically syrup-selling organizations and bottling operations located in many different countries. In some cases, regional businesses within part of a country are also separately incorporated. Each such business has a distinct value. If Coca-Cola made known all the facts about each of these companies, Coca-Cola's overall value could be determined by adding together these values, plus any other assets that Coca-Cola owned at the parent company level, less the value of any debt and other liabilities.

5. *Valuers of assets, portions of businesses, businesses, and whole companies will do the same sorts of adjustments when other types of assets are owned together.*

   Whether you are talking about an asset that includes total ownership of a company or the opposite (plus any other permutations of holders and holdings), valuers will take into account the value of what is owned, less any liabilities, when considering the total value of the asset, an activity, a portion of a business, a business, or a whole company.

6. *While valuers will take such ownership circumstances into account, value may be discounted where either the transaction costs to realize the value are high or the results are uncertain.*

As an example, consider the hypothetical case of a public company that owns an 89 percent stake in another public company. Because the transparency of value is high in such a situation, you might imagine that the value translation into the parent company shares might be almost 100 percent. Such a valuation is too high, however, if the price for the 11 percent of tradable shares is artificially inflated by the small supply of public stock. In such a circumstance, valuers may only add a premium of 50 to 80 percent of the apparent extra value reflected in the public shares of the partially owned public company to the parent company's share price.

7. *If the value of such cross-ownership positions is small enough, the cost of analysis may discourage any work being done, as well as any credit being received.*

   For instance, if the owner has 500 of such ownership positions and none is bigger than 0.5 percent of the enterprise's total value, valuers will probably ignore all these positions. In such a case, owners could hope to offset part of this disregard by shifting the values into some other forms that can be more easily valued, such as combining cash flows received by the owners into a few larger equity stakes.

So how can all of this information be successfully applied to increase value for stakeholders? *Where stakeholder values are much smaller than the most valuable entity in the stakeholder universe and stakeholder actions can greatly improve the entity's value, it will be possible to add substantial value for each stakeholder by providing access to increasingly valuable ownership in the most valuable entity, conditioned on taking actions that greatly expand the entity's value.*

Since we are thinking in terms of increasing the overall ownership value by 20 times beyond what the usual approaches to expanding profits and cash flow can accomplish, in such a circumstance there's a substantial opportunity to assist many stakeholders. Let me quantify this opportunity with a hypothetical example:

Most valuable entity's current value: $1,000,000
Expected value increase in this entity from operating breakthroughs: $20,000,000
Average employee net worth before entity value increases: $5,000
Average customer net worth before entity value increases: $3,000
Average end user net worth before entity value increases: $300
Average community resident net worth before entity value increases: $100
Average supplier net worth before entity value increases: $20,000
Average distributor net worth before entity value increases: $1,000
Average shareholder net worth before the entity value increases: $333,333

Expected entity value increase if an average employee is more productive: $200,000
Expected entity value increase if an average customer doubles purchases of offerings: $20,000
Expected entity value increase if an average end user doubles consumption: $ 20,000
Expected entity value increase if an average person in the community improves the business environment: $ 2,000
Expected entity value increase if an average supplier reduces costs and prices by 50 percent: $200,000
Expected value increase if an average distributor doubles sales: $200,000

As you can see from this example, there's a high potential for increasing the value of the most valuable entity by nonshareholding stakeholders taking the right value-enhancing actions.

If bargains are struck such that stakeholders receive stock options, or something similar, equal to half of the value they add through their ac-

tions before the $20,000,000 gain occurs from still other actions, net worths can soar for every stakeholder.

Let me demonstrate this point with a hypothetical illustration:

> 50,000 end users holding pre-value-increase stock options expand their consumption by 100 percent.
>
> (50,000 end users)($20,000) = $1,000,000,000 in additional value
>
> Entity value goes from $1,000,000 to $1,021,000,000 after the other value-enhancing actions are taken. That's an increase of 1,020 times. From such a value increase, it's easy to expand all stakeholder net worths by 20 times, assuming that each stakeholder has an equity stake or option before the change occurs. In the case of the end users, receiving $6,000 of the $20,000 in value increase provided by each one would expand their net worths by 20 times. Doing so leaves a surplus value increase of $700,000,000 that could be distributed to the other nonshareholding stakeholders, even if they provided no new benefits.
>
> If, in addition, other stakeholders make valuable changes, the increased values for everyone can become much greater.

Conversely, if the value improvements from stakeholder changes are small, cross-ownership doesn't do much to help increase stakeholder net worths, unless all stakeholders are very poor compared to the most valuable entity's initial value.

What's the key lesson? *Finding ways for entities to increase value by an additional 20 times creates a foundation for developing opportunities to expand stakeholder value still further through value-based incentives that stimulate helpful stakeholder actions. By increasing cross-ownership by all stakeholders, you can expand value faster and reward all stakeholders with greater value increases than would otherwise occur.*

Your Lesson Thirty-One Assignments

1. Determine ways that the value of the most valuable entity could be expanded by 20 times without changing any stakeholder ownership, attitudes, or behavior.

2. Identify how changing stakeholder actions in new ways could cause more value improvement for the most valuable entity.

3. Consider the size of the potential benefits from such changed actions compared to the net worths of those you want to encourage to act.

4. Provide ownership incentives for those stakeholders who can help the most and see how well the incentives work.

5. Adjust incentives to encourage even more valuable behavior changes.

6. If the advantages are large and appear to be sustainable, build onto and expand the use of successful programs.

Lesson Thirty-Two

Finance Growth with Customer Advances

"So you ought to have deposited my money
with the bankers, and at my coming
I would have received back my own with interest."

— Matthew 25:27 (NKJV)

Many organizations and their financial officers limit themselves to the following sources of financing: borrowings, leases, and equity offerings of securities. Increasingly, savvy leaders are also doing as much as possible to gain needed operating funds by securing advance payments from customers. If you doubt that observation, consider how hard various organizations tried in recent months to interest you in buying or giving various payment and gift cards. Others, including perhaps your vehicle insurer, expected you to pay for all of the service you would receive in the following year before you even began receiving the service. Add the number of organizations that asked you to buy "memberships" before you receive any benefits. For instance, many people belong to a wholesale goods operation, which requires such a membership. From the day I first bought my car, the manufacturer and dealer have been pounding me with offerings to buy an extended warranty, even though my current warranty is still in force.

This financing strategy can be more helpful if you also have a very high-value entity or asset for stakeholders to participate in owning. In total, I see the following seven benefits from such a strategy.

1. Providing the opportunity to have a very high-value entity or asset
2. Accelerating growth
3. Adding ways to shift more value to stakeholders
4. Sooner serving and involving more stakeholders
5. Cutting costs more rapidly
6. Eliminating many investments
7. Increasing credibility with investors

I address each of these points separately so that you will be sure to understand what the opportunities are.

But before looking at the seven points, let me briefly summarize how such a financing strategy works. The basic idea is to obtain *all* the cash needed to operate the business from customers. Here are several ways to do so:

- Require advance payment of the total sum involved in the transaction when an order is placed.
- Obtain a deposit at the time of taking an order.
- Be paid at the time of delivery.
- Receive full payment long before suppliers require being paid.
- Charge for any special investments needed to support a given customer, such as molds or programming.
- Offer special advantages for those who purchase memberships or pay for offerings well in advance of when payments are normally due.

Okay, let's look now at how such arrangements can help increase stakeholder value by 20 times.

Financing with customer advances provides or enhances the opportunity to own a very high-value entity or asset. As we explored in Lesson Thirty-One, one of the most effective and simplest ways to add much value for all stakeholders is to provide opportunities to own some of an extremely high-value entity or asset before the biggest portion of value enhancement occurs. Financing growth with customer advances can improve the opportunity to enhance such an asset or entity value expansion. Here's why:

- Such a unit can operate with no net investment when customer advance payments provide for all of the fixed assets and working funds that are needed to operate. As a result, such an entity or asset will have an infinite return on no shareholder investment, other than whatever retained earnings remain in the business as non-operating investments (such as holdings in short-term, cash-equivalent investments). Such an entity will have very high value as well as attract much interest from investors who like high-return opportunities.
- While first operating, such an asset or entity tends to lose a little money due to start-up costs. As a consequence, the initial valuation of such an entity or asset is usually low compared to what it will be later after substantial operating income is being received and a large cash generation is established. When the entity or asset grows to a large size, the shift from losing a little money to high-margin profitability on no net investment is rapid and dramatic, causing value to grow even more quickly than profits and cash flow do.
- Because a fully mature operation financed with customer advances can have no operating need for using the cash, a high rate of dividends can be paid. As a result, those who place a high value on discounted free cash flow and dividends are strongly attracted to such assets and entities.
- Any portion of a business entity that is totally financed by customer advances is often worth more than the entire business that is not so financed. As a result, value-form arbitrage is available to enable assets requiring a net investment to be held

in forms that maximize their value, while the free cash flow is held in forms that maximize its value. As a result, the combined approach of having two or more entities may well create more value in total than a combined entity would have in the public markets.

Financing with customer advances provides or enhances the opportunity to accelerate growth. In businesses that can be financed by customer advances, the cash flow of the operation is always positive. As a result, business leaders can be more aggressive in market- and business-expanding opportunities, knowing that more growth means more financial safety due to increasing free cash flow and potentially by holding large cash balances.

If business conditions change so that the cost of capital for competitors increases (interest costs go up for debt and price-earnings multiples go down for equity), a business that is totally financed by customer advances will find competitors to be more vulnerable to new initiatives and less able to respond with new investments and offerings. This is particularly true if customer advances can be applied to permit more development of advantaged new offerings, due to the reduced risk of not finding customers who will pay to have them developed. As we know, faster growth is good for valuation, so such results will accelerate the value growth of whatever entities and assets are established.

Financing with customer advances provides or enhances the opportunity to shift more value to stakeholders. A business that is financed with customer advances can engage in many different kinds of activities and establish many different value structures for stakeholders to participate in. Each time another value form is added, there are more ways for stakeholders to participate. Here are some examples of value forms that can be created:

- Royalty-receiving asset or entity
- Product-producing asset or entity
- Land-owning assets or entities

- Equipment-owning assets or entities
- Distributor-owning assets or entities
- Management-company assets or entities
- Service-related assets or entities

Dell, the PC maker, has been financed almost totally by customer advances. Let's look at how it might have used such structures. Many people don't know it, but Dell has developed hundreds of patents. This intellectual property could have been segregated into a patent-owning unit that licensed them in exchange for royalties to a product-producing entity. Dell produces its products in huge factories. The land, buildings, and equipment could have been put into different entities to allow stakeholders to specialize in one of those holdings. Dell has a huge online presence. That organization could have been formed as a distributor and made available for investment. The various entities could also have contracts with management companies in which stakeholders could invest. Finally, Dell has a huge service operation that could have been set up as a separate entity or series of entities. By creating so many assets and entities, a stakeholder could have been provided with more choices and ways to participate in value expansion, allowing for more gains to have been experienced and more stakeholders accommodated.

Financing with customer advances provides or enhances the opportunity to sooner serve and to involve more stakeholders. While at first blush the growth of a firm financed with customer advances mostly seems to expand revenues and customers served, the expansion in number of stakeholders is actually much greater, due to there being so many more owners of various entities and people affected who live in the communities served by the much more rapidly expanding customer-financed enterprise.

Here's a brief example to illustrate that point. If a conventionally financed company operation were established in 5 locations, the total owners might be 5, the number of employees might be 100, the number of customers might be 4,000, and the number of community residents affected might be 40,000. In a customer-financed operation with 500 larger locations, the total owners might be 50,000, the number of employees might be 200,000, the number of customers might be 6,000,000, and the number of community residents affected might be 100,000,000, simply due to the advantages of combined scale.

Financing with customer advances provides or enhances the opportunity to cut costs more rapidly. Most costs decline with either scale effects (spreading fixed and semi-fixed costs over more volume) or experience (learning how to perform more effectively). Since a customer-financed operation is going to expand more rapidly, such scale and learning effects sooner become significant and remain larger.

Such effects will often be experienced in a given geography. For instance, the administrative costs in a market with 100 times more volume might only need to be three times the level of an operation that is 1 percent of that size. As a result, administrative costs on a per-unit basis go down by 97 percent. Similar efficiencies would show up in many overhead-related costs. Similar benefits would be enjoyed in reducing per-unit marketing costs.

Financing with customer advances provides or enhances the opportunity to eliminate many investments. Due to scale effects, fewer assets will be needed. During a tour of a Dell factory, I was told that with an increased investment of only 5 percent the organization could double production capacity in that facility, just by adding a second story for which the building already had the necessary foundation and structure in place.

Financing with customer advances provides or enhances the opportunity to increase credibility with investors. Because customers are willing to finance growth, investors don't have to worry nearly as much about excess finished inventories, sales hiccups, and product obsolescence ... particularly if the organization produces its offerings to order, as Dell does. Consequently, investors will pay more for the earnings, cash flow, and dividends that are generated, knowing that they are more reliable and sustainable in the future than for competitors that finance conventionally.

What's the key lesson? *By using customer advances to finance growth, you can expand value faster and have more ways to reward all stakeholders through value increases than would otherwise occur.*

Your Lesson Thirty- Two Assignments

1. Determine ways that financing growth with customer advances could enhance the performance of your entities and assets for stakeholders.

2. Evaluate how various structures of customer-financed entities could cause more value improvement for the most valuable operations and assets.

3. Consider the size of the potential benefits from such changed actions compared to the net worths of those whom you would like to encourage.

4. Provide incentives for those stakeholders who can help the most and see how well the incentives work.

5. Adjust incentives to encourage even more valuable behavior changes.

6. If the advantages are large and appear to be sustainable, expand the successful programs.

Lesson Thirty-Three

Minimize Taxes for All Stakeholders

Render therefore to all their due:
taxes to whom taxes are due,
customs to whom customs,
fear to whom fear,
honor to whom honor.

– Romans 13:7 (NKJV)

Romans 13 (NKJV) reminds us that we are to submit to governmental authority because God has placed such people into these positions. While we are encouraged to be generous in contributing to churches, those in need, and people who ask for help (including our enemies), references to doing more than the minimum for the government are missing, except in Jesus' direction to go the extra mile beyond what Roman law required if ordered to carry a soldier's gear. If you aren't sure about whether you should pay more in taxes than what is required, I encourage you to do your own Bible studies and to pray for guidance in this regard.

You may be wondering why this topic is included. After all, don't almost all companies try to minimize taxes? Well, yes, that's true. However, few organizations seek to minimize taxes for more than just the firm and its shareholders. The other stakeholders might just as well not exist in terms of the tax planning done by most financial executives.

Organizations that don't seek to minimize taxes for all stakeholders miss great opportunities to become more successful. This financial strategy is also consistent with having a very high-value entity or asset for stakeholders to participate in. In total, the following seven benefits can be derived from such a strategy.

1. Providing the opportunity to have a very high-value entity or asset
2. Accelerating growth
3. Adding ways to shift more value to stakeholders
4. Sooner serving and involving more stakeholders
5. Cutting costs more rapidly
6. Eliminating many investments
7. Increasing credibility with investors

I address each of these points separately so that you will be sure to understand what the opportunities are.

Before looking at the seven points, however, let me briefly summarize how such a strategy works. The basic idea is for stakeholders to pay as few taxes as possible while fully complying with all laws and regulations.

Some may argue that such an approach violates the principle of increasing stakeholder value by 20 times by cutting down what the government receives. I disagree with that conclusion because any government that levies taxes should be serving its citizens and legal residents (and in some cases the illegal residents) as its sole purpose. If the people who live in that governmental area see their benefits from an organization grow in value by more than 20 times, the test of expanded stakeholder value has been met. It doesn't matter if those benefits come from paying taxes or in some other way. Do you see what I mean?

There are a number of ways to add value for everyone who lives in a governmental area, one of the best being to increase the economic activity that the organization does by at least 20 times so that more people are employed, more valuable offerings are made and used by more people, and those who have an ownership stake increase their wealth so that they can further enhance the economic well-being of those in the community. If you would like to go into this subject in greater detail with me, just send me your comments and questions to askdonmitchell@yahoo.com/, and I'll be glad to address your concerns and issues.

Here are several of the more obvious ways to minimize taxes for the company and all stakeholders:

- Earn profits in places where profits are taxed either little or not at all.
- Pay dividends in forms that either avoid or delay taxation, or don't pay dividends.
- Place assets in places where assets are either taxed very lightly or not at all.
- Avoid transactions that trigger tax payments.
- Pay for services and goods in ways that will defer or minimize taxes for employees and suppliers.
- Provide tax-free or tax-deferred benefits to stakeholders.
- Help customers and end users receive the benefits they seek in ways that do not incur sales, value-added, and use taxes.
- Negotiate with governments for special tax treatment as a substitute for receiving direct payments to encourage moving to or investing in a particular governmental area.

Okay, let's look at how such arrangements can help increase stakeholder value by 20 times.

Minimizing taxes for all stakeholders provides or enhances the opportunity to have a very high-value entity or asset. As we explored in Lesson Thirty-One, one of the most effective and simplest ways to add substantial value for all stakeholders is to provide opportunities to own some of an extremely high-value entity or asset before the biggest portion of value enhancement takes place. Paying no taxes from the entity or through transactions with stakeholders can enhance the opportunity to provide and to enhance such an asset or entity expansion. Here's why:

- When such a unit can operate with no taxes paid by it or its stakeholders, it will have a much higher return on the profits and cash flow earned by its shareholders' investments, while the absolute levels of earnings and cash flow before considering taxes will also be higher due to spending less to compensate or reward stakeholders. Such an entity will have very high value as well as attract much interest from investors who like higher-return opportunities.

- While first operating, such an asset or entity tends to lose a little money due to start-up costs. As a consequence, the initial valuation of such an entity or asset is usually very low compared to what it will be later after substantial operating income is being received and a large cash position may be built. When the entity or asset grows to a large size, the shift from losing a little money to high-margin profitability on relatively little investment is rapid and dramatic, causing value to grow even more quickly than profits and cash flow do.

- Because a fully mature operation should generate lots of cash, the absence of needing to pay taxes increases the ability to pay dividends (or their equivalents in various tax-advantaged structures). As a result, those who place a high value on discounted free cash flow and dividends are strongly attracted to such assets and entities.

- Any portion of a business entity that has more favorable tax treatment for it and its stakeholders is often worth more than the entire business that doesn't have such advantages. As a result, value-form arbitrage is available to enable assets requiring a net investment to be held in forms that maximize their value while the free cash flow is held in forms that maximize its value. As a result, the combined approach may well create more value in total for the individual units than a combined entity would enjoy in the public markets.

Minimizing taxes for all stakeholders provides or enhances the opportunity to accelerate growth. In businesses that pay no taxes and whose stakeholders pay no taxes, the cash flow of the operation is almost always going to be positive. As a result, business leaders can be more aggressive in engaging in market- and business-expanding opportunities, knowing that more growth means more financial safety due to increasing free cash flow.

If business conditions change so that the cost of capital for competitors increases (interest costs go up for debt and price-earnings multiples for equity go down), a business that pays much less in taxes (and whose stakeholders also enjoy the same benefit) will find competitors to be more vulnerable to new initiatives and less able to respond with new investments and offerings.

This is particularly true if funds that would otherwise be spent on taxes (or payments to stakeholders to cover their taxes) can be applied to permit more development of advantaged new offerings, due to the reduced risk of not finding a profitable market for them by using funds that incur no tax or tax-related costs.

As we know, faster growth is good for valuation, so such results will accelerate the value growth of whatever entities and assets are established.

Minimizing taxes for all stakeholders provides or enhances the opportunity to add ways to shift more value to stakeholders. A business and its stakeholders that pay no taxes can engage in many different kinds of activities, and establish many different value structures for stakeholders to participate in. Each time another value dimension is added, there are more ways for stakeholders to participate. Here are some examples of value forms that can be created:

- Royalty-receiving asset or entity
- Product-producing asset or entity
- Land-owning assets or entities
- Equipment-owning assets or entities
- Distributor-owning assets or entities
- Management-company assets or entities
- Service-related assets or entities

Many international online businesses and their stakeholders pay few or no taxes. Let's consider how such enterprises might be organized to take advantage of these reduced costs. Many such entities could develop or now own valuable trademarks, service marks, and copyrights. An intellectual-property-owning unit could license the right to use such intellectual property to a product-producing entity in exchange for royalties. If any products are produced in company facilities, the land, buildings, and equipment could be put into different entities to permit stakeholders to specialize in one of those three types of holdings. Those facilities could be located in jurisdictions where taxes would not be incurred from earnings, sales, payments to stakeholders, or dividends. The online portion of the organization could be formed as a distributor, domiciled in the most tax-advantaged locations, and made available for stakeholders to invest in. The various entities could also have contracts with management companies that stakeholders could invest in. Finally, if there is a service activity, that could be set up as a separate entity or series of entities. By establishing so many assets and entities, each stakeholder could be provided with more choices and ways to participate in value expansion so that more gains could be experienced and more stakeholders accommodated.

Minimizing taxes for all stakeholders provides or enhances the opportunity to sooner serve and involve more stakeholders. While at first blush not having to pay taxes at the company or the stakeholder level mostly seems to expand revenues and customers served, the expansion in how many stakeholders are affected is actually much greater. That's primarily because there will be so many more owners of various entities and people affected who live in the communities served by the much more rapidly expanding tax-free enterprise.

Here's a brief example to illustrate that point. If a conventionally financed company operation were establishing 10 locations, the total owners might be 10, the number of employees might be 200, the number of customers might be 8,000, and the number of community residents affected might be 80,000. In a tax-free global operation with 1,000 locations, the total owners might be 100,000, the number of employees might be 400,000, the number of customers might be 12,000,000, and the number of community residents affected might be 200,000,000 simply through combined scale effects that make it attractive to involve more people.

Minimizing taxes for all stakeholders provides or enhances the opportunity to cut costs more rapidly. Most costs decline with either scale effects (spreading fixed and semi-fixed costs over more volume) or experience (learning how to perform more effectively). Since a tax-free system is going to expand more rapidly, such scale and learning effects sooner become significant.

Such effects will often be experienced in a given geography. For instance, the administrative costs in a market with 100 times more volume might only need to be three times the level of an operation 1 percent of that size. As a result, administrative costs on a per-unit basis go down by 97 percent. Similar efficiencies would show up in many overhead-related costs. Similar benefits would be enjoyed in reducing per-unit marketing costs.

In addition, by helping customers, employees, suppliers, and other stakeholders also become free of taxes, less will have to be paid to them. As a result, prices can be lower (while still enjoying higher profits) or marketing can be much more substantial so that growth will be even further enhanced.

Minimizing taxes for all stakeholders provides or enhances the opportunity to eliminate many investments. Due to scale effects, fewer assets will be needed. In addition, the prices paid for land, buildings, and equipment will be reduced due to a higher-value (or lower-cost) source of capital and sellers needing less in payments due to their also not having to pay taxes.

Minimizing taxes for all stakeholders provides or enhances the opportunity to increase credibility with investors. Because no one is paying taxes, investors have an extra margin of safety in difficult times. During good times, returns will be even higher. Because wealth can be transferred to investors in tax-free ways, investors will pay a premium for that benefit as well. As a result, they will pay more for whatever earnings, cash flow, and dividends are generated.

What's the key lesson? *By establishing a company that doesn't have to pay taxes and doing the same for stakeholders, you can expand value faster and have more ways to reward all stakeholders through value increases than would otherwise occur.*

Your Lesson Thirty-Three Assignments

1. Determine ways that not being required to pay taxes could enhance the performance of your entities and assets in rewarding stakeholders.

2. Evaluate how various structures of tax-free or tax-deferred entities could cause more value improvement for the most valuable operations and assets.

3. Consider the size of the potential benefits from such changed actions compared to the net worths of those whom you would like to encourage.

4. Provide incentives for those stakeholders who can help the most and see how well the incentives work.

5. Adjust incentives to encourage even more valuable behavior changes.

6. If the advantages are large and appear to be sustainable, expand the successful programs.

Lesson Thirty-Four

Turn Volatility to Your Advantage

"The heavens and earth will shake;
But the LORD will be a shelter for His people,
And the strength of the children of Israel."

— Joel 3:16 (NKJV)

Joel 3:16 (NKJV) tells us that God will protect His children when everything around them is shaking, undoubtedly increasing danger and causing fear. Similarly, when we are prepared to increase the value of a company for the benefit of all stakeholders, we will be able to do so whether the values involved are temporarily much lower or higher.

Most organizations and their financial executives see volatility as a problem, rather than as presenting valuable opportunities. When such a misperception occurs, an organization will miss some of the best ways to increase stakeholder value.

Let me begin by pointing out that customer demand and the level of financial markets are usually well above or below their annual averages. Consider toys. Just before Christmas, many purchasers will spend more on toys than they will in total during the subsequent eleven months. And in February, purchasers will spend almost nothing, due to having just bought Christmas presents and picked up any "must have" items that were sold out before Christmas. Planning for such volatility is critical if a company is going to make the most profit and hold its economic value. Otherwise, someone could simply come along every February and buy all publicly held toy companies for very little.

In addition, even publicly held companies whose sales and profits aren't very volatile during the course of a year usually see the value of their securities trade at a 20 percent premium and discount to the annual average price for at least a few days during a year.

Subject to certain limitations (which vary from country to country and from time to time), companies are legally allowed to purchase their own securities and to issue new ones at times of their own choosing. By concentrating these purchases when prices are low and issuances when prices are relatively high, the number of shares outstanding can potentially be reduced at no net cost after a cycle of repurchase and reissue has been completed. As a consequence, the value of the remaining shares will be higher due to their representing an increasing proportion of the total company's ownership.

Some people object to such a strategy, observing that those who pay high prices for shares are going to lose money. While that's true for an organization whose value doesn't grow, a public company that's using the methods of *Business Basics* and *Advanced Business* will be expanding in value quite rapidly, thus not causing anyone to lose money by such an approach.

Here's a hypothetical example of spending $1 million a year to buy shares at low prices and issuing an equal value of stock at higher prices annually during several years of rapid stock-price growth to make the point clearer:

Year	Average Price	Purchase at 20 Percent Discount	Sell at 20 Percent Premium	Shares Available
Zero				1,000,000
One	$10.00	125,000	83,333	958,333
Two	20.00	62,500	41,667	937,500

Three	40.00	31,250	20,833	927,083
Four	80.00	15,625	10,417	921,875
Five	160.00	7,812	5,208	919,271

As you can see from this example, simply buying and selling using the same total amount of money for each annual transaction can shrink shares outstanding by 8 percent over five years during a period of rapidly increasing security prices. If share prices grow more slowly, the percentage reduction will be greater.

Now let's consider the potential effect of greater volatility in security prices from year to year and concentrating much larger purchases and sales during the more extreme price fluctuations:

Year	Average Price	Purchase at 20 Percent Discount	Sell at 20 Percent Premium	Shares Available
Zero				1,000,000
One	$10.00	500,000	0	500,000
Two	80.00	0	41,667	541,667
Three	40.00	125,000	0	416,667
Four	160.00	0	20,833	437,500

With more volatility in security price from year to year, waiting longer for optimal times to buy and sell, and spending four times as much money on the initial purchase, the same approach can instead reduce shares outstanding by 56 percent at no net cost.

Let's look next at an even simpler case where extremely large security purchasing is concentrated in the beginning and sales are concentrated at the highest prices during a four-year period:

Year	Average Price	Purchase at 20 Percent Discount	Sell at 20 Percent Premium	Shares Available
Zero				1,000,000
One	$10.00	950,000	0	50,000
Four	160.00	0	39,583	89,583

By waiting for greater shifts in prices and spending almost double the amount of money on the final purchase compared to the second example, the same approach in the third example can instead reduce shares outstanding by 91 percent at no net cost. The effect of such a change would be to increase the value of the remaining shares by over 1,000 percent, before any increases in economic performance.

If you are the owner of a private company, you may be thinking that such an example doesn't apply to you. Don't be too hasty in drawing such a conclusion. In many countries, there are major economic incentives for all companies to establish employee pension plans that involve ownership in the enterprise. Typically, the timing of when such trusts are established is determined by the company's management. In addition, owners can decide when to set up similar trusts for other classes of stakeholders, including customers, suppliers, and distributors. It is also often legal to make tenders to purchase the shares in such trusts at the current "fair" market value. The cash that is acquired by the trust can be paid out to trust owners or used to purchase shares in other organizations, so that ownership risk can be diversified. Timing of such purchases and sales can be used to enhance overall shareholder value, as well as the value of trust holdings. For instance, one trust might tender to buy shares from another trust that holds the company shares.

Beyond this example, there is also the highly relevant issue of making acquisitions. Whether the acquired entity is publicly or privately held, the purchase price can be below the average of what might be paid for it. When such an acquired entity also increases economic performance for the acquiring company, the per-share value (of a private or a public company) also expands.

If you combine the effects of purchases and sales of securities at no net cost with also making acquisitions (and selling businesses) in such a way that the acquisitions don't cost anything, you can use volatility to greatly expand stakeholder value ... well beyond 20 times. What could be nicer?

I won't go into all of the other ways to take advantage of volatility, but I do want to caution you to be sure that any such purchasing and sales are done in ways that do not harm the economic interests of any stakeholders. For instance, you shouldn't sell securities at such a high price that those who buy the securities will lose money on the purchases over the long run (as happened to shareholders in so-called dot-com companies in the late 1990s and in homebuilders worldwide around 2007 and 2008). Notice that in the second and third hypothetical examples, those who bought shares at a premium to $160 per share in year four would need to see further appreciation in subsequent years to avoid what could be a substantial temporary loss from "normal" volatility for such businesses. Consequently, it makes the most sense to make such transactions in advance of major value-improvement programs.

With an enterprise that is expanding according to the excellent, value-improving moves we have been studying, such harmful share sales are much less likely to occur. But be mindful anyway. Extreme market volatility could still unexpectedly harm stakeholders, at least temporarily. Naturally, any such transactions should also be done in the most ethical way possible. Avoid taking actions that cause people to buy or sell who may be better off not doing so. In addition, be sure that you are fully disclosing all that is or could be coming to the best of your understanding. Be especially careful when selling shares, since it could take a few years before those purchasers will benefit. Always be guided by whatever the Holy Spirit, the Bible, and thoughtful conversations with other believers indicate that Jesus would be likely to do.

What's the key lesson? *By appropriately buying and selling company or unit shares at times of extreme forms of volatility in business value, you can improve business performance and also cause value to expand more rapidly on a per-share basis. Buying and selling businesses provide similar opportunities. By so doing, you create more ways to reward stakeholders who can add further gains to your economic performance by their actions before considering the effects of such transactions.*

Your Lesson Thirty-Four Assignments

1. Determine ways that volatility in values could be used to enhance the operating performance of your entities and assets for stakeholders on a per-share basis.

2. Evaluate how different types of transactions could cause more value improvement for the most attractive operations and assets during periods of volatility.

3. Consider the size of the potential benefits from such changed actions, compared to the net worths of those whom you would like to encourage.

4. Provide incentives for those potential stakeholders who can help the most and see how well the incentives work.

5. Adjust incentives to encourage even more valuable behavior changes.

6. If the advantages gained are large and appear to be sustainable, expand the successful programs.

Lesson Thirty-Five

Use Futures Contracts to Enhance Attractiveness

For I know the thoughts that I think toward you,
says the Lord,
thoughts of peace and not of evil,
to give you a future and a hope.

— Jeremiah 29:11 (NKJV)

God wants your future to be good and for you to experience hope until desirable events He intends occur. Futures contracts are one way that God has provided for us to do so. Futures contracts are another way that you can employ volatility to your advantage (the subject of our preceding lesson). I have rarely met anyone who thought about futures contracts for enhancing the attractiveness of businesses, assets, and securities. Instead, most organizations see futures contracts primarily as a mechanism for protecting budget performance by "locking in" assumptions about prices and costs.

Futures contracts have nine other valuable uses:

1. Gaining higher prices now than will prevail in the future
2. Reducing costs below what they will be in the future
3. Getting paid for volatility in the price of what you sell

4. Enhancing profits and cash flow above what the current market environment would provide on its own
5. Making future earnings and cash flow more certain
6. Providing funds that can be used to provide more value for stakeholders
7. Opening the door to faster market expansion
8. Permitting opportunities to purchase competitors at lower relative prices compared to your organization's equity value
9. Being able to offer customers extra value at no increased cost in exchange for longer-term commitments

Notice that each of these uses also makes businesses, assets, and securities more attractive and valuable.

Although these opportunities are attractive, they are not without risk. If your estimates of future prices are wrong, you may "lock in" selling prices well below what the market will later pay or purchase raw materials and other inputs at prices well above where the market will be.

In making such evaluations, however, you have two sources of strength on which to draw:

1. Just seek an advantage over competitors in gaining relatively better prices and lower costs.
2. Tie your futures contract transactions to fulfilling customers' contractual requests, so that you are, in effect, sharing the risk with a customer.

In addition, you can choose to be very conservative in your purchases and sales of futures contracts so that the risk of being wrong is unusually low in historical terms, by comparing the current economic situation to what has occurred before.

I am often told by clients that they don't want to "tie-up" capital in such contracts. Let me address that concern in these four points:

1. Over a full economic cycle, the capital requirements will probably be about a wash with extra cash being generated when prices for your offerings are about to begin falling (a good time to have extra cash) and extra cash being needed to purchase inputs after a long period of costs dropping (the effect of which will probably have added cash).

2. After considering the extra profits you will earn, these contract purchases and sales should be looked at as investments that will have a more than acceptable rate of return. Why wouldn't you want to invest to make a reasonable profit?

3. As an organization that is growing very rapidly with low costs and little need for added cash to operate on a larger scale, cash should be plentiful for this purpose.

4. By using long-term puts and calls rather than futures contracts, the cash cost of taking such positions can be much smaller. Most large brokerage firms offer such options.

Let's assume that you want to be very prudent and always have an advantage by being more attractive to investors than the alternatives in your industry: Consider splitting your assets, businesses, and securities in two parts that stakeholders can own, with one part not using any futures contracts and the other part making the best possible use of futures contracts. In this way, if you are wrong about either taking or not taking futures positions, investors can still find a haven in the part of your organization where the "right" decision has been made. Naturally, making such a split can be a complication for a very small organization, but your enterprise should rapidly increase to quite a large size. In such an environment, split offerings are much more affordable and sensible.

Such a split approach gives you an extra margin of safety: You can use the asset, business, or security from the part that's benefiting from taking or not taking futures positions to purchase positions in the assets, businesses, or security that are being harmed. This principle is in accord with Lesson Thirty-Four, where we consider how to take better advantage of volatility.

I won't develop the point further, but I'm sure you'll agree that it would be wonderful to sell your product for double the current market price simply due to having sold future contracts while the price was rapidly rising, or to purchase the materials and other inputs you need at half the current market price due to having bought call options (the right to purchase quantities at a fixed price) for future delivery dates when prices were lower.

Why then will such assets, businesses, and securities be more attractive to stakeholders, independent of the improved economic performance? Here are three reasons:

1. The predictability of future performance will be greatly enhanced in ways that stakeholders can calculate and depend on.

2. The likelihood is increased of sustained outperformance compared to competitors, making a relationship with your organization more attractive.

3. The futures and options positions you take will provide clear signals of what your organization thinks about the future environment, making it easier to gauge when to buy and sell your organization's assets, businesses, and securities.

What's the key lesson? *By establishing a company that seeks to buy and sell futures contracts and options to take advantage of price and cost volatility for your offerings and inputs, you can improve business performance and also cause value to expand more rapidly on a per-share basis while making ownership positions more valuable, separate from any economic improvements. By so doing, you create more ways to reward stakeholders who can add further gains to your economic performance before considering the effects of such transactions.*

Your Lesson Thirty-Five Assignments

1. Determine ways that volatility in prices and costs could be used through futures contracts and options to enhance the operating performance of your entities and assets for stakeholders on a per-share basis.

2. Evaluate how different types of transactions could cause more value improvement for the most valuable operations and assets.

3. Consider the size of the potential benefits from such changed actions compared to the net worths of those whom you would like to encourage.

4. Provide incentives for those potential stakeholders who can help the most and see how well the incentives work.

5. Adjust incentives to encourage even more valuable behavior changes.

6. If the advantages are large and appear to be sustainable, expand the successful programs.

Lesson Thirty-Six

Offer Convertible Securities

And in this mountain
The L*ORD* *of hosts will make for all people*
A feast of choice pieces,
A feast of wines on the lees,
Of fat things full of marrow,
Of well-refined wines on the lees.

— Isaiah 25:6 (NKJV)

God intends for His children to enjoy the best of what He has created. Unfortunately, all of that plan won't be fulfilled until Jesus returns. In the meantime, His plan does include ways to generate more value that will enable us to expand His Kingdom and glorify Him by making good use of the best of what is currently available for such purposes.

I was reminded of the potential usefulness of convertible securities for expanding value while thinking about how hard it is to find convertible securities that an investor could use to execute superior investment strategies. You may remember that Carol Coles, Robert Metz, and I write about this approach in *The 2,000 Percent Solution*, citing the example of Avon Products. That once high-flying direct-sales cosmetics company had fallen on hard times and could no longer afford to pay the generous dividend that had long attracted many investors to the stock just a couple of years after the company's CEO, Hicks Waldron, had promised that he would never cut the dividend. What was a responsible CEO to do under such circumstances?

A convertible security turned out to be an answer that might have appealed to King Solomon when faced with two women claiming to be the mothers of the same child. Avon Products announced it would have for three years two classes of stock: a regular common stock paying a small dividend and a convertible preferred stock that would pay the same dividend as the current common stock. Common stock shareholders could swap their common shares for the convertible preferred stock and be assured of continuing to receive their dividends at the current rate for three years. At the end of three years, the convertible stock would be automatically turned into the same number of shares of common stock at whatever the price was for the common at the time.

In the meantime, those who held the common stock would see higher earnings per share ... and potentially more appreciation. And anyone who needed a higher dividend had three years to find a replacement security before selling the convertible preferred stock. In this way, Avon Products avoided having the common shares plunge in price due to panic selling, so the dividend-sensitive investors didn't lose money ... but the parent company could immediately cut its total dividend payments by a large percentage.

As this example demonstrates, we live in a time of "make-up-your-own" convertible securities. That's a relatively recent phenomenon.

Prior to 1960, many companies only provided investors with the opportunity to purchase common stock. A few large companies with weak balance sheets might also have some preferred shares outstanding that paid a fixed dividend. Most borrowing was done from banks, except for a handful of large, very creditworthy companies.

Beginning around 1960, a few companies started to become interested in borrowing more money to substitute for equity capital. Many banks didn't want to lend to them, but the rapid growth of mutual funds and pension funds meant that there was a rapidly increasing public market for higher-quality debt securities.

Some companies began to acquire lots of other companies. The accounting rules at the time meant that by paying with common stock you could expand earnings per share very rapidly if you bought low-earnings-multiple companies. The result of such a focus was to create unmanageable messes called "conglomerates." For a while such stocks soared, but the ugly performance reality began to set in before 1970 and many of these stocks dropped in value by more than 90 percent.

Such organizations still had an "urge to merge" and began to look for a new way to finance such purchases. They began to issue convertible debt. Because these securities were convertible into common stock, they weren't as risky for investors as straight debt issuances. Because there weren't very many such securities available, issuers were able to get away with paying well below the current market rates of interest. Typically, the conversion was dependent on the common stock rising by a certain amount (often 20 percent). Until converted, such securities didn't affect earnings per share very much because the interest rates paid were so low. As a result, almost any acquisition immediately boosted earnings per share. The merger mania continued for another couple of years before collapsing in a puddle of broken dreams filled with the remnants of shattered fortunes. Stock prices then languished for the next fourteen years.

Companies still wanted to make acquisitions ... while some also wanted to retire lots of low-multiple stock through share repurchases. Neither banks nor the public markets wanted to lend to most companies for such purposes. Selling equity was a loser's game because stock-price multiples were so low.

Into the gap strode Michael Milken from a small Wall Street firm few had heard of called Drexel, Burnham, Lambert. With interest rates at incredibly high levels, savings and loan associations (S&Ls) were going bankrupt as they paid depositors high, short-term rates to lend at low rates for long-term mortgages. Seeking high-yield investments, S&Ls became customers for high-yield ("junk") bonds.

Milken provided historical evidence that the risk of default for many such borrowers had been low ... and many people bought his story. Most organizations would initially borrow this way and refinance with lower-cost funds just as soon as they could. It worked for a while ... especially since those who issued such securities often had secret agreements to buy from other issuers to illegally prop up the market prices.

In the process, the leveraged buyout was born due to equity prices being so low that you could pay a big premium for the stock, pay too much in interest to borrow, borrow too much money, and still repay the loans. Billionaires were made.

Interest rates then began a decades-long tumble to today's artificially depressed levels. Through those years, common stock prices soared. Issuances of convertible debt became commonplace as did straight debt and equity issues.

Today, we stand near or at the beginning of a period when interest rates may well rise for many years and common stock prices will languish for many companies. Such a market is ripe for new types of convertible securities that boost common stock values and provide access to lower-cost equity.

Here are five examples:

1. A convertible bond issued in 2015 may not ever have to be redeemed for common stock because the common stock won't rise very much from today's levels. If that occurred, the company issuing such a bond will benefit from paying way below market interest rates for many years.

2. Many people today are consumed by the idea that gold, silver, oil, and other commodities are ideal inflation hedges during a time when governments are printing too much money and spending more than they can afford. In such an environment, companies might issue equity and debt that's convertible into commodities on some fixed ratio. The issuer could hedge any

further increases in such commodity prices by purchasing options, futures contracts, and physical goods. The issuer could also hedge any decrease in the prices with puts (guarantees to be able to sell at a fixed price) and short sales (selling securities now and paying back with securities bought later). During the inevitable ensuing volatility, the issuer could profit greatly from paying lower interest costs and any changes in commodity prices. Such arrangements would work best for those organizations that regularly produce such commodities.

3. Some visionary companies might realize that they could use today's high-priced stock and low-cost debt to repurchase company shares at much lower prices in a few years. Convertible issuances might guarantee a fixed conversion at 80 percent of the current prices after a period of five years. Thinking what a bargain that could be, many investors would pay a premium price for such securities. By issuing at current prices whatever the convertible security would be, cash could be acquired in two ways now at bargain costs. The cash could be used later to retire whatever is issued before the time of conversion at a lower price, providing access to "free" funds.

4. Other companies might issue zero-coupon, inflation-adjusted securities now, which would probably command a huge premium. The cash from such issuances could be used to retire more conventional debt and common stock in ways that would greatly expand future performance.

5. In such an environment, a value-improvement-oriented company that was always expanding the value of its securities could take advantage of today's market environment to issue lots of convertible securities that would benefit from rapid equity-price increases. For instance, a new equity convertible might present the opportunity to be converted for a number of years into var-

ious forms of low-cost debt where there is little principal risk for investors. Here's an example of what I mean:

a. Start by selling convertible debt at a fixed coupon that's convertible into money-market preferred stock (a very valuable security for regulated financial companies such as banks and insurance companies) whenever the return on money-market preferred reaches above a certain level (where the value of the convertible fixed-rate debt would start to swoon).

b. Add a second convertibility feature to the money-market preferred that permitted swapping it for common stock that has appreciated by 80 percent. Such a feature would lower the initial coupon rate on the convertible debt to a tiny level and allow ultimate redemption in much higher-priced common stock. The amount of "free" money acquired by the company would be huge.

A company focused on expanding stakeholder value by 20 times would be able to credibly provide various convertible instruments that would provide lower risk for investors, a boost in the financial results reported by the company, and a lower cost of capital for the company. This is a win-win-win solution.

In looking for new forms of convertible instruments, you can use the same tools described in Part Eight to determine what investors and stakeholders are looking for that they cannot obtain enough of from the public market. Then, use your superior knowledge of the outstanding future results you will deliver to construct low-cost convertible instruments that will provide more wealth for everyone during a time of change in the market psychology when most people expect to see their equity and debt holdings decline in value.

What's the key lesson? *By creating and offering the right convertible securities for the circumstances and volatility, you will increase prof-*

its, profitability, cash, and cash flow, and gain and retain a higher multiple value of equity for your economic performance. If you can also use the improved results and the extra value premium to create some other strategic and economic advantages, you can be well on your way to expanding value by 20 times more than would otherwise be the case. In addition, you can provide a safe haven for investors and stakeholders who are risk averse.

Your Lesson Thirty-Six Assignments

1. Find out what investing risks concern your potential investors, current investors, and stakeholders.

2. Determine where they believe they have too-limited choices for reducing or managing such investing risks.

3. Estimate the lowest end of your equity values over the next few years.

4. Learn how public perceptions of future equity values differ from what you expect.

5. Design new convertible securities that deal with such concerns and provide less risk while enhancing company performance and value.

6. Test the appeal of such convertible securities through the ways described in Part Eight.

7. Formally offer for sale or swap the most attractive convertible securities at optimal times to provide profitable opportunities for the company and all stakeholders.

Lesson Thirty-Seven

Pay Extraordinary Dividends In Low Interest-Rate Environments

In the morning they are like grass which *grows up:*
In the morning it flourishes and grows up;
In the evening it is cut down and withers.

— Psalm 90:5-6 (NKJV)

Psalm 90:5-6 (NKJV) reminds us that our lives on Earth are brief and end in physical death, while God endures forever. These verses should also remind us that the usefulness of financial strategies depends on the market, economic, and interest-rate environments. Such a caution should be especially valuable after having read in the previous lesson about the difficulties that a generous dividend caused for Avon Products after its business performance weakened. You've also just been told that interest rates might soon begin to rise and could keep doing so for some time to come.

So the obvious question is why even consider paying extraordinarily high levels of dividends? Well, it's entirely possible that low interest rates will persist due to extreme central bank and government actions, or quickly return after a rise in rates stifles economic growth. Whatever happens, it's important to remember that paying a large portion of earnings in dividends is not always a way to add value. Such an approach can be a dead weight, instead.

For years, the Federal Reserve has been hinting that interest rates would have to rise from an artificially low level. Such hints have continued, while rates have remained low.

Traditionally, high dividend yields (dividends paid divided by the price of the underlying security) were primarily attractive to small investors, especially older ones, who saw such cash payments as a way to reduce risk, to receive more retirement income than bonds and banks offered, and to offset inflation as dividends climbed over time.

For organizations with typical profitability from their activities, dividends are usually limited to being between 1 to 60 percent of earnings ... depending on the rate of capital reinvestment required to meet the growth in customer demand. The limit is usually whether the financial policies could be sustained without adjustment.

As a result of this financial perspective, it was often viewed as harmful to valuation to be paying very generous dividends as a percentage of earnings. Many institutional investors saw such dividends as a sign that an organization didn't plan to and couldn't afford to grow very much. As a result, forecasts of future performance improvement (the basis of most valuation methods) were modest.

If dividend payout rates (the percentage of the last five years' annual earnings paid in dividends) were too high, many investors assumed that the company was ... or soon would be ... in trouble. The typical conclusion was that the dividend was about to be reduced ... or eliminated.

Such a negative conclusion would be drawn even for businesses where the accounting rules required using depreciation schedules that reduced asset values much more rapidly than the assets wore out or had to be replaced. Propane distribution companies are a good example. The depreciation rules for accounting in the United States are much too high for such companies and the rules reduce earnings well below what's going on in an economic sense (rather than what is demonstrated by applying the overly conservative accounting rules).

In terms of financial theory, such views didn't make a lot of sense, but that's the way the equity markets traded ... until a few years ago.

What changed? Five important things:

1. Interest rates dropped to unusually low levels in many countries compared to the local inflation rate (the "real" interest rate). Previously, the so-called low-risk, real interest rate would be about 2 to 3 percentage points above the rate of local inflation in a given country. For much of the last decade in many countries, interest rates have instead been 2 to 3 percentage points (and sometimes more) *below* the rate of local inflation. That's a swing of 4 to 6 percentage points that made it very cheap to borrow money. Most countries allow a tax deduction for the cost of the interest, and you paid back the loans with currency that had much less purchasing power.

2. Equity markets came to be dominated by hedge funds and other investors employing dozens of dollars of debt for every dollar of equity in their investments.

3. Hedge funds began looking for a certain kind of investment:

   a. Buy something that would go up rapidly in price (such as commodities temporarily in short supply ... copper, corn, wheat, and cotton have been examples in recent years).

   b. Borrow the money at a very low interest rate.

   c. Borrow with an agreement to pay back the loan in a currency whose value was likely to fall compared to other "hard" currencies during the term of the loan.

4. New types of securities were established that made it easier and cheaper for anyone to take a long or a short position (and

with plenty of debt leverage). Many of such securities were in the form of ETFs (Exchange Traded Funds).

5. Discount brokers began lending large amounts of money to anyone who wanted a margin account at very low interest rates.

   One television advertisement sticks in my mind. It showed cash registers kicking out money from their cash drawers while a voice intoned that central banks were printing too much currency. The announcer noted that you could borrow $1 million at 0.5 percent interest for every $200,000 in an equity margin account. The tag line was the hundreds of U.S. stocks were paying dividends providing yields in excess of 5 percent.

   The underlying, tacit message was that while a debt-free investor could earn 5 percent a year in dividends in a market where equity prices were stable, a debt-leveraged investor could earn over 20 percent a year (a high return) from the same investing approach ... simply by borrowing lots of money.

If interest rates are about to rise, you might think that there would be a limited opportunity to benefit from being a high dividend-return stock. Normally, what would happen is that such stocks would start to drop in price as interest rates rose ... due to investors wanting a bigger yield compared to interest rates.

I believe that the opportunity will only be different this time for companies that have accomplished the first three complementary breakthroughs (accelerated market growth by 20 times, reduced unit costs by 96 percent, and eliminated 96 percent of investments needs). Here are five reasons why:

1. Such firms will be able to pay over 100 percent of earnings without harming growth prospects while carrying moderate amounts of debt.

2. The dividends can grow at the same rate as the earnings ... very rapidly.
3. By creating a special class of stock with a guaranteed minimum redemption price, risk of reduced value for the underlying shares could be eliminated.
4. If desired, a class of stock could be created that could have double or triple the payout ratio of a traditional high-payout common stock.
5. Due to collapsing currency values in some low interest-rate countries, borrowing costs are still going to be low in hard currency terms even after interest rates rise quite a bit.

Let me explain what I have in mind. One obvious alternative is to simply raise the dividend near to the highest level that can be safely sustained with prudent borrowing. In doing so it will be important to demonstrate why this high level can be sustained and rapidly increased. The combination of a high payout ratio and rapid growth in dividends will be so unique to investors that many will be attracted. Because they can afford to borrow to purchase such shares and still earn back their cost of interest relative to future dividends, there should be immense demand. If investors believed that such performance would be long sustained, the potential value would be astronomical.

An even more attractive choice is to create a convertible debt security that can be turned into an even higher-paying preferred stock at a fixed conversion price. If you set the conversion terms so that earnings per share will be higher than the preferred dividend, this conversion will actually expand the rate of earnings and cash flow per share growth.

As a result, you could use such a security to purchase regular common stock shares ... further bolstering measures of per-share growth. Because then you are only paying such interest and/or dividends on far less than all of your shares, you could pay a lot more interest for these shares ... making them even more desirable to own and to hold. For example, if you do this with 20 percent of your shares, you could potentially pay out more than five times the earnings on these few shares and keep the whole company in balance. With rapid-enough growth, there would be per-share earnings dilution for fewer than 18 months. If you also used some cash to retire other shares, the dilution could be totally eliminated at the start.

Realizing how attractive these shares would be, there would be a mad scramble to purchase the regular common equity if that were the only way to obtain some of these shares. That scramble would push up the value of the enterprise even faster.

If stakeholders had been granted an opportunity to own common stock earlier, the net effect would be to greatly accelerate their accumulation of added value.

What's the key lesson? *By making extraordinarily rich dividends or interest payments available in low-interest rate environments, you will increase profits, profitability, cash, and cash flow, and gain and retain a higher multiple value of equity for your economic performance. In addition, you will give investors a sense that such improvements are coming long before they arrive, adding a premium to the organization's value that can be good for all stakeholders. If you can also use the improved results and the extra value premium to create some other strategic and economic advantages, you can be well on your way to expanding value by 20 times more than would otherwise be the case.*

Your Lesson Thirty-Seven Assignments

1. Identify what classes of investors aren't attracted to your securities now.

2. Determine how extraordinary dividends might attract those classes of investors while making your securities more attractive to investors who already like your shares.

3. Test your assumptions with anonymously sponsored investor interviews.

4. Implement any new directions that pass the tests of the effect on your verified correlation, what relevant case histories show, and what anonymously sponsored investor interviews tell you. These tasks are described in Part Eight.

Part Seven

Communications Procedures for Value Expansion

Having many things to write to you,
I did not wish to do so *with paper and ink;*
but I hope to come to you and speak face to face,
that our joy may be full.

— 2 John 1:12 (NKJV)

Would you rather learn about important news by e-mail or face to face from someone you know, like, and respect? In today's world, almost everything possible is used as a substitute for in-person communications, so much so that individual meetings may now be as endangered as the long thoughtful letter to a friend became in 1965 when color television became widely available. 2 John 1:12 (NKJV) indicates that John wanted to share important information, so important that he preferred that it not go into a letter. By sharing the news face to face, he expected that their mutual joy would be fuller. Now isn't that a lovely thought?

Most efficient-market theorists would argue that it doesn't matter how relevant company news gets out. The market will react just the same way. In my experience, that observation is a simplifying assumption rather than an accurate statement of fact. Most so-called information needs a lot of explaining before anyone can hope to discern its relevance and make an appropriate investment decision. Certainly, that point is even truer with the large sums that can be made by owning securities in a company that has made four complementary 2,000 percent solutions to expand value.

In this part of *Advanced Business*, I describe ways of communicating that are more like developing lasting, mutually beneficial friendships with highly esteemed people than traditional methods of investor and stakeholder "communications." As background for applying this process, we begin in Lesson Thirty-Eight by considering the value effects associated with the ratio of how much stock is practically available to trade compared to how much trading actually occurs. By taking the ratio of trading to available shares to much higher levels, a firm can greatly expand the multiple that investors pay for company performance.

Since having more investors who will hold a stock through thick and thin expands the company's stock-price multiple, it's obviously useful to attract and retain more of such individuals and institutions. Lesson Thirty-Nine describes a process for doing so.

Valuers play a key role in determining your organization's and your credibility for doing what you say you will do. Lesson Forty describes how to apply the Golden Rule in communications to help valuers accurately understand your future prospects.

If you improve communications and reveal that management is performing poorly, you'll be worse off. In Lesson Forty-One, we look at how to be more candid about problems and what you are doing to resolve them, as well as strengthening management and company performance. Doing so will increase the confidence of valuers and stakeholders that you will accomplish more.

In Lesson Forty-Two, we look at continually adding special-situation reasons to own a stock so that the short-term focus of the huge hedge funds that dominate market trading will cause them to act like long-term investors. As a result, valuations can be greatly expanded.

Lesson Forty-Three addresses the importance of having all stakeholders know what the issues are and what's being done about them, as well as engaging stakeholders to make faster and more effective improvements. Such communications create a highly transparent view of the company for its stakeholders. This lesson also describes the special opportunities of privately held firms in these regards.

Continually attracting new stakeholders who can contribute to expanding organizational effectiveness is the topic of Lesson Forty-Four. We focus primarily on opportunities with potential customers, suppliers, and distributors, as well as uninvolved experts.

Lesson Thirty-Eight

Create and Maintain a Perfect Balance of Investors

It is *God who arms me with strength,*
And makes my way perfect.

— Psalm 18:32 (NKJV)

Psalm 18:32 (NKJV) points out that God gives us the strength to proceed and also clears the way so that the strength we receive from Him can be most effectively used. While such praise in the Bible is often associated with overcoming enemies during warfare, I believe that it also applies to developing a community of investors who are part of the committed stakeholders to your organization. In this lesson, you will learn a way that God has provided for you to work with shareholders so that their support will be more valuable to the company and to all the other stakeholders.

Creating and maintaining a perfect balance of investors is much easier to accomplish in conjunction with the kind of business and financial strategies that we have been examining in *Advanced Business*. Let me explain what I mean by a perfect balance of investors by first visiting the Netherlands in 1637, soon after tulips were introduced. During this time, the prices of tulip bulbs soared to unimaginable levels ... estimated to have equaled as much as a skilled craftsman would earn in ten years for a single bulb called the "Viceroy." Although there undoubtedly had been speculative markets that went too high in price prior to this instance, so-called Tulipomania is the first well-documented example. Prices quickly collapsed, and many Dutch people went bankrupt because of having borrowed vast sums to speculate in owning tulips.

Such a collapse is what normally happens when excess speculation occurs: Prices go too high relative to economic value (what financial benefits can be produced) and eventually fall like a brick thrown from the top of a tall building. Clearly such excess happens because many people are drawn to purchase by stories of how much "wealth" others have gained. In addition, many people employ an investing strategy called "momentum" investing where they buy during the upward price trend ... until the trend breaks. In the process, most of the purchasing is done by people who do not know or don't care about the economic value of what is being purchased. Following the peak, prices may fall more than 10 times faster than they rose. Few want to buy on the way down. It's hard to sell without incurring losses at that point. Naturally, such spikes are only guaranteed to help those who sell before or at the beginning of the collapse, hardly a recipe for increasing stakeholder value by 20 times on a sustained basis.

Mitchell and Company studied such excesses that occurred in more recent times to better understand how stock-price premiums are created. From that work, we developed a helpful new measurement: trading volume/available float. Let me define these terms for you. *Trading volume* is simply the sum of all the shares traded during a given period of time. *Available float* is the total number of shares that have not been continuously held by the same investors throughout the last three years. For a publicly held company, trading volume is reported daily for each type of security. To determine the amount involved, you simply add each day's trading volume to the others in the same time period (usually three months). With an Excel spreadsheet, this calculation is easy to do.

Calculating the denominator in the ratio requires more work. You start by examining the shareholder list to see which investors have continuously held shares for the last three years and what the minimum amount held was during those years. You then add up the minimum holdings of all such investors during each measured time period. Subtract that total of minimum holdings from the shares outstanding, and the remainder is the available float.

From making many such calculations, we noticed that it was helpful to then perform statistical regressions comparing the ratio of trading volume to available float with some popular value ratios, such as price/earnings, price/cash flow, price/free cash flow, and price/book. The pattern varies from security to security, but typically the relationship shows a long relatively flat section at lower ratios of trading volume to available float where the effect of increasing the ratio of trading volume to available float is fairly small.

At some point, however, an inflection point is reached where the valuation ratio begins to climb rapidly, as the ratio of trading volume to available float further increases. We call that inflection point the beginning of the "sweet spot" (a reference to making solid contact with a ball by using a golf club or tennis racquet).

The "perfect balance" range can be determined by looking at this regression to identify ratios of trading volume to available float where the security is trading at a desirable valuation multiple that can be sustained through encouraging sufficient long-term holdings to keep the available float low enough to ensure the relationship to trading volume stays continually in that desirable range.

Once having identified the sweet spot, you should obviously take reasonable steps to reach and stay there. What can be done?

Although there are some things that can be done to increase trading volume, it's usually much easier to reduce the amount of available float. Let me explain.

Although many financial theorists believe that everyone has full and equal knowledge of financial markets and the same ability to draw accurate conclusions from what is known, in practice such a belief is more accurate as a description of what's possible rather than of what actually occurs. For instance, a Mitchell and Company survey identified that fewer than 10 percent of major institutional investors usually had enough current knowledge about any major equity security to make an informed buy or sell decision. Even for an extremely large company that is relatively easy to analyze (such as Coca-Cola), this percentage of knowledgeable institutional investors rarely exceeded 50 percent.

There's good news in this relative lack of effective knowledge: A company can seek and educate investors who prefer to buy and hold securities rather than to trade them frequently. When enough of such investors buy and hold the shares, the available float declines.

But that's not all that a company can do to attract more long-term shareholders. A company can also seek out long-term investors who would only buy if the price/value ratios drop somewhat. In this way, should available float become too large or trading volume drop, new long-term investors will rush in to remedy such deficiencies.

If all else fails, a company can seek to attract traders who will find buying in a certain range to be "a good value."

Financial strategies can help, too. Share purchases by companies retire available float, permitting a fast recourse to increasing trading volume while reducing available float. If open market purchases do not work fast enough, the company can in many countries tender to purchase larger quantities of its own shares. If cash and debt capacity are not available to fund such share purchases for almost any reason, a company can offer exchanges of existing shares for new classes of securities that will not expand very rapidly in value, but that are attractive to own and hold for other reasons (such as by offering more generous dividends).

Here's another option: If a company's available float for a subsidiary's public shares is too small to attract most potential investors, such a swap of high-value subsidiary shares for company shares can be used to increase float in the subsidiary while reducing the float for the parent's securities. Think back to the prior discussion of having partially public subsidiaries. You can now see another reason why such units often enjoy premium prices for their securities: The available float is quite small (because the parent company still owns almost all of the shares) while the demand for shares is usually above average due to the strong performance of many high-value subsidiaries that are taken partially public.

You may be wondering how any of this analysis applies to a privately owned company. I believe that any organization that's developing such fine solutions will eventually become public. But in the meantime, shares in "hot" private companies such as Facebook and Twitter have often been traded on private exchanges long before their public offerings. The same lessons apply in such circumstances.

Further, a private company can position itself to go public in a higher-value way by selling some shares to employee trusts, as well as to trusts established for other types of stakeholders, in such a way that available float will be reduced. The valuations for such transactions should be adjusted, in part, to reflect how normal supply and demand would affect security prices without a perfect balance of investors. Analysis can be made of similar public companies and the effect of reduced float and increased trading volume to develop a more accurate valuation. By doing so, stakeholders can obtain shares at more advantageous prices.

What's the key lesson? B*y creating a perfect balance of investors, you can establish and maintain a premium valuation for your firm's securities well above what economic performance alone would justify. By doing so, you increase and protect your ability to reward stakeholders who can add further gains to your economic performance.*

Your Lesson Thirty-Eight Assignments

1. Determine what the historical relationship has been between price/value and trading volume/available float for your securities and for similar companies.

2. Identify which securities have the best potential for sustained premium expansion.

3. Develop a set of goals for levels of price/value and trading volume/available float.

4. Investigate how well-informed stakeholders and investors are about the value potential of each business and its securities.

5. Identify investors you want to attract as long-term holders.

6. Identify any attractive financial strategies to use for meeting your goals for price/value and trading volume/available float.

7. Determine how you can interest desirable long-term holders in purchasing or being ready to purchase during dips in valuation.

Lesson Thirty-Nine

Identify and Attract Supportive Investors

And they delivered the king's orders
to the king's satraps and the governors
in the region *beyond the River.*
So they gave support to the people
and the house of God.

— Ezra 8:36 (NKJV)

After Judah had been captured and the captives sent to Babylon, it looked bad for God's people. However, God was faithful in fulfilling His promise that their descendants would return to the Promised Land. True to His word, God affected Cyrus so that he funded and sponsored the return of these exiles. Ezra 8:36 (NKJV) describes how Ezra was able to employ the king's orders to obtain the resources needed to start rebuilding Jerusalem and the Temple.

We can never expect to have human supporters as reliable as God is. However, when we engage in advancing His Kingdom, we can have God's support to attract investors who can expand the value of the enterprise for all the stakeholders. Let's look at some ways to do so.

Although we have addressed attracting more stakeholders and why investors decide to purchase securities in the past, we have not yet looked into how proactive investor relations can identify and attract more investors. While this approach by itself will probably not create a 20 times increase in valuation for a security, it certainly can be a valuable aspect of accomplishing such a result by favorably shifting supply and demand for securities, as well as by doing so into more supportive hands.

The material we reviewed on creating and maintaining a perfect balance of investors in the previous lesson provides one perspective on what types of investors are needed. Let me expand here on what was written there.

For the purposes of this discussion, all classes of investors can be assigned to one of the following nine categories:

1. Founders, their families, and their foundations
2. Executives and managers
3. Other employees
4. Employee trusts
5. Other stakeholders
6. Individuals
7. Passive institutions (indexed funds and buy-and-hold, long-term investors)
8. Active institutions (banks, hedge funds, insurance companies, mutual funds, and pension funds)
9. Involuntary owners (debt holders converted from other securities in bankruptcy, governments that provided bailout funding, and suppliers who weren't paid)

Let's now define a supportive investor and identify where one can be found:

> A *supportive investor* is any security holder whose behavior contributes to expanding securities' value beyond where they would otherwise be.

Generally, behavior can contribute in either active or passive ways. Let's list the five more valuable forms of active contributions, which include:

1. Voting for proxy resolutions favored by management
2. Purchasing more securities
3. Publicly speaking on behalf of what the company is doing
4. Suggesting useful actions to strengthen the valuation of company securities
5. Buying when most others are selling

Now, let's look at the most valuable forms of passive contributions, which include these four:

1. Holding securities for many years without trading
2. Not voting proxies
3. Not taking positions in favor of what critics or opponents propose
4. Not commenting negatively about the company or its securities

I'm sure you understand what forms of action could have negative consequences, so I won't bother to spell those out.

Founders, founders' families, and founders' foundations are usually quite supportive unless the founders (or the founders' family members) are feuding with the current management. When such a split appears to be developing, it's a good idea to arrange for either the founder group or the management group to be bought out. Otherwise, harmful attacks will continue for some time. Ideally, the group that is in a better position to lead the company well should prevail.

When executives and managers gain too much authority, attention can shift from adding stakeholder value to feathering their personal nests.

Other employees are usually positive contributors, putting their money behind their desire for the organization to prosper. By providing incentives for them to purchase, these holdings can be helpfully increased.

Employee trusts are usually controlled by management. Be sure that too much power doesn't accumulate in this manner, so that management isn't insulated from valid concerns.

Investments by other stakeholders can make a big impression on outsiders, seeing that such stakeholders don't need to make such investments ... but choose to do so. Such investments are viewed as signs of good times to buy in many peoples' eyes.

Individuals usually make long-term investments and support management on proxy issues.

Passive institutions give stability to a stock because they rarely sell, and they are usually buying a little along the way.

Active institutions are a mixed bag. Many (especially hedge funds and momentum-favoring mutual funds) often move in and out at awkward times. Such investors are often antagonistic toward a company and its management when actions don't create instant valuation gains. Unless buyers are waiting in the wings to replace them, much downward value risk can come from such investors. Contrarian and special-situation investors are possible counterbalances.

Involuntary holders are going to dump their securities just as soon as they can. As a result, they put a predictable lid on the valuation of securities until they finish selling.

So where do the better investor replacements come from? Here are the primary six options:

1. If the company isn't part of any sponsored indexes, seek to be included in some.

2. Special programs can be put in place to encourage more management, employee, and other stakeholder ownership where those levels are below the optimum size. In some countries, there are tax benefits that can be obtained by putting such incentives in place.

3. Other stakeholders can also be encouraged to buy more by performance-based incentive programs.

4. Increasing dividend payments for a class of securities will attract more individual holders.

5. The company can stand prepared to purchase securities from those who want to make a quick exit from ownership (such as founders or managers who have decided to exit the relationship, involuntary owners, and hedge funds).

6. The organization's investor relations department can have active institutions lined up to purchase in circumstances where many active investors are selling.

It's in this last category that identifying and attracting supportive investors become important. Let me outline a nine-step process that can be used for this purpose (you will find more details about how to do these analyses in Part Eight):

1. Correlate purchases and sales of company securities by each major active institution to various company, industry, financial, and economic variables. From such correlations, you will be able to somewhat anticipate under what circumstances and when various active institutions will probably buy and sell.

2. Find securities in other companies that have similar verified-valuation correlations (are sensitive to the same variables, and with similar or higher price multiples to value).

3. Identify which active institutional investors are making major buys and sells in the other firms' securities that aren't doing so in your securities.

4. Anonymously interview investment decision makers at such institutions to find out why they buy the other securities ... but not yours.

5. Where ignorance or misunderstandings of your organization are limiting factors, spend time educating these active investors.

6. Ask such investors when they are most likely to buy and to sell your securities.

7. Find out what such current and potential investors do and don't like about what you are doing.

8. When you believe that investors' preferred circumstances for buying and selling will soon arise, alert the institutions that will be most supportive.

9. Have an eager reservoir of potential purchasers at supportive institutions continually available that represents likely purchases of at least twice what the near-term sales are likely to be.

What's the key lesson? *By having a surplus of active investors well prepared and eager to buy your securities when major sales are imminent, you will gain and retain a higher multiple value for your economic performance. If you can also use that extra premium to create some other strategic and economic advantages, you can be well on your way to expanding value by 20 times more than would otherwise be the case.*

Your Lesson Thirty-Nine Assignments

1. Examine and learn from your current and potential investors what will trigger purchases and sales of securities.

2. Continually build a larger reservoir of active potential purchasers to replace expected sellers.

3. Alert potential sellers and buyers when optimal conditions for them are coming so that you will be better able to manage the transition into a new, more supportive group of security holders.

Lesson Forty

Influence Expectations

He answered and said to them,
"Well did Isaiah prophesy of you hypocrites,
as it is written:

'This people honors Me with their lips,
But their heart is far from Me.'"

— Mark 7:6 (NKJV)

Perhaps the most amazing aspect of the Bible for some is how God made promises and spoke through prophets to foretell what would happen centuries in advance. In this verse from Mark 7 (NKJV), Jesus is recalling how Isaiah had predicted the rise of religious followers who would honor God in appearance only. Believers can be heartened while reading Old Testament texts to see details of what Jesus later faced. Similarly, while leaders of companies are supposed to be representing investors and other stakeholders, they often do so very poorly. In this lesson, we consider how communications can be improved to help stakeholders more correctly understand and appreciate a company's future.

Perhaps the most important point to share with you is that although many owners and managers will seek to promise any result that they think will help valuation, most attempts by owners and managers to influence expectations to improve value won't work very well.

Let me share seven points to open the discussion:

1. *Those who value assets, ownership in a business, a business itself, or an entire company ask owners and managers about their plans in order to improve the accuracy of valuations.* During such contacts, valuers get a sense of what the owners and managers are like, how successfully they accomplish what they have committed to do in the past, how aware they are of the circumstances they are in, and whether their plans are appropriate. In many cases, valuers also make some personal judgments about the character of the owners and managers in terms of qualities such as honesty, candor, commitment, and selfishness.

2. *Most owners and managers don't understand how their responses to valuers' questions will be used to value assets, ownership in a business, a business itself, or an entire company.* Perhaps the biggest source of misunderstanding is about what valuers hope that owners and managers will say. In dealing with their own subordinates, owners and managers usually seek to lift promises to higher levels that subordinates must meet to gain a promotion, earn a performance-based bonus, or obtain a raise in base pay. Many owners and managers transfer that mentality to valuers and assume that valuers will prefer larger performance promises to smaller ones. As a consequence, owners and managers often make statements about future accomplishments that they fail to meet, causing a lower valuation than would have occurred by meeting a more modest promise.

3. *It's easier for an owner or a manager to destroy credibility with valuers than it is for an owner or a manager to build credibility.* There is a brief "honeymoon" period when an owner or a manager first begins making statements to valuers during which time the owners and managers are given the benefit of the doubt. In other words, their statements are taken at face

value as being accurate and credible at first. If actions taken and performances match what the owners and managers have said, that presumed credibility is maintained. If actions taken and performances do not match what the owners and managers have said, owners and managers are now assumed to be wrong by the same amount as they were in the past ... and much of what they have to say is heavily discounted. If, as a result, an owner or a manager shifts to being much more conservative in describing future performance, valuers will then discount what is being said below the lowered prediction. As a result, a loss of credibility can easily lead to a substantial undervaluation of an asset, ownership in a business, a business itself, or an entire company.

4. *In the interest of making a good impression, some owners and managers start to play games with valuers by promising so little compared to what they can do that valuers realize that they are being manipulated.* Here's an example of what many public company CEOs do: They ask their financial executives to produce very conservative earnings for several quarters, using that time to build contingent reserve funds concerning future risks. Then, if there's a short-term problem with producing earnings, the CEOs ask the financial executives to use some of the contingent funds to produce "earnings" to cover the short-fall. Many CEOs think that no valuers realize what is going on. What the CEOs don't appreciate is that the changes in reported financial results may make no sense, giving everyone a clear picture of extreme manipulation. For instance, if a company "grows" earnings by 15 percent in some time period during which revenues declined and costs were rising rapidly, it doesn't take a Ph.D. from Harvard to figure out that most of those earnings came from reversing some accounting reserves. When that happens, valuers may lose all faith in the owners, the managers, and the numbers ... and tell others why they

feel that way. The result is not very helpful for improving valuations to the proper levels.

5. *In trying to affect expectations, some owners and managers will deliberately make disclosures that they expect to be misinterpreted.* I cannot mention the name of the company, but for many years this was true of a well-known large organization. Most of the company's earnings growth came from sources that valuers didn't take very seriously. As a result, the company didn't provide very many details about where its earnings growth came from, knowing that valuers would make mistakes in their assumptions. Such a "rigged" game is a little like playing roulette with an unbalanced wheel favoring zero and double zero. When those low-probability roulette numbers come up too often, even the dumbest bettor will eventually figure out that he or she would be better off taking any money left and running away from the crooked game. Under such circumstances, valuers may be totally unwilling to use the organization's numbers for anything until disclosure becomes more transparent.

6. *Beware of backlash from those who get burned.* Valuers, despite their inevitable mistakes and shortcomings, take themselves very seriously. In addition, those who rely on their views hold valuers accountable in extreme ways. For instance, someone who loses too much money for others because of a mistake in valuation may not be able to ever again attract an audience of people who will invest based on the valuer's view. Someone who has just seen a fine or a promising valuation-based career go down in flames due to something that an owner or a manager did will feel justifiably angry with the owner or the manager. If the person is at all vindictive, such a valuer may feel justified in bringing enormous public opinion and legal pres-

sure to bear on the owners and managers who led to her or his downfall.

7. *Don't condescend to valuers.* The CEO of a well-known company decided that he didn't want to make a formal presentation to some valuers. He felt that he had better ways to spend his time. While attending a luncheon where he was the only speaker to over 100 valuers who brought their own brown-bag meals, he sat down in a chair and said, "Ask me anything." At that point, he began to ramble and say things that weren't true ... which everyone knew were untrue. The valuers couldn't decide whether the man was insane, stupid, or thumbing his nose at them. Whatever it was, they didn't like it. They complained loudly to board members, and the CEO was forced to resign from the company three weeks later. He never held another important job during the rest of his life. Now, he was a very bright guy ... but he made a very dumb mistake. Don't repeat it.

Here are seven rules to keep in mind that will help you avoid some of these mistakes:

1. Treat valuers like deeply admired and and respected royalty.

2. If you don't know something, tell them that you don't know ... but that you will find out just as soon as you can and then get the answer to them. Show sincere disappointment in yourself for not being able to do better.

3. If you think someone may be taking what you said or published the wrong way, caution the person to be careful.

4. If there's something unusual about what has been shared, point it out.

5. Don't try to convince someone that the commonsense conclusion is wrong.

6. Share what you know in as open, as candid, and as helpful a way as you possibly can.

7. Promise exactly what you think you are 90 percent likely to deliver (and explain this point) — and no more and no less. Don't hide any plans you have that could lead to greater or lesser results.

I can wrap up this list of rules with a simple principle: Treat valuers the way you would like to be treated if you were a valuer. Sounds like the Golden Rule, doesn't it? You're right!

There are three corollaries that are important to keep in mind in applying the Golden Rule. The three are:

1. Review and comment on valuers' work before they publish it. In this way, you can keep them from making big mistakes. They will thank you for the help.

2. Many valuers will misinterpret your intentions in terms of what you will do with the asset, the ownership in a business, a business, or an entire company. Be sure you know what valuers think your intentions are. Whenever you find that there's a misunderstanding, immediately let everyone know.

3. Ask valuers what you can do to help them be more successful in their work. Take a serious look at whether you can, in fact, help them. If you can, make the change. If you can't, give a very good reason why you can't (and it had better be that it's illegal or something similarly strong).

Follow these rules, and you can expect that the valuation of your asset, ownership in a business, a business, or an entire company will be more accurate than it would otherwise be. Given that most assets, ownership in businesses, businesses, and entire companies are consistently undervalued, that's a good result.

The lesson I would like you to draw from this thinking is that *owners and managers should seek an accurate valuation based on a solid understanding of the current position and future plans as the goal for their work with valuers.*

What's the key lesson? *Influence expectations by providing highly accurate and reliable information in a helpful way.*

Your Lesson Forty Assignments

1. Find out who your valuers are and learn about them and what they do.

2. See what you can do to help them be more accurate in their work.

3. Tell them how you plan to communicate with them and ask for their reactions to your plans.

4. Keep checking with them to see how you are doing.

Lesson Forty-One

Inspire Confidence

It is *better to trust in the LORD*
Than to put confidence in man.

— Psalm 118:8 (NKJV)

The verse that follows Psalm 118:8 (NKJV) says that it's better to trust in the LORD than to put confidence in princes. In today's business context, it's not hard to see that verse as warning against putting confidence in those in power, such as CEOs, instead of God. Everyone knows that people are fallible, as this verse so well reminds us. What are the communications implications of human fallibility for a value-improvement program?

Perhaps the most important point to share with you is that valuers realize that difficulties will arise and believe that timely, appropriate responses by management can make a big difference. As a result, valuers attach a premium value to assets, ownership in a business, a business itself, or an entire company that they view as having outstanding management. Valuers will, instead, attach a discount to assets, ownership in a business, a business itself, or an entire company that they view as having ineffective or unresponsive management.

Let me share seven points to open the discussion. These points will be familiar from the preceding lesson, but I've shifted my comments about them to address inspiring confidence in management. In doing so, I want to separate the useful concept of inspiring confidence in management from the bad practice of trying "to put lipstick on the pig" by promising too much or turning attention away from obvious problems.

1. *Those who value assets, ownership in a business, a business itself, or an entire company ask owners and managers about their plans in order to improve the accuracy of valuations.* During such contacts, valuers get a sense of what the owners and managers are like, how accurately they accomplish what they have committed to do in the past, how aware they are of the circumstances they are in, how candid they are in sharing information, and whether their plans are appropriate. In many cases, valuers also make some personal judgments about the character of the owners and managers in terms of desirable qualities such as honesty, sensitivity, candor, responsiveness, and selflessness.

   Pointing out all the problems that valuers already know about and raising red flags (warning valuers) about problems that could arise that valuers should be concerned about increase, not decrease, confidence. By sharing these perspectives, valuers can appreciate that you understand the situation you are in, you are seeking problems to address before they become significant, and you are open about what you know and what you are working on.

   As an analogy, imagine that you have an office manager who takes care of your business while you are away on a vacation. In reports from the office manager while you aren't there, you want the office manager to bring up all the subjects that should be covered and no others. If the office manager skips something or doesn't tell you about anything other than what you ask about, you'll soon be left thinking that this office manager isn't up to the task, and you'll worry about how your business will fare until you return. Valuers have similar reactions to how company leaders report to them.

2. *Most owners and managers don't understand how their responses to valuers' questions will be used to value assets, ownership in a business, a business itself, or an entire company.* Perhaps the biggest source of misunderstanding is about what valuers hope that owners and managers will say. Valuers are very interested in what managers know about any problems or opportunities, when action began or will begin to address those areas, what the actions are, how any results are changing so far, and what the reasonable range of future performance is going to be (and have the results eventually fall in that range, unless something major occurs out of the blue ... such as a major earthquake that disrupts operations).

3. *It's easier for an owner or a manager to destroy credibility with valuers than it is for an owner or a manager to build credibility.* There is a brief "honeymoon" period when an owner or a manager first begins making statements to valuers during which the owners and managers are given the benefit of the doubt. In other words, their statements are taken at face value as being accurate and credible at first. If actions taken and performances match what the owners and managers have said, that presumed credibility is maintained. If actions taken and performances do not match what the owners and managers have said, owners and managers are now assumed to be wrong by the same amount as they were in the past ... and much of what they have to say is heavily discounted.

   Credibility can, however, be built to even higher than the initial levels. That improvement occurs when management does some combination (hopefully all) of the following five things:

a. Leaps quickly and successfully into grasping great unexpected opportunities.
b. Finds unusual solutions to common problems.
c. Eliminates persistent problems.
d. Routinely takes the action that a fully informed valuer would see as optimal.
e. Never engages in a controversial action without plenty of evidence.

4. *In the interests of being honest and above board, owners and managers do their best to provide accurate, timely information – before they are asked to do so.* Here's an example from what a client of mine once did. The company's CEO had announced a plan to develop a new technology that was expected to turn around the sales and profits of its largest, and often faltering, division. As the project proceeded, the CFO (Chief Financial Officer) insisted that valuers be given up-to-date status reports. These reports were never good. The cost of the technology kept rising. The expected sales and profits kept falling. Eventually, the project was halted ... but not before many millions had been futilely spent. Valuers, however, were so pleased with the candor that they perceived about this project that they increased the company's valuation quite a lot based on the belief that the management would eventually find something good to do with the struggling business. And you know what? The management did. Good call!

5. *In trying to be fair to valuers, some owners and managers will deliberately make disclosures they don't have to in order to save valuers from making serious mistakes.* I cannot mention the name of the company, but for many years it was a leader in its industry and highly regarded. The firm's management realized that three of its valuers were routinely making mistakes in drawing conclusions from its published material. The man-

agement arranged to study the valuers' methods in detail to see where the errors were coming from. In response, the company made some additional voluntary disclosures, including 20 years of history in those areas, and spent time with everyone who valued the company explaining how to use the new information. The accuracy of forecasts greatly improved a result, and the management gained some enthusiastic valuers as fans.

6. *Sometimes you are just wrong. What you do about it matters.* A client company was the largest in the world in its product lines. Due to unusual industry conditions, many valuers expected that there would be a tight squeeze on capacity leading to enormous increases in prices. Right on schedule prices started to rise ... for a while. Eventually, excess inventories began to build and customers found ways to reduce their consumption. Prices and sales collapsed. The company's CEO who had believed in the optimistic scenario was diagnosed with what eventually became a lethal case of lung cancer. Barely able to stand, he visited all of the valuers who had gone down in flames with him, apologized for being wrong, described what he intended to do next, and sat there and took whatever abuse they wanted to dish out. It was a mark of great character, and valuers remained firmly committed to his plans for the company.

7. *Be available to and friendly with valuers.* They are at least as important to you as a good customer. Treat them accordingly. They know you are busy, but they have problems, too. If you can help them out, do so. Some CEOs overdo this approach and make themselves available when someone else could provide better information. In such a case, the CEO should accept the telephone call or call the valuer back and connect the valuer with the right person so that great information flows. Sometimes, doing this means that a press release has to be put

out right away for a public company so that no one is treated unfairly. Give out the information in a press release.

Let me repeat the seven rules from Lesson Forty to keep in mind that will help you avoid some mistakes:

1. Treat valuers like deeply admired and and respected royalty.

2. If you don't know something, tell them that you don't know ... but that you will find out just as soon as you can and get the answer to them. Show sincere disappointment in yourself for not being able to do better.

3. If you think someone may be taking what you said or published the wrong way, caution the person to be careful.

4. If there's something unusual about what has been shared, point it out.

5. Don't try to convince someone that the commonsense conclusion is wrong.

6. Share what you know in as open, as candid, and as helpful a way as you possibly can.

7. Promise exactly what you think you are 90 percent likely to deliver (and explain that point) — and no more and no less. But don't hide any plans you have that could lead to greater or lesser results.

I again wrap up this list of rules with a simple principle: Treat valuers the way you would like to be treated if you were a valuer. Sounds like the Golden Rule, doesn't it? You're right!

As previously noted, here are three corollaries that are important to keep in mind in applying the Golden Rule:

1. Review and comment on valuers' work before they publish it. In this way, you can keep them from making big mistakes. They will thank you for the help.

2. Many valuers will misinterpret your intentions in terms of what you will do with the asset, the ownership in a business, a business, or an entire company. Be sure you know what valuers think your intentions are. Whenever you find that there's a misunderstanding, immediately let everyone know.

3. Ask valuers what you can do to help them be more successful in their work. Take a serious look at whether you can, in fact, help them. If you can, make the change. If you can't, give a very good reason why you can't (and it had better be that it's illegal or something similarly strong).

Follow these rules, and you can expect that the valuation of your asset, ownership in a business, a business, or an entire company will be more accurate than it would otherwise be. Given that most assets, ownership in businesses, businesses, and entire companies are consistently undervalued, that's a good result.

The lesson I would like you to draw from this thinking is that *owners and managers should have as their goal expanding an accurate valuation based on working with valuers to develop a solid understanding of the current position and future plans and by showing that the organization can produce superior results while delivering unparalleled transparency about what they are doing.*

What's the key lesson? *Build on accurately influencing expectations through providing highly reliable information in a helpful way that demonstrates superior management qualities so that valuers can build in accurate expectations of what you are doing, as well as improvements that you haven't started working on yet, haven't told anyone about yet, but are going to accomplish.*

Your Lesson Forty-One Assignments

1. Find out what valuers like and don't like about the way your organization is managed.

2. Evaluate making changes where valuers have a good point to make about the need for improvements.

3. Tell valuers what changes you are going to make, keep them apprised of what you are doing, and let them know your progress along the way.

4. Keep checking with them to see how you are doing as a management team.

Lesson Forty-Two

Continually Attract Investors to Special-Situation Opportunities

For you, brethren, have been called to liberty;
only do not use *liberty as an opportunity for the flesh,*
but through love serve one another.

— Galatians 5:13 (NKJV)

In Galatians 5:13 (NKJV), the Apostle Paul discusses the proper use of free will. Due to the evil one, all kinds of temptations are around us. Whenever our attention is diverted by what we should not focus on, it's helpful to have someone remind us what we should do. At a moment when an enterprise is about to experience unusually substantial improvement, many will be attracted by the opportunity if they hear enough about it to understand what's coming. That's an opportunity for better communications to attract stakeholders, especially those who want to become investors.

Although we have addressed attracting more stakeholders and why investors decide to purchase securities in previous lessons, we have not yet looked into how following a strategy and business model of continually adding special-situation opportunities can help. While this approach will probably not create a 20 times increase in valuation for a security, it certainly can be a valuable contributor to such a result by favorably shifting supply and demand for securities.

The material we reviewed on creating and maintaining a perfect balance of investors (Lesson Thirty-Eight) provides one perspective on what types of investors are helpful to attract. Let me expand here on what was written there by defining a "special situation." According to www.investopedia.com it is:

> Particular circumstances involving a security that would compel investors to trade the security based on the special situation, rather than the underlying fundamentals of the security or some other investment rationale. An investment made due to a special situation is typically an attempt to profit from a change in valuation as a result of the special situation, and is generally not a long-term investment.

A special situation that could prompt investors' attention might be a large public company spinning off one of its smaller business units to become its own public company. If the market deems that the soon-to-be-spun-off company will have a somewhat higher valuation in its new form after the spinoff, an investor might buy shares in the larger company before the spinoff in an attempt to gain a quick price increase. There are many other circumstances that could be referred to as special-situation investment opportunities, such as tender offers, mergers and acquisitions, and bankruptcy proceedings.

This definition of a special situation may make you wonder why it would be attractive to seek such a "temporary" advantage. Well, while investors may look at the situation as temporary, I'm thinking of creating a series of nonstop special situations that go on and on for increasing value.

Let me explain what I mean. Start with the example above. If I intend to totally spin off a somewhat higher value part of the company to be its own public company, any valuation benefit from such an action for the parent company shares disappears after the spin-off. That's the kind of special situation that many investors look for.

Let me change just two things in the example: Let's make this a partial spin-off of a much higher value part of the company, rather than a total spin-off of a somewhat higher value part. In such a transaction, the parent company still owns almost all of the operation that has been taken partially public. If the price of the parent company shares falls too low in comparison to what the partially public unit sells for, special-situation investors will swoop in to buy parent company shares ... helping to put a floor under the value of that stock. As long as this circumstance pertains and is significant to the parent company's total value, the parent's shares will be considered a special-situation investment opportunity.

Do you see the difference in how the two methods would affect value?

Here are some more of the typical temporary causes of a special situation:

- A tender offer has been received from a potential purchaser of the company and higher bids are expected to follow.
- The company is tendering to purchase a large quantity of its own shares.
- The company is being acquired for a fixed number of stock shares, and the value of the acquiring company's shares is rapidly rising.
- The company is in bankruptcy proceedings, but it is expected to emerge with some value being retained by shareholders in excess of the current price level of the common shares.

Why are special situations important to a company's valuation? The primary five reasons are:

1. Academic studies show that potential investment gains under a given set of circumstances are much larger than potential investment losses.
2. Academic studies show that the size of the potential gain is substantial.
3. Academic studies show that the gains occur in a relatively short period of time.
4. Academic studies show that the historic frequency of gains occurring is much higher than that of losses being suffered.
5. Other financial instruments can be used to reduce risk of loss (such as calls, puts, short sales, and currency and other futures contracts).

As a result of such knowledge, many of the better-educated and -informed investors seek such circumstances, knowing that they can enjoy above-average gains by concentrating their investments where such favorable past patterns and situations exist today. To diversify risk, most special-situation investors will seek to invest in every single qualifying special situation they can find.

If a company manages to continually present new special situations to potential investors, the result is to bring into the stock short-term investors who will stay with it, from one special circumstance to another, so that they are acting as though they were long-term investors even though that is not their intention.

Here are some of the methods that companies have used to continually attract special-situation investors:

- Frequently announcing attractive transactions that are so significant in size that they qualify as "special situations"

  As an example, a company with little or no debt and lots of cash might announce repurchases of a large percentage of outstanding stock every few months and continue doing so for years.

- Making many large acquisitions for stock that extend the company's business model in appealing ways

  This method is particularly easy for technology companies to do because there are usually so many more alternative technologies being developed by other companies than any firm can hope to master for itself.

- Establishing joint ventures with high-performing organizations that are likely to succeed and help to eliminate or to reduce large near-term losses and cash expenditures

  This approach works particularly well if the other company in the venture has good access to the highest-potential customers for what is being developed. Many of the early Corning joint ventures displayed this characteristic.

- Taking high-value operations partially public before they accelerate performance improvement

  When such entities demonstrate that the break-up value of the parent is greatly more than its current market value, many investors are attracted by such an opportunity to benefit from seeing the discount from break-up value reduced.

Special-situation investors are more important now in most nations than ever before. Since the nineteen nineties, investment trading has gone from being dominated by large mutual funds and pension funds to becoming primarily driven by large hedge funds that borrow enormous sums to increase the size of their bets. Without an ability to attract and retain hedge-fund investors, most securities will frequently trade well below their potential value. That's because hedge-fund investors are typically focused on making special-situation investments.

By finding out and doing what will attract buying and reduce selling through creating a continual special-situation profile, a company can attract many more higher-value purchasers and increase valuation. This point will also be true of private companies that want to go public.

What's the key lesson? *By giving special-situation investors reasons to pay attention to and to invest in your securities, you will gain and retain a higher multiple value for your economic performance. If you can also use that extra premium to create some other strategic and economic advantages, you can be well on your way to expanding value by 20 times more than would otherwise be the case.*

Your Lesson Forty-Two Assignments

1. Examine the academic literature to identify what kinds of company actions are now attracting special-situation investors.

2. Continually ask special-situation investors how they see your company in terms of whether any of your actions qualify your securities for special-situation investing.

3. Continually study what other actions you could take that would improve your business performance while raising your special-situation appeal.

Lesson Forty-Three

Clearly Signal What's Coming

Now the appointed signal between the men of Israel
and the men in ambush was that they would
make a great cloud of smoke rise up from the city,
whereupon the men of Israel would turn in battle.

— Judges 20:38-39 (NKJV)

Judges 20 (NKJV) describes the combat between Israel and the tribe of Benjamin after members of that tribe abused and killed a Levite's concubine. In the ensuing battles, the Benjaminites had the better until God presented His plan. The Israelites attacked and fell back, as if in defeat. While the Benjaminites chased them, other Israelites fell on the city that Benjamin had left behind. At the sight of the smoke rising from the Benjaminite city, the retreating Israelites counterattacked, the other Israelites attacked from the city, and Benjamin was destroyed between the two Israelite forces. The unmistakable signal made the timing of such difficult coordination much easier to accomplish. In addition, realizing that their homes were burning caused the Benjaminite forces to despair, making it easier to defeat them.

Companies should be equally clear in helping valuers and stakeholders to know what's coming next on a timely basis. Most organizations confuse stakeholders in unintended ways that reduce confidence in the organization's future performance, leading stakeholders to make bad investment decisions.

Let me briefly summarize how signaling affects stakeholder perceptions and actions. Most people believe that companies only communicate with stakeholders through documents such as the government requires (10Ks, 10Qs, proxies, and other similar documents in the United States), voluntary disclosures (press releases and public announcements of all sorts), and public speeches (that are often also included on a company's Web site). While those means of communications are the most visible, they form only the tip of the iceberg (almost all of an iceberg is under water) in terms of what is actually observed.

In addition, companies leave visible clues about what might happen next. One example comes in the form of what external observers say. Sophisticated investors know that organizations often speak privately with security analysts, institutional investors, and journalists. During such meetings, outsiders ask probing questions (often including ones that they know the company cannot legally answer) and carefully watch for clues to the answers in the body language of the people who answer. Later, many such people are interviewed by journalists concerning their "opinions" about what's coming next at the company. Knowledgeable observers know that such comments are often simply mirroring what company spokespeople have said in private conversations and the impressions they have created in their listeners.

Companies also leave public footprints in other kinds of government filings. For instance, a new pharmaceutical product will be highly regulated and much of such regulation is accompanied by filings that the public can read. Similarly, lawsuits are in the public record and often disclose details about company activities, plans, and vulnerabilities.

Stakeholder disclosures can also reveal a lot about what's going on. For instance, an organization that supplies a key component will often know what the customer organization's sales trends are by simply tracking what the orders from the customer organization have been. If such a supplier comments that big customers are slow-ing down their orders, it will be inferred that *all* big customers are selling fewer items.

Observant local stakeholders can also discern fine details that others might miss. How full is the employee parking lot? Is the grass being maintained as well as it was in the past? How do help-wanted ads compare to previous ones?

As a response to being so closely observed, many companies pay as much attention to secrecy as do some counterespionage agencies of major countries. The effect of being secretive is to amplify the importance of every hint that is received.

In such an environment, I believe there's a major opportunity for breakthrough companies that are regularly creating 2,000 percent solutions to expand markets, to slash per-unit costs, and to reduce investments to increase value by deliberately sending signals that reinforce a well-informed internal outlook concerning what's coming next. As a result, the organization's situation and prospects will be better understood by stakeholders, who can then make more appropriate contributions.

Since many companies are not publicly held, let me focus on how private companies can signal their circumstances and prospects more accurately and frequently to stakeholders. Here are seven suggestions:

1. *Use so-called open-book accounting*. After your major 2,000 percent solutions are well defined and tested, you could make this change. By following this approach, any stakeholder inside or outside of an organization can look at the company's financial statements to see how the organization has performed. While many owners and company leaders are frightened by the idea, research has shown that employees work more effectively when they know exactly how their organization is doing. When problems arise, more effective attention is aimed at them. Some research has suggested that such financial transparency works well with suppliers. Stakeholders who hold investments in the organization gain advantages by knowing more about how the underlying performance is going. Such information can encour-

age better timing of purchases and sales in the organization's securities, businesses, and assets.

2. *Regularly disclose future-performance-related information.* Such information might include the current sales level, backlogs, new contracts, and progress in developing new and improved offerings. Many owners and managers have a deep fear of having anyone know such details. I believe that such fear is usually unfounded. As a CEO once said to me, "If I had each of my competitor's detailed plans for the next five years, I wouldn't know what to do with them." Unlike warfare where moves and countermoves cost and save lives, in business an organization's customers determine its success and failure much more than competitors do. If you disclose more about how well you are doing, you'll encourage competitors' best employees to seek jobs with you or to leave the industry while retaining more of your top talent. Potential customers will probably be more interested in working with you, as well. As a result, I believe that such disclosure will improve performance versus competitors.

3. *Let stakeholders know what other stakeholders are buying and selling among the organization's securities, businesses, and assets.* There's an old American saying, "Put your money where your mouth is." The idea behind the saying is that the action of spending your own money is a better indication of your true opinion than anything you might say. If stakeholders see that other stakeholders are predominately buying or selling a given security, business, or asset, that's a way for a stakeholder to know that something different is going on. The price has gotten too high or too low ... or performance is about to surge or falter. As stakeholders, individuals are often in a position to contribute to accomplishing more. A heavily invested customer, for example, might see weak sales by its supplier as an opportunity to place a large order, realizing that faster and better

service should be expected, as well as an increase in the value of the customer's stake.

4. *Share persistent problems and progress toward solving them.* One of the biggest issues for many organizations is having the same limitations holding them back, year after year. When such issues are out in the open, they attract more attention and better solutions. Morale also improves because no one feels as if the organization is trying to pretend that it operates perfectly.

5. *Alert stakeholders to issues and opportunities that lay just over the horizon.* No one likes to be blindsided. That's a reference to being hit by a person or vehicle coming from a direction that provides no warning. So much trust can be lost at such a time that prior levels of confidence may never be regained. Lawyers hate this kind of disclosure. They fear that mentioning what hasn't happened yet will increase litigation and liabilities. I suspect that the opposite will usually be the case: People will realize that an organization is making its best efforts to do the right things and be more forgiving.

6. *Be very open about disclosing mistakes, apologizing, and describing remediation.* Organizations are simply groups of people, and many mistakes are to be expected. It's also a very human reaction to deny that anything is wrong and to seek to shift blame to some other person or organization. If you know that an organization will seek to do the right thing, mistakes don't bother you as much. In addition, if you know that an organization is committed to doing the "right" thing, you'll be less likely to seek a windfall from a goof-up.

7. *Regularly ask stakeholders what they believe is coming next.* When such views are at odds with what management thinks, first investigate to determine if stakeholders know some things that management doesn't. Once satisfied that different infor-

mation isn't the source, check to see what communications (or lack thereof) might have contributed to any misunderstandings. Then change your communication practices to help narrow the gap between perceptions and a reasonably accurate view of what's coming next.

What's the key lesson? *By establishing a company that more accurately signals what's coming next, you can improve business performance and cause value to also expand more rapidly, providing still more ways to reward all stakeholders through value increases than would otherwise occur.*

Your Lesson Forty-Three Assignments

1. Determine ways that more accurate signaling could enhance operating performance for stakeholders.

2. Evaluate how different signaling could cause more value improvement for the most valuable operations and assets.

3. Consider the size of the potential benefits from such changed actions compared to the net worths of those whom you would like to encourage.

4. Provide incentives for those stakeholders who can help the most and see how well the incentives work.

5. Adjust incentives to encourage even more valuable behavior changes.

6. If the advantages are large and appear to be sustainable, expand the successful programs.

Lesson Forty-Four

Continually Draw in New Stakeholders

"Go therefore and make disciples of all the nations,
baptizing them in the name of the Father and
of the Son and of the Holy Spirit,
teaching them to observe all things
that I have commanded you; and lo,
I am with you always, even *to the end of the age."*

— Matthew 28:19-20 (NKJV)

In the Great Commission (Matthew 28:19-20, NKJV), Jesus charged His followers to take the Gospel message everywhere to all people, so that It would attract fully informed new believers. Similarly, an organization seeking to advance God's Kingdom should be seeking to add new stakeholders of all kinds and to engage them in increasing fruitfulness for God's Kingdom.

Unfortunately, most organizations see the boundary between stakeholders and nonstakeholders as being relatively fixed and unimportant. When that perception occurs, an organization will find that it is losing the bulk of potential benefits by not adding as many valuable contributors as would be desirable to solve problems and open the doors to better opportunities.

In lessons found in *Business Basics* as well as those in this book, we have often considered ways to engage nonstakeholders, such as by interviewing people who are familiar with offerings but don't buy them, attracting ideas from different people outside the organization who can help solve problems such as through global contests, encouraging more nonholding investors to commit their financial resources, making potential suppliers less reticent in proposing solutions that they think the organization will reject, and uncovering hidden problems that customers don't even realize they are experiencing based on the behavioral observations of expert third parties such as cultural anthropologists.

Only in this lesson do we focus on attracting new stakeholders through communications as a major strategy. The potential benefits are enormous: Most of the people in the world aren't yet one of your organization's stakeholders. Bring enough of such people into your stakeholder fold to work on the right tasks, and you will dramatically and decisively shift the balance of effectiveness in your organization's favor.

You might also think that it's unlikely that you can make much progress in this regard. If you consider the kind of advanced strategies we have been exploring for how to increase stakeholder value by 20 times, I'm sure you'll agree that the potential rewards from this activity for stakeholders should certainly cause many more people to consider establishing a value-creating connection with your organization.

While I don't want to discourage your thinking and ideas, let me propose a few potential programs that might help start your thinking.

Let's look first at *those who aren't yet, but could become, customers.* In many industries, suppliers better understand the pros and cons of what purchasers do than what the purchasers themselves understand, often just asking their buying departments to obtain the lowest price for a given set of specifications. In many cases, such buyers lack the ability to assess how an offering with different qualities could enable large improvements for their organization. In many cases (as Carol

Coles and I observe about Ecolab in *The Ultimate Competitive Advantage*), suppliers offer free "studies" of their potential customers' practices to identify improvement opportunities that may have little or nothing to do with purchasing the supplier's goods and services. After realizing from receiving such studies how much expertise the supplier has, many noncustomers choose to become customers. It's possible to make such improvements because suppliers see so many excellent, average, and poor practices among their customers and noncustomers that suppliers can easily measure and quantify the value of making desirable changes for any given organization.

I suggest that organizations seek to widen their base of knowledge by routinely measuring the practices of as many noncustomers as possible. In addition to providing the resulting information for free to noncustomers, I suggest that organizations also encourage any noncustomers who participate in such regular measurements to become stakeholders who can invest in the organization's activities. While such investment opportunities need not be as substantial as those provided for customers, I believe that making such incentives available will greatly expand useful knowledge about noncustomer practices, help identify which of the noncustomers to attract first, and lead to developing many successful new offerings.

Let's look next at *uninvolved experts*. You may remember from *The Ultimate Competitive Advantage* how Goldcorp used a global contest to attract great ideas from gold mining experts and how that practice has become an industry standard. You are less likely to remember that Procter & Gamble (P&G) has taken that practice much further, seeking the bulk of its solutions to difficult problems, innovative ideas, and new products from outside P&G.

Although such innovative programs are financially rewarding for those whose solutions are accepted, the bulk of those who participate receive nothing other than a "thank you" from the sponsoring organization. I don't believe that such a way of rewarding experts will work well in the long run. Why should large numbers of the most talented people and organizations participate?

I believe that the following adjustments could greatly expand the appeal and effectiveness of such methods:

- Design the competitions to become highly desirable "fun" as leisure-time activities. This approach might mean polling potential entrants to learn their leisure preferences and engaging talented designers to provide what the potential entrants most enjoy.

- Create a mechanism for measuring participation for all entrants through the quality of what an entrant provides. Reward all of those who show potentially helpful approaches, even if they aren't selected. Based on such measures, offer preferred opportunities to invest in the organization, much as stakeholders would be allowed to do under the methods we have been exploring. In the process, make it easy for participating experts to gain stakeholder status and its privileges for increasing the value of their stakes in the organization.

Now consider *potential suppliers.* Having highly knowledgeable and experienced organizations assess your organization (as Ecolab does) is highly desirable. Yet in many cases, such organizations aren't engaged in providing such excellent evaluations and directions.

After your organization has found a way to make such work highly effective in attracting new customers, you can offer a training program to help potential suppliers learn how to do something similar that makes sense for them. Then, allow those who supply the evaluations of your organization to be treated as stakeholders when it comes to making preferred investments that will rapidly increase in value.

Finally, let's look at *potential distributors.* Many organizations limit their potential by only considering distribution methods that have been tried and found to work in their industry. Chances are, however, that untried methods by other organizations may be valuable supplements to or substitutes for what is usually done.

Rather than only consider what has always been done, seek out distributors to engage in tests of potential methods that could widen availability. Even if such tests "prove" that the methods won't work, treat those who work with you to do the tests as stakeholders and reward them with the preferred methods of making investments that only stakeholders can do now.

I could go on, but I'm sure that you have the idea by now: *Consider who doesn't connect to your organization today, find potential benefits from working together, and begin to seek such benefits through collaborations of all sorts. Reward those who dream, hope, and act effectively with you as stakeholders through access to your highly favored ways of providing investment-growth opportunities.*

What's the key lesson? *By reaching out to those with no connection to your organization in ways that encourage them to contribute their skills, talents, and resources, you can improve business performance and also cause value to expand more rapidly. When you reward those who attempt to contribute as stakeholders, the opportunity to increase their stakeholder value by 20 times will expand the efforts and their effectiveness on your behalf.*

Your Lesson Forty-Four Assignments

1. Determine ways that drawing in new stakeholders could enhance the operating performance of your entities and assets for stakeholders.

2. Evaluate how involving new stakeholders could cause more value improvement for the most valuable operations and assets.

3. Consider the size of the potential benefits from such changed actions compared to the net worths of those whom you would like to encourage.

4. Provide incentives for those potential stakeholders who can help the most and see how well the incentives work.

5. Adjust incentives to encourage even more valuable behavior changes.

6. If the advantages are large and appear to be sustainable, expand the successful programs.

Part Eight

Identifying the Optimal Value-Improvement Program

But Moses' hands became *heavy;*
so they took a stone and put it *under him,*
and he sat on it.
And Aaron and Hur supported his hands,
one on one side, and the other on the other side;
and his hands were steady
until the going down of the sun.

— Exodus 17:12 (NKJV)

During the exodus from Egypt, God often supplied supernatural power through the rod that Moses carried. In the instance described in Exodus 17:12 (NKJV), the Israelites were battling the Amalekites in Rephidim. Whenever Moses held the rod over his head, the Israelites under Joshua prevailed. If his hands lowered the rod, the Amalekites had the better of the battle. Finally, Aaron and Hur supported Moses' hands until the battle was won at the end of the day. Similarly, a company that wants to develop the optimal value-improvement program is going to need to identify one that has God's blessing and is going to be supported by all stakeholders.

While teaching value improvement, I often begin with the material in Part Eight. I do so because so many executives have limited attention spans for a new subject. Only after they appreciate that there's a safe way to identify an optimal value-improvement program are they interested in learning more about what to do.

In this part, I describe each of the steps needed to identify such a program. As the final lesson, I focus on next steps for getting started with implementing what you've learned in this book.

Lesson Forty-Five describes how to organize a planning activity for identifying the optimal choices and sequence of actions for increasing value. In this lesson you'll also find the social-science tests and methods described that CEOs and financial executives usually skip in developing their strategies. Unfortunately, many of those who are deemed "expert," such as investment bankers, are also deficient in knowing about and applying these methods. After reading this lesson, you'll be one of the most knowledgeable people on Earth about how to identify such a value-improving strategy.

In Lesson Forty-Six, we consider how statistical analysis and stakeholder conversations can identify value-improvement choices that your management may not realize have high potential. You will also learn what questions to ask during the interviews.

We next validate statistical correlations that are consistent with stakeholder responses. With this information in hand, we can begin to identify which changes in performance, what kinds of actions, and what order of these actions will most help or hurt valuation of the company's securities. In Lesson Forty-Seven, we continue the consideration begun in Lesson Forty-Six to add these perspectives.

Lesson Forty-Eight describes the work involved in identifying comparable case histories that can inform you about the size of risk and its likelihood due to taking actions that stakeholders and correlations favor.

In Lesson Forty-Nine, you will see how to combine what you did in the prior lessons in this part to come to sound conclusions concerning what actions to take, under what circumstances, and in what sequence. You will also learn how to double-check for risk that you've inadvertently ignored.

Lesson Fifty provides cautions about bad practices that have derailed many well-meaning leaders who were seeking to improve value for all stakeholders as part of the next steps for implementing what you've learned in this book.

Lesson Forty-Five

Plan a Value-Improvement Program

"In My Father's house are many mansions;
if it were *not* so, *I would have told you.*
I go to prepare a place for you.
And if I go and prepare a place for you,
I will come again and receive you to Myself;
that where I am, there *you may be also.*
And where I go you know,
and the way you know."

— John 14:2-4 (NKJV)

As John 14:2-4 (NKJV) tell us, even Jesus had to make preparations for the next step in expanding God's Kingdom. I'm sure your head is filled with good ideas for expanding value, but you are probably wondering how to organize those ideas into their most effective combination. Relax. The next few lessons explain what to do.

Implementing this method for improving stakeholder value requires understanding many of the business and financial strategies in *Business Basics* and *Advanced Business*. If the method wasn't so strongly connected to those strategies, I would have begun with this topic.

You might be wondering why I would devote a whole lesson to planning a value-improvement program, rather than just assuming that such planning will take place. The reason I do so is because I never meet people who know how to do such planning before I teach them.

Before describing what I have in mind, let me begin by describing and commenting on three perspectives that I often see CEOs and CFOs apply to the subject of how to plan for value improvement:

1. For those who believe that discounted cash value is what should be optimized, the task seems to be quite simple: Look at the operationally interesting choices, calculate discounted values for each one, and implement the directions with the highest values.

   Let me politely disagree. As we explored in earlier lessons, discounted cash flow isn't the way that many stakeholders determine value. To assume so can be to make a large mistake that will put decisions at odds with what stakeholders want. In addition, calculating discounted cash flow is more art than science in most organizations, due to ether forecasting future performance being very difficult or improper methods being applied. Further, many managements are unaware of their best value-improvement alternatives and obviously don't even consider the ones that they don't notice.

2. For people who like to get advice, the problem seems even easier to solve: Just contact a professional in the field and ask for recommendations. This approach is most often done by asking investment bankers and valuation experts to explore and document alternatives.

   While many people like to believe that such organizations and individuals have deep expertise, my experience has been that the expertise is usually based on having much experience performing incorrect analyses. For instance, an investment bank will also do discounted cash flow analysis, but often less accurately than the organization it is studying could due to not knowing as much about the industry and the company's situation. The investment bank will often also show the "track record" of everyone who has recently taken a similar action, regardless of comparability to the client organization. Further, investment banks don't make much money doing such work. They make the bulk of their profits by doing transactions, so there is often a bias towards actions that earn the most money for the investment bank. Valuation experts, by comparison, do their best work in setting prices for buying and selling whole businesses in the current environment. If some other action needs to be evaluated, valuation experts often lack the expertise to do so.

3. Some managements and owners don't want to consider value implications at all. They simply want to make decisions based on their own sense of what's the best strategic or operational alternative and simply assume that good value results will follow.

   While I would never recommend that an organization choose value-based strategies that would be either competitively or financially risky or counterproductive, my experience has been that the bulk of those who ignore value dimensions select strategies that reduce the value of their organizations while also usually failing to strengthen them relative to competitors or financially.

Having explained the problems with what some other people do, let me now explain *what you should do*. I'll begin by explaining the three rules concerning information that need to be followed:

1. Any accurate value-investigation method requires *using at least three independent sources of information*, *at least one* source of

which needs to be *totally based on information about current conditions.*

It's this observation that shows the most important limitation of discounted cash flow analysis: It's just one method, and it's not totally based on information about current conditions.

2. While there are many different independent sources of information that can be applied, I have found that *the most reliable sources* are:

    a. *Multivariate correlations of the organization's past security prices to variables that most current stakeholders are using to make their decisions to buy and sell securities*

    b. *Recent case histories of similar transactions done by organizations whose past and current security prices are similarly correlated to the securities of the organization under study*

    c. *Anonymously sponsored interviews with investors and conversations with stakeholders about how their purchases and sales of securities would be affected by the potential actions that an organization could take.*

3. *In looking at the three independent sources of information for value investigations*, I have found that the following rules are essential:

    a. *Assume that the company's forecasts are wrong.*

    b. *Test all the conclusions to see if they leave the company better off regardless of future economic conditions and organizational performance.*

    c. *Only take actions that are neutral or positive in terms of what each of the three information sources indicates, and that are also positive for strengthening competitive and financial performance.*

Where do these rules come from? They are standard controls employed by any rigorous application of social-science evaluation methods. Unfortunately, most people who work with value assessment were solely trained in either finance or business and are ignorant of statistical and decision-making methodologies used to produce reliable conclusions.

An obvious advantage of planning a value-improvement program is that an organization is likely to have taken the time and applied the effort to assemble the useful data needed to accurately consider how valuation will be affected by various decisions.

A less obvious advantage from such an approach is to consider more alternatives and more thoroughly. For instance, the stakeholder interviews can be conducted in such a way that millions of permutations are tested. In my experience, by casting such a wider net the organization will locate more and better value-improvement alternatives. In fact, of the ten best alternatives for what actions to take next, it is rare that management will have been considering eight of the actions before learning about stakeholder reactions.

Perhaps the most significant advantage is that the optimal sequencing of attractive actions is essential to gaining the most benefit from the time, money, and effort involved.

I also see another advantage: Managements won't impulsively take actions based on too little information and thinking. With the right data in place at all times, most spur-of-the-moment opportunities can be correctly evaluated within 72 hours. This quick-response capability means that major value mistakes can be avoided.

In the following lessons, I explain more about how to gather the right information and to perform the analyses I've been describing to grasp great unperceived opportunities and to avoid errors.

What's the key lesson? *By developing good value-based information and planning your optimal choices based on it, you can establish and sustain a more premium valuation for your firm's securities. By doing so, you increase and protect your ability to reward stakeholders who can add further gains to your economic performance.*

Your Lesson Forty-Five Assignments

1. Schedule a planning activity for making value-improvement decisions.

2. Use the next few lessons to develop the information needed to conduct such planning.

Lesson Forty-Six

Start Your Value-Improvement Program with Stakeholder Conversations

Listen to counsel and receive instruction,
That you may be wise in your latter days.

— Proverbs 19:20 (NKJV)

One reason new leaders often get better results than the leaders they replace is that many new leaders take time to listen to anyone who might be able to provide useful information or advice. Present leaders need to refresh their listening with an open mind if they are to gain as much insight. I think it's significant that King Solomon, to whom God gave immense wisdom, exhorted us all to listen to counsel, as well.

In Lesson Forty-Five, I introduce how to plan a value-improvement program. I want to use this lesson and the two following to explain how to implement that method. Let's begin by rereading the information rules for using the method:

1. Any accurate value-investigation method requires *using at least three independent sources of information, at least one* source of which needs to be *totally based on information about current conditions.*

   It's this observation that shows the most important limitation of discounted cash flow analysis: It's just one method, and it's not totally based on information about current conditions.

2. While there are many different independent sources of information that can be applied, I have found that *the most reliable sources* are:

   a. *Multivariate correlations of the organization's past security prices to variables that most current stakeholders are using to make their decisions to buy and sell securities*

   b. *Recent case histories of similar transactions done by organizations whose past and current security prices are similarly correlated to the securities of the organization under study*

   c. *Anonymously sponsored interviews with investors and conversations with stakeholders about how their purchases and sales of securities would be affected by the potential actions that an organization could take.*

3. *In looking at the three independent sources of information for value investigations*, I have found that the following rules are essential:

   a. *Assume that the company's forecasts are wrong.*

   b. *Test all the conclusions to see if they leave the company better off regardless of future economic conditions and organizational performance.*

c. *Only take actions that are neutral or positive in terms of what each of the three information sources indicates, and that are also positive for strengthening competitive and financial performance.*

Let me explain more about the logic of the method. There are several important advantages to starting this method with stakeholder conversations and investor interviews. Perhaps the most significant is that this information gathering helps eliminate a lot of unnecessary work that's slow, expensive, and difficult to do. At the same time, this information gathering is also very powerful for turning up the right agenda of actions to consider.

But there is one bit of homework that needs to precede the stakeholder conversations and investor interviews. Let me identify what that homework is: You will be using data to determine the underlying causes of stakeholder behavior. If you are not familiar with how to use statistics for such work, please ask someone to help you. Chances are that someone in your organization who works in market research or quality analysis will have the necessary knowledge and skill. If you don't have anyone with such skills, a college professor of statistics can usually be hired relatively inexpensively to provide the same expertise.

Whether your organization is publicly held or a private firm, you need to understand on what public valuations for your kind of business are most often based. To do this, you'll need a powerful statistics program with full multivariate correlation capabilities. I prefer the basic version of SPSS, but you should use any software you want of similar or greater capability.

For analytical purposes, you need to pick the public companies (in addition to yours, if your company is publicly held) that perform activities most like your own. Ideally, these will be firms that engage in only one activity, the same one you do. Few such firms may exist.

If a public firm does something similar to what you do in only a small portion of the organization, exclude such a firm from your analysis. You should only analyze those companies where the firm's main activity is the same as yours, and that activity accounts for at least 40 percent of revenues, profits, and cash flow. If no firms meet that test in your country, check out the most similar firms in other countries with valuation levels most like yours. If no public companies anywhere fit, you won't be able to do this analysis.

The best firms to study will be those that have been public continually for at least 20 years. Don't bother to study any that have been public for less than 15 years because the analytical results won't be reliable.

If a study company meets these tests, you should calculate as many economic, industry, product, and company variables as you can think of that might be relevant, including at least the following, on an annual basis (be sure to match data to the same time periods ... some organizations don't use a calendar year for their financial reports):

- Average annual stock price (closing price every trading day added together and divided by the number of trading days in that year – many online sources provide the daily stock prices for free, such as Yahoo Finance)
- Equity per share (these and other company financial ratios can be determined from looking at online sites and company financial reports that can be downloaded from the Internet)
- Earnings per share
- Cash flow per share (you may need to use a variety of definitions)
- Revenues per share
- Profit margin (after-tax profits divided by total revenues)
- Return on equity (after-tax profits divided by total equity)
- Debt/equity ratio
- Dividends per share

Using your statistical software, load all these data and develop the best multivariate correlations to average annual stock price you can that make logical sense. The results will be tested during your investor interviews.

In applying the strategies for value improvement that we have been considering, a goal is to encourage all stakeholders to purchase some of the various securities that your organization makes available. To make such sales successful, the securities need to be attractive to stakeholders and then increase in value.

I encourage you to have personal conversations with each stakeholder who is critical to your success. If there are too many for you to handle personally, ask other trustworthy people in your firm to help.

I prefer that such conversations be relatively unstructured so that stakeholders have an opportunity to tell you what they have in their hearts and on their minds, rather than constraining their answers into some predetermined set of potential responses. But I also suggest that you be prepared to prompt people if they don't mention something that you care about.

Start each conversation by explaining that you want to understand the stakeholder's perspective on what your company is doing or might do in order to create more value for the stakeholder and for your organization. Ask for permission to take notes so that you don't miss anything that the person wants to tell you. Promise the person that his or her specific responses will not be disclosed to anyone other than whoever combines all the answers for analysis. Keep your word.

I suggest these ten questions, but feel free to revise them to make more sense to your stakeholders and ask clarifying follow-up questions where you don't understand a response:

1. What are the five most important things that our organization can do to add value for you (and your organization, if applicable)?

2. What are the five most important things that you (and your organization) can do to add value for our organization?

3. What are the five most important ways that you (and your organization) add value for your own benefit?

4. What are the five most important ways that our organization should add value for itself?

5. What are the major actions that you expect our organization to take in the next twelve months?

6. Which of those actions do you believe will add value, which will be neutral in value effects, and which (if any) will harm value?

7. What are the major actions that you believe our organization should take instead, but will not take, in the next twelve months to add value?

8. If you were offered an opportunity to purchase securities in our organization, what factors other than the price would you consider in deciding if you were interested?

9. Investors in some companies similar to ours appear to make investment decisions in part by considering factors such as [list variables that were most important in the multivariate correlations that the stakeholder did not mention in answering question 8]. Which of those factors do you think are important enough that you would use them in making your decision about purchasing our company's securities?

10. What other advice do you have for our company in adding more value to you (and your organization) and to our company?

Finalize the conversation by thanking the person for providing such helpful assistance. Ask for permission to contact the person again if need be to clarify specific answers.

Tabulate the answers in a way that weights the responses according to how important the stakeholder is (customer responses, for instance, might be weighted by the percentage of total company profits provided by each customer).

Please note that in the case of shareholders and potential shareholders for public companies, due to disclosure laws in your country it may be more appropriate to have your interviews done by a trustworthy third party to maintain confidentiality about your sponsorship. To do so, be sure to ask about at least 10 reasonably similar companies in total. Validate the effectiveness of the disguise by asking interviewees who they think sponsored the interview. If your organization is directly asked if you have been the sponsor, it will help to have already adopted a policy that you don't comment on surveys. Then you can decline to comment without telling a falsehood or misleading anyone.

In your investor interviews, be sure to include a statistically valid sample of those who own or have owned the most similar public companies to your own. Attracting their interest is extremely important to developing an effective value-improvement program. Separately tabulate the responses of current shareholders from the potential shareholders.

In the next lesson, we turn our attention to looking more closely at developing and using a stakeholder-confirmed multivariate correlation to develop a value-improvement program.

What's the key lesson? *By conducting stakeholder interviews after developing multivariate correlations for your firm and similar publicly held companies, you can begin to establish the essential data to develop and to maintain a more premium valuation for your firm's securities. By doing so, you increase the ability to reward stakeholders who can make possible further gains in economic performance.*

Your Lesson Forty-Six Assignments

1. Perform any appropriate multivariate correlations.

2. Interview all influential stakeholders, as well as a statistically representative sample of all categories of stakeholders.

Lesson Forty-Seven

Determine Your Valuation Correlations and Sensitive Actions

And He Himself gave some to be
apostles, some prophets, some evangelists,
and some pastors and teachers,
for the equipping of the saints
for the work of ministry,
for the edifying of the body of Christ,
till we all come to the unity of the faith and
of the knowledge of the Son of God,
to a perfect man, to the measure of the stature
of the fullness of Christ;
that we should no longer be children,
tossed to and fro and carried about
with every wind of doctrine, by the trickery of men,
in the cunning craftiness of deceitful plotting,
but, speaking the truth in love,
may grow up in all things into Him
who is the head — Christ —
from whom the whole body,
joined and knit together

by what every joint supplies,
according to the effective working
by which every part does its share,
causes growth of the body
for the edifying of itself in love.

— Ephesians 4:11-16 (NKJV)

In Ephesians 4:11-16 (NKJV), the Apostle Paul creates a vivid image of how different roles for believers contribute to one unifying effect: all coming to Christ in full knowledge of Him. Similarly, different kinds of information reveal aspects of what we need to know to expand value in ways that increase God's Kingdom through our businesses.

In the previous lesson, we focused on holding and tabulating stakeholder conversations and investor interviews. In this lesson, I finish explaining how to identify the correct multivariate correlations that reflect what stakeholders are using. You may recall that I began the discussion in the previous lesson by describing one bit of homework that needs to precede the stakeholder conversations. Here is that information again in the following paragraphs:

> Whether your organization is publicly held or a private firm, you need to understand on what public valuations for your kind of business are most often based. To do this, you'll need a powerful statistics program with full multivariate correlation capabilities. I prefer the basic version of SPSS, but you should use any software you want of similar or greater capability.
>
> For analytical purposes, you need to pick the public companies (in addition to yours, if your company is publicly held) that perform activities most like your own. Ideally, these will be firms that engage in only one activity, the same one you do. Few such firms may exist.

If a public firm does something similar to what you do in only a small portion of the organization, exclude such a firm from your analysis. You should only analyze those companies where the firm's main activity is the same as yours, and that activity accounts for at least 40 percent of revenues, profits, and cash flow. If no firms meet that test in your country, check out the most similar firms in other countries with valuation levels most like yours. If no public companies anywhere fit, you won't be able to do this analysis.

The best firms to study will be those that have been public continually for at least 20 years. Don't bother to study any that have been public for less than 15 years because the analytical results won't be reliable.

If a study company meets these tests, you should calculate as many economic, industry, product, and company variables as you can think of that might be relevant, including at least the following, on an annual basis (be sure to match data to the same time periods ... some organizations don't use a calendar year for their financial reports):

- Average annual stock price (closing price every trading day added together and divided by the number of trading days in that year – many online sources provide the daily stock prices for free, such as Yahoo Finance)
- Equity per share (these and other company financial ratios can be determined from looking at online sites and company financial reports that can be downloaded from the Internet)
- Earnings per share
- Cash flow per share (you may need to use a variety of definitions)
- Revenues per share

- Profit margin (after-tax profits divided by total revenues)
- Return on equity (after-tax profits divided by total equity)
- Debt/equity ratio
- Dividends per share

Using your statistical software, load all these data and develop the best multivariate correlations to average annual stock price you can that make logical sense. The results will be tested during your investor interviews.

In the previous lesson's discussion of stakeholder conversations and investor interviews, you may remember that you were directed to ask the following two questions:

8. If you were offered an opportunity to purchase securities in our organization, what factors other than the price would you consider in deciding if you were interested?

9. Investors in some companies similar to ours appear to make investment decisions in part by considering factors such as [list variables that were most important in the multivariate correlations that the stakeholder did not mention in answering question 8]. Which of those factors do you think are important enough that you would use them in making your decision about purchasing our company's securities?

You were then told to weight the tabulations of the answers according to how important the stakeholder is. (Customer responses, for instance, might be weighted by the percentage of total company profits provided by each customer.)

At this point, you should take the most common responses to questions 8 and 9 and consider which of the most statistically significant multivariate correlations and correlation variables that you ran earlier best match the responses you received in the various shareholder interviews and stakeholder conversations.

In making this comparison, be aware that the answers may not be homogenous in pointing towards a single correlation and set of correlation variables. Be open to identifying more than one correlation and set of correlation variables. In fact, it's entirely possible that a number of major stakeholders from the same organization may each respond to a different set of correlation variables.

Since your purpose is to interest stakeholders in investing in various securities for different value forms of your organization, those differences matter. Don't be afraid to identify a number of multivariate correlations to which stakeholders with significant resources and interests in your organization pay attention.

Once you have identified all of the multivariate correlations that are used by either a substantial stakeholder or stakeholders, you should do some simulation work to understand under what external circumstances and types of company performance one set of correlations will yield substantially higher or lower valuations for the organization than the other correlations that are verified by stakeholder comments.

Then, identify by name which stakeholders are associated with which correlations. Separately tabulate their interview responses to the other eight questions from Lesson Forty-Six to determine what actions are favored by those who are most closely associated with each verified multivariate correlation. Double check the logic of assigning stakeholders to one correlation versus another for identifying what actions are favored by that group.

Here's an example of what I mean: If a stakeholder's answers are very similar to more than one multivariate correlation, assign that stakeholder to the most logical connection. Let's assume one stakeholder is sensitive to the variables of both cash flow per share and dividends per share. In looking at favored actions, let's assume this stakeholder strongly prefers paying more dividends rather than paying down debt levels. I would interpret such a pattern as describing someone who is probably using a dividend-correlation valuation. The mentions of cash flow per share only come up because higher levels of performance in that dimension make it easier to pay more dividends per share.

Does that example make sense to you? If it doesn't, please send me your questions, and I'll see if I can help you better understand the example and the activity that is being described here.

From what we learn by looking at these multivariate correlations and stakeholder preferred actions, we next consider recent case histories to determine which actions will be most helpful and harmful to improving valuations in the perceptions of your stakeholders, the topic of the next lesson.

What's the key lesson? *By looking at the results of shareholder interviews and stakeholder conversations to identify multivariate correlations for your company and the actions that stakeholders who are associated with each type of correlation prefer, you can determine which stakeholders will boost or hold down valuations under a variety of company performance and external circumstances and identify which actions to evaluate through looking at recent case histories to identify the ones that will help to develop and to maintain a more premium valuation for your firm's securities. By doing so, you increase your ability to reward stakeholders who can add further value gains.*

Your Lesson Forty-Seven Assignments

1. Compare multivariate correlations to stakeholder responses to identify which correlations and variables best approximate how the most significant stakeholders and clusters of stakeholders value your enterprise.

2. Run scenarios of external circumstances and organizational performance to see which stakeholders and variables will be most important under which circumstances in pulling valuation of the organization's securities up or down.

3. Look at the preferred actions that can most help or hurt valuation to identify which actions should be studied through examining recent case histories of similarly valued companies.

Lesson Forty-Eight

Prepare and Analyze Relevant Case Histories for Sensitive Actions

Having confidence in your obedience, I write to you,
knowing that you will do even more than I say.
But, meanwhile, also prepare a guest room for me,
for I trust that through your prayers
I shall be granted to you.

– Philemon 1:21-22 (NKJV)

In Philemon, the Apostle Paul writes to his friend and fellow believer to beg his indulgence on behalf of Philemon's escaped slave, Onesimus, who had been faithfully serving Paul in prison. Paul asks Philemon to forgive Onesimus and to treat him as though he were Paul. In the verses quoted above, Paul goes on to share his belief that Philemon will do more than Paul asks. He also states that Philemon's prayers will lead to God freeing Paul so that he may visit Philemon.

Although the Bible doesn't tell us, one possible interpretation of Paul's confidence can be found in assuming that he has spent so much time with Philemon in somewhat similar situations that Paul feels comfortable projecting those actions onto the current situation. If so, what Paul was doing is similar to the task of preparing and analyzing relevant case histories for sensitive actions affecting your company's valuation.

The first step in preparing and analyzing relevant case histories for sensitive actions is to decide what actions to study. Begin by looking at the tabulations of the stakeholder conversations to see which actions would cause substantial amounts of purchasing compared to the security sales that would occur. In doing so, pay particular attention to what nonholding investors like. I typically focus on just those actions where there will be three times as much purchasing as selling, after weighting responses by the relative potential purchasing power of those who were interviewed. Applying this ratio helps counterbalance the tendency for some people to overstate their intent to purchase and to downplay their intent to sell as a way of pleasing the interviewer.

Next, also consider what actions should expand the value of securities based on the multivariate correlation work that you did. For instance, if the correlation is strongly influenced by increasing dividends, that would be an action you would consider. In this example, cutting dividends would be an action you would not consider.

Then check what the multivariate correlations suggest for which actions to take against what the stakeholder interviews indicated so that you don't study any action where there is more selling indicated than buying for all stakeholders, as the minimum standard for doing additional data preparation and analysis.

Combine your two lists of actions to study into one list. For each action, you next need to identify all the publicly held companies that have done what you are studying in stock market conditions that are similar to the current time. In many countries, there are services that provide such lists. If you cannot find the lists, you can probably screen through historical databases to look for large shifts in reported numbers that are normally associated with the action you are studying. In the United States, for instance, *Value Line* publishes data histories over many years that reveal major changes in shares outstanding that can be used to identify when large share repurchases occurred. Zacks also provides special data studies that are pretty inexpensive.

Now, take your list of public companies and eliminate the cases that are the most different from your organization (size, mix of business activities, profitability, balance sheet ratios, business performance during the time of announcement and thereafter, and so forth).

With the remaining cases for each action, begin running simple, one-variable correlations on the most common factors found in the multivariate correlations you developed relative to average annual stock price for public companies (book value per share, dividends per share, cash flow per share, and earnings per share) for at least 15 years prior to the year when the action was taken that you want to study.

Retain only the cases where the strongest of those four correlations is the same as the strongest correlation to your company ... or to those companies you located that are public and most similar to yours if you are a private company. So if your correlation (or the surrogate from other public companies) is to book value per share, you'll only keep the cases where the correlation fit of average annual stock price is closest to book value per share among the four variables tested.

At this point, you may have no cases or as many as seven or eight. If you have no cases, there's nothing more to be done. But if you have at least one case, work remains.

Take whatever cases remain and develop the highest multivariate correlation you can for each case for the 15 years prior to the year of the action being announced. You will probably have to dig into sources of old press releases or call the company to find the announcement date.

Now, recreate the financial results for each company as though the action had not been taken. So, in the case of a dividend increase, you go back to what the prior dividend level had been, decrease debt or increase cash on the balance sheet to reverse how the dividend increase was funded, and make any adjustment needed to earnings (such as by reducing interests costs for borrowed money or adding interest income for larger cash balances).

After that, plug into the correlation for the company the recreated financial results that simulate the action not being taken, keeping constant any price premium or discount to the multiyear correlation that had existed in the year prior to the action having been announced.

Take all such calculations for the case histories and see how well the stock prices did compared to what such a continuation of the correlation and premium or discount would have indicated over the next three years from not taking the action.

If the stocks in all cases were either helped by the action or the effect was neutral, the action can be considered. If some of the effects for individual cases were substantially negative, don't take the action.

In the next lesson, we look at how to combine the information from the three sources described in lessons forty-six, forty-seven, and forty-eight to assemble a highly effective value-improvement program for stakeholders.

What's the key lesson? *By looking at the stock-price results of similar case histories for companies that are publicly held for various actions that stakeholders who are associated with each type of correlation prefer and are suggested by the verified correlation, you can determine if it's safe to consider taking actions to develop and to maintain a more premium valuation for your firm's securities. By doing so, you increase and protect your ability to reward stakeholders who can add further gains to your economic performance.*

Your Lesson Forty-Eight Assignments

1. Identify which actions to study.

2. Develop the required information to estimate the effects of the actions on stock price for the relevant case-history companies.

3. Determine which actions helped, which were neutral, and which were risky for seeking a more premium stock-price valuation.

Lesson Forty-Nine

Analyze Stakeholder Conversations, Verified Correlations, and Case Histories to Create a Value-Improvement Program

Consider the work of God;
For who can make straight what He has made crooked?
In the day of prosperity be joyful,
But in the day of adversity consider:
Surely God has appointed the one as well as the other,
So that man can find out nothing that will come *after him.*

— Ecclesiastes 7:13-14 (NKJV)

In Ecclesiastes 7:13-14 (NKJV), King Solomon reminds us that there will be difficulties we can't change, good times, and bad times, as well. With clear-eyed realism, he says that we should remember that they all come from God and serve a purpose. In this lesson, we draw on these cautions to consider how to develop a value-improvement program that will hold up under the future's unanticipated difficulties and opportunities.

In developing a value-improvement program, I've found that many companies fail to consider how dependent the accuracy of their decisions is on the future performance of their organizations. As a result, *I encourage you to first test the potential actions that you studied through the stakeholder conversations, correlations, and case histories to see how dependent each one is on future company performance and the financial markets.*

Almost any action you might take will change your company's performance along the lines of measurements such as revenues per share, earnings per share, cash flow per share, dividends per share, book value per share, and return on equity. *You need to understand under what circumstances such shifts turn unfavorable for valuation.* Let me explain what I mean through an example of a share repurchase.

Let's start with revenues per share. A share repurchase reduces shares outstanding while leaving revenues untouched. As a result, revenues per share increase after *any* repurchase above 1 percent of the outstanding shares, regardless of how much or how little you spend for the shares. Naturally, you gain more value benefit for the expenditure if the price paid is lower.

Something similar occurs with dividends per share. Unless the amount you spend on share repurchases eliminates all the cash and debt capacity for paying any dividend, the effect of a share repurchase is to let you pay out the same amount of money in dividends on fewer shares, thus potentially increasing dividends per share.

Return on equity is somewhat similar. The accounting treatment is to reduce the company's equity account by the amount spent on the repurchase. As a result, earnings usually stay about the same (being reduced only by interest income on the cash you spend for repurchasing or the interest cost of any funds you borrow for this purpose). As a result, most times return on equity increases.

Cash flow per share is a little trickier to increase. You can actually pay such a high price for shares that cash flow goes down due to reduced interest income or increased interest cost. That result happens more often when interest rates are high. The effects on earnings per share are similar.

Book value per share is quite a different story. If you purchase shares at a price above the current book value per share, this value goes down and stays down until retained earnings or future stock sales accumulate enough on the reduced number of shares to exceed the prior level of book value per share. If, however, you buy under the current book value per share value, there's an immediate and longer-term increase in book value per share.

Why is any of this important? Unless you have a very unusual valuation pattern, one of the ratios I just reviewed has a large influence on what stakeholders will pay for your securities. So, depending on which influences are important (and in some cases, how much you pay), an action may or may not make sense at the current time and price. That doesn't rule out taking the action. It just means that the timing may have to shift, or you may have to consider if you want to reduce value today in the interests of a higher value down the road.

In making such valuations, *you also should analyze value sensitivity to subsequent company, operating unit, or asset performance.* A company that's sensitive to book-value-per-share, for instance, should wait to make share repurchases until after it has done any necessary write-offs of common equity and ended any period of losing money (which also depress book value per share). At such times, the cost of repurchase will usually be less.

The analysis obviously becomes more difficult if factors such as interest rates, inflation, offering prices, and performance of newly acquired companies, operations, and assets are also involved. A good way to approach such circumstances is to understand how much each of the variables can change before the value effect is negative.

Ultimately, you have to make a judgment about what future performance will be in the appropriate dimensions. In making such judgments, I encourage you to consider how bad the value effects would be in a very negative value environment for your organization. As a result, you'll probably become more patient in waiting for the optimal time to make certain value-improving actions.

My experience has been that excellent value opportunities to do virtually any action occur at least once a decade for any organization. Keep that observation in mind when people argue for taking action while values are high and the economy has been strong for a long time. Such moments more often precede declining value environments than increasing ones. Don't assume that today goes on forever. If it's bad now, it will get better later. If it's good now, it will get worse at some later point.

The second step is to consider the risk limits of taking such value-improving actions, assuming that there's a weak business and value environment in the future. My experience has been that companies usually take much too much risk in implementing value-improvement programs. It's more important to avoid having a disaster than to push matters so that you do the maximum you can absorb if all turns out well. I particularly encourage you to consider the effects on:

- Debt ratings
- Debt covenant limits
- Cash balances
- Ability to improve day-to-day operations
- Management credibility for making good decisions

The third step is to examine the proper sequence of actions. I encourage you to begin by considering at least one full economic and value cycle. Such cycles include a full sequence of up-and-down or down-and-up until the current levels are reached again. A full cycle is usually about eight years.

In looking at proper sequencing, it often makes sense to evaluate how the other actions affect the benefits of a given action you are studying. For example, a share repurchase often doesn't have all that large of a value effect if that's all you do. But if you do the same share repurchase as the first of ten effective, value-improving steps, the benefits of such a share repurchase may be increased by 20 or 30 times as the other benefits accrue to a smaller set of shares outstanding.

I also encourage you to think in terms of doing parallel actions where that makes sense. For instance, a share repurchase at a low price that's followed by an equal currency-value share issuance at a much higher price usually increases the company's value while leaving financial and value risk unchanged. Be open to using such opportunities to your organization's and your stakeholders' advantages.

The fourth step is to plan entry points for stakeholders to benefit from the value-improvement program. In doing so, I encourage you to look for multiple entry points that should be appealing to each stakeholder and perspective, based on what the conversations revealed.

When you are done developing your value-improvement program, I encourage you to share it with me. I'll be glad to comment on it. I've done a lot of this work, and my experience may help me spot issues that are easy to miss. I also advise you to have other people outside your organization check your thinking. It's very easy to become overly optimistic and overreach. The resulting fall can be quite painful.

What's the key lesson? *By looking at the results of stakeholder conversations, value correlations, and similar case histories for companies that are publicly held for various actions that stakeholders who are associated with your type of correlation prefer and are suggested by the verified correlations, you can develop a superior value-improvement program to reach and maintain a more premium valuation for your firm's securities while providing access for stakeholders to benefit. By doing so, you increase and protect your ability to reward stakeholders who can add further gains to your economic performance.*

Your Lesson Forty-Nine Assignments

1. Study only the actions that are indicated to be positive or neutral for value and company competitive and financial health in very difficult economic and value times.

2. Determine the circumstances under which such actions would be harmful.

3. Only engage in actions that give you an enormous margin of safety for sustaining all aspects of company and stakeholder economic health.

4. Plan an optimal value-improvement program over an entire economic and value cycle by putting the actions in the ideal sequence to add value without increasing risk.

5. Test your thinking with outsiders.

6. Double check your thinking for risk just before taking any of the actions.

7. Track how well the value decisions turn out compared to your expectations.

8. Correct any bias that's revealed for taking on undesirable risk or missing desirable low-risk opportunities.

Lesson Fifty

Next Steps for Implementing Your Value-Improvement Program

So Jonah went out of the city
and sat on the east side of the city.
There he made himself a shelter
till he might see what would become of the city.
And the LORD *God prepared a plant and*
made it come up over Jonah,
that it might be shade for his head
to deliver him from his misery.
So Jonah was very grateful for the plant.
But as morning dawned the next day
God prepared a worm, and
it so damaged the plant that it withered.
And it happened, when the sun arose,
that God prepared a vehement east wind;
and the sun beat on Jonah's head,
so that he grew faint.

— Jonah 4:5-8 (NKJV)

Jonah was a reluctant prophet. It was only after he was swallowed by a great fish (NKJV) that he finally relented and went to Nineveh to warn the people there to repent. When they repented, Jonah was annoyed. In these verses from Jonah 4:5-8 (NKJV), Jonah is pouting and God is preparing a lesson for him: We should depend on the Lord for our needs and be grateful for whatever He brings our way, whether seemingly good or bad.

Reading a book like *Advanced Business* can give you a false impression: Explaining clearly what needs to be done can make the work seem simpler and less risky than it actually is. I would feel I had done you a disservice if I didn't describe some of what can go wrong.

Let me begin by noting that *many organizations refuse to believe that their performance results can fall by as much as they later do*. I well remember the company that was planning a large share repurchase, as well as a substantial dividend increase. In the sensitivity testing, I warned the leaders that if earnings would ever actually fall, the stock price would be hurt by taking these actions. Based on many years of uninterrupted high growth, they assured me no such thing could occur. Within a year, their profits were crushed by about 40 percent. They had no inkling in advance.

My advice is to check disaster scenarios and imagine yourself stuck in one of them, much as Jonah was while in the great fish. If you take that risk seriously, I'm sure you'll be less aggressive in what actions you take that can weaken your firm in terms of cash, cash flow, and stock price during a vulnerable time.

What else can go wrong? *It's completely predictable that some of your company's investment bankers, lawyers, and accountants will disagree with what you are about to do*. Such reactions are even more likely to be the case if most of your plans don't generate large fees for investment bankers. If such advisors have substantial credibility with your board of directors, you could be in for quite a battle. If you don't properly prepare in the face of such opposition, you may not be authorized by the board to do what you think is right for value expansion.

My advice is to ask for your board's consent before starting work on the value-improvement program and to then candidly discuss with the members how they would like to handle any disagreements about what to do among the company's advisors. Show your work at each step in the process to the board members and encourage their questions and suggestions so that they feel fully briefed and comfortable with what you are doing. If you have advisors whose opinions you trust, check with them for their issues before presenting your conclusions to the board. Their points may be valid and might just switch what you do by pointing out an issue or two that you missed.

Another risk is in explaining the program to stakeholders as immutable, rather than as subject to change depending on what conditions are encountered and what the performance results are. *Stakeholders will expect you to do exactly what you said you would do*. Disappointing them can cause much lost credibility, trust, and goodwill.

Consequently, tiptoe into any announcements you make. For instance, if step one should be a share repurchase of a certain size, consider if you can announce less than that and later make a second, or even a third, announcement of an additional repurchase. Such an approach might allow you to pay less for the shares and permit affording to buy more. If your business performance started to weaken while this was going on, you could also string out the repurchases for a much longer time at still lower prices without putting as much pressure on your balance sheet or cash flow.

Realize that case histories don't tell the whole story. First, there may be very few of them. Second, you may be able to implement better than those managements did. Third, there may be some different influences going on now that you haven't considered. Fourth, the action you announce may have a different meaning to stakeholders than did the parallel actions by these other companies.

My advice is to study how any case histories were implemented to see how you can do a better job than the other companies did. You might find one useful idea from one case history, and another good one from a different case history. By combining both ideas, you might present something far more desirable than stakeholders have ever seen. Should such be the case, your success might open the door to opportunities that you didn't expect to have. Do enough work on having more success than you expected at a given stage to know what to do next and to be ready to do so.

Many company managements have such a high opinion of their skills and knowledge that they fall into mistakes without having anyone objective check on their thinking. I wish I had a dollar for every time I cautioned a management team about something and they told me that they knew better ... but they could provide no evidence to support their views. To me, taking such an approach is a lot like Jonah running away from God's calling on his life. You have all the help you need at hand to get the right result. Why would you want to ignore it?

One of my clients expected that an action under consideration would be very controversial. The executives were so concerned that they make the right decision that they hired not one, but two organizations to come up with independent recommendations without knowing what the company was thinking. Both firms (ours was one) affirmed the company viewpoint. The action was taken with great results. Their humility allowed them to be bold in the face of potential controversy and disapproval.

Some people are inclined not to do enough stakeholder interviews to obtain a statistically valid sample. Because of their inexperience in this kind of work, they don't realize that the answer they get is inaccurate with too small of a sample. I've even had difficulty convincing my staff to do enough interviews for some assignments.

Doing enough interviews is so important because the answer patterns shift until you have a big-enough sample. I know because some clients have insisted that I give them interim tabulations while we were working on reaching the minimum samples. I've seen the answer sway into as many as six incorrect directions before permanently settling into the correct one. I also tested several times to see if the answers would keep swinging back and forth after the minimum sample was reached. I've never seen that happen. So do enough interviews!

Some leaders do not believe in acting on answers that differ from what they think stakeholders should *want.* One reason I encourage leaders to conduct themselves as many of the interviews as they can is so that any different information from what the leaders believe can be directly received. Some leaders have had so much exposure to financial theory that they find it difficult to believe that anyone thinks differently from what such theory says that rational individuals "should" think.

I encourage leaders to be open to finding out that others think differently than they, themselves, think, as well as what people have expressed to them in the past. In particular, stakeholders will say different things when not asked directly than in responding to a precise question. Otherwise, there's a tendency to "go along" with management and focus on pleasantries.

Finally, I notice that many management teams are remiss in not updating their information as time passes. They seem to think that information doesn't change, but it does. Don't be that way.

Thanks for reading the book. I hope you will find it easy to apply what you have learned. Keep an eye open for the next book in the Advanced Business series, *Advanced Business for Innovation: Stimulate Competitor Innovation and Copying.* It will add even more value for you and your stakeholders by showing you how to encourage competition in ways that will stimulate more value-adding innovation by your organization.

Appendix

Donald Mitchell's Testimony

He will lift you up.

Humble yourselves
in the sight of the Lord,
and He will lift you up.

— James 4:10 (NKJV)

Let me share with you how I became a Christian so you'll know where I'm coming from with regard to encouraging you to become a Christian and to be fruitful in Godly contributions for creating and implementing breakthrough solutions.

There has been a long commitment to the Lord in our family. For example, I remember my great-grandmother, Edith Foster, reading the Bible every day. As a youngster, my mother regularly took me to Sunday school. It was my least favorite activity; sleeping was much preferred. I did enjoy listening to sermons, but it was frowned on to take youngsters to the adult services where the sermons were given.

If I pretended to be asleep, mom would sometimes let me stay home on Sundays. I was pretty good at pretending, and I soon was the biggest backslider in my Sunday school grade. Fortunately, it was an evangelical church so my classmates were always cooking up schemes to get me to attend again. Because of my high opinion of myself, I would always return if invited to play my clarinet for the congregation.

By the time I turned thirteen, I was pretty full of myself. There wasn't much room for God in there alongside my exaggerated opinion of myself.

One day at home while my family was away for a drive, I felt really sick. By the time they returned, I was delirious. Within an hour, I was in the hospital where I would stay for two weeks as I barely survived a bad case of double pneumonia.

My physician, Dr. Helmsley, was an observant Christian and worried about my soul because my life was in jeopardy. He talked to me about our Heavenly Father, Jesus, and the Holy Spirit twice a day when he stopped by to check on me. These conversations were when I first learned how to become a Christian through being born again. I also came to realize that I couldn't stop sinning on my own. I needed a Savior, Jesus Christ! After I recovered, he took my mom and me to a tent revival meeting.

Having recovered from the illness, I soon pushed God out of my life again. During the next year, I was, instead, very caught up in athletics. When I was in ninth grade, I desperately wanted to make a contribution to our junior high track team, which had a remote chance of winning the big meet. Our coach, Mr. Layman, told each of us exactly what had to be accomplished for the team to win. I was determined to do my part. I had to come in first!

But that wasn't likely to happen. Based on past performances, there were at least two people who could out leap me in the standing broad jump, my main event. To make such a jump, you stand on a slightly raised, forward-tilted board and spring outward as far as you can into a sand-filled pit. After two of the three jumping rounds, I knew it was hopeless. I was in sixth place and four of the competitors' jumps were longer than I had ever gone before. I also didn't like the board we were using.

Remembering that we should call on God when we need help, I thought of praying ... but what I wanted was so trivial in God's terms that I didn't think it was worthy of prayer. So I decided to make God an offer instead: "Dear God, help me win this event, and I'm yours forever." After all, if He came through, any doubts I had about God would be dispelled.

I stepped onto the broad-jump board and felt very calm. I did my routine and took off into the air. Instantly, I felt light as a feather cradled in a large, gentle hand that was lifting me. I was dropped softly at the far end of the pit. I had outleapt everyone and gone more than six inches past my best previous jump. I couldn't believe it. Then I remembered my promise to God, thanked Him, repented my sins, accepted Jesus as my Lord and Savior, and ran off to tell everyone on the team.

Even more remarkable, I was the only person on the team who performed up to the plan. Knowing what had to be done had probably given us performance anxiety, and people underperformed because they didn't believe they could do what the team needed. I also suspect that God wanted to make a point with me that I needed Him.

After a few days, I started to think that perhaps I'd just developed a new broad-jump technique and God didn't have a role at all. God soon dispelled that thought by making sure that my jumps for the rest of my life were much shorter than I had jumped when He lifted me up.

Since then, God has been speaking to me on a regular basis through the Holy Spirit. I've learned to pay attention and act promptly. When I pursue my own ideas, things don't go so well. When I follow His directions, things work out great. That's my secret to high performance, and I just wanted to share it with you so you could benefit, too. He knows the answers, even when you and I don't ... which is most of the time.

As a management consultant, the Holy Spirit has often filled me with knowledge about what the consequences of one set of actions would be compared to another for my clients. Naturally, I always recommended as the Holy Spirit directed me. Clients often told me that they were impressed by how certain I was of my conclusions and of how persuasive I could be in describing the advantages of whatever recommendations were made. Once again, the explanatory words came from the Holy Spirit, rather than from me.

Unfortunately, I wasn't comfortable in my younger days sharing my faith with clients, and I wrongly gave many people the impression that I was the author of the solutions rather than merely the transmitter. I wish I had been more faithful in this regard. I apologize to my clients for having missed so many great witnessing opportunities.

I didn't always listen as well as I should in making decisions that primarily affected me, but God would always do something to get my attention. Here's an example. I made an investment that I hoped would reduce my taxes in addition to making some money. I didn't have a good feeling from the Holy Spirit at the time, and I shouldn't have invested.

My tax return was later audited by the Internal Revenue Service concerning that investment. It turned out I was in the wrong for the deductions I had taken. Anticipating a big tax bill plus penalties and interest, you can imagine my astonishment when the revised tax return showed me owing no additional money to the government even though I had lost on the audit issues. I knew that result was a gift from God, and I was overwhelmed by His wisdom and power in protecting me. Praise God for His mercy!

I rededicated my life to Jesus in 1995, and I have enjoyed great peace since then. I have also done a lot better in being obedient to the Holy Spirit and to what the Bible tells us to do in all aspects of my life. Many blessings have been mine since then.

After being told by God to start The 400 Year Project (demonstrating how everyone in the world could make improvements twenty times faster and more effectively than normal with no additional resources) in 1995, I continued to receive His instructions. In 2005, for example, God told me to start explaining to people how to live their lives by gaining more joy from what they already have.

In the summer of 2006, I began to see how The 400 Year Project could be brought to a successful conclusion (as I reported in *Adventures of an Optimist*, Mitchell and Company Press, 2007). Realizing that perhaps I had devoted too much of my attention to this one challenge, I began to seek ways to rebalance my life. One of those rebalancing methods was to spend more time communing with God through prayer, Scriptural studies, attending church services and Bible classes, and listening more to the still, small voice within.

For several years I had been enjoying the devotionals sent to me daily over the Internet by evangelist Bill Keller. One of those devotionals speared me like an arrow that summer. The evangelist reminded his readers that our responsibility as believers is to share our faith with others through our example and sharing the Gospel message from the Bible. Not feeling well equipped to do more than try to be a good example, I began to pray about what else I should be doing.

The next day, my answer came: I was to launch a global contest to locate the most effective ways that souls were being saved and be sure that information was shared widely. This sharing would be a blessing for those who wished to fulfill the Great Commission to spread the Good News of Jesus as commanded in Matthew 28:18-20 (NKJV):

> And Jesus came and spoke to them, saying, "All authority has been given to Me in heaven and on earth. Go therefore and make disciples of all the nations, baptizing them in the name of the Father and of the Son and of the Holy Spirit, teaching them to observe all things that I have commanded you; and lo, I am with you always, *even* to the end of the age."

The contest winners were Jubilee Worship Center in Hobart, Indiana, and Step by Step Ministries in Porter, Indiana. You can read their stories and learn amazingly effective ways to help unsaved people choose to accept Salvation in *Witnessing Made Easy: Yes, You Can Make a Difference* (Jubilee Worship Center Step by Step Press, 2010) by Bishop Dale P.

Combs, Lisa Combs, Jim Barbarossa, Carla Barbarossa, and me. Six of the many other worthy ideas and practices from the contest for leading more people to learn about and some to be moved by the Holy Spirit to pledge their lives to Jesus are described in a second book, *Ways You Can Witness: How the Lost Are Found* (Salvation Press, 2010) by Cherie Hill, Roger de Brabant, Drew Dickens, Gael Torcise, Wendy Lobos, Herpha Jane Obod, Gisele Umugiraneza, and me.

Let me tell you another interesting thing about my life with Jesus. When my daughter was about a year old, I suffered what resembled a stroke that caused me to start to become paralyzed. As I could feel my face's muscles freezing, I immediately prayed to Jesus to stop the paralysis and He did. I was left with a lot of pain and numbness on the left side of my body and was very weak for over a year.

Part of that pain continued for the next twenty-two years until, on November 8, 2009, I asked two of my pastors during a communion service to pray in the name of Jesus that the remaining pain be removed. During the prayer, the pain started leaving immediately and was totally gone within a half hour. As I felt the pain leaving me, through some power traveling inch by inch down my body, I was overcome with gratitude and fell on my knees in thanks.

That wasn't the only time He recently healed me. Encouraged by that miraculous experience, I came forward again on December 19, 2010, during another communion service to request prayer for relief from the pain in my wrists that was making it difficult for me to write books to serve Him and to do my other work. Knowing that my mother had been plagued with arthritis, I assumed it was a similar onset for me. My pastors were occupied with prayers for other members of the congregation. This time an elder of the church and his wife anointed me with oil and prayed for me. Almost immediately, my whole body shook violently in a way that I couldn't stop. Gradually, the shaking was reduced until it stopped after about half an hour, and my wrist pain was totally gone. It has not returned. I was even more overwhelmed that He had healed me again. Can anyone appreciate all the goodness that God has in store for us?

Let me share yet another miraculous healing (not the last that I've experienced). I've always been troubled with many respiratory and food allergies and sensitivities. In my sixties, these problems had grown worse. I finally reached the point where it was difficult to be in the same room with another person, due to my reactions to any deodorants and scents they were using. During still another communion service on January 16, 2012, two pastors again prayed for me to be relieved of these problems so that I could be a better witness for Him. Once again, power filled my body. My allergies and sensitivities were gone in a few minutes. Since then, they haven't returned. It has made a huge improvement in my life and in my witnessing.

I have also been saved by God from what I believed to be certain death on twelve occasions, most recently on July 2, 2013. I won't go into all of these events, but I did want you to be aware that He is always touching all aspects of my life in beneficial ways.

While it's up to God to decide if and when He wants to heal us or to protect us from harm, it's certainly reassuring to know that He has the ability and power to do anything He wants.

Glory be to God! Praise Him always! His miracles, grace, and mercy never end. I am so happy and honored to be His servant and witness to you.

www.ingramcontent.com/pod-product-compliance
Lightning Source LLC
Chambersburg PA
CBHW060316200326
41519CB00011BA/1749
9780692413876